LIFE WITH QUEEN VICTORIA

Marie Mallet at the time of her marriage, July 1891

LIFE WITH QUEEN VICTORIA

Marie Mallet's letters from Court
1887–1901, edited by
VICTOR MALLET

JOHN MURRAY · LONDON

First published April 1968
Reprinted April 1968

Printed in Great Britain for
John Murray, Albemarle Street, London
by Butler & Tanner Ltd, Frome
and London
7195 1783 4

*I dedicate this book
to my eight grandchildren in the hope
that one day they may care to read
about their great-grandmother*

CONTENTS

ILLUSTRATIONS

PREFACE

Marie Mallet's letters from Court to her mother Lady Elizabeth Biddulph and her husband Bernard Mallet are the basis of this book. I have selected from them those which seem to throw light on the lives of the men and women who served Queen Victoria in the last few years of her long life, and have omitted much that was purely ephemeral or personal. I have, however, included a good deal that is of family interest, as otherwise the picture of my mother would be incomplete. The letters were kept in a black tin box by my father, and by luck escaped the 'blitz' which destroyed most of my family papers and almost all of Marie's huge output of excellent water-colours, which had occupied much of her spare time. I have not attempted to alter her punctuation, but have added footnotes to explain briefly who some of the personalities were. In this I have been greatly helped by various books. First, *Lady Lytton's Court Diary* edited by Mary Lutyens (Rupert Hart-Davis, 1961), a delightful book which covers much of this period. Next, Lady Longford's *Victoria, R.I.* (Weidenfeld and Nicolson, 1964), which is a mine of accurate information for those who look for a complete portrait of the Queen, and has greatly helped me in getting perspective for Marie's letters. Arthur Ponsonby's *Henry Ponsonby: Queen Victoria's Private Secretary* (Macmillan and Company, 1942) is also a valuable guide.

By most gracious permission of Her Majesty the Queen I have quoted a few of Queen Victoria's own short notes and letters to Marie now in my possession; and also Marie's letter to the Duchess of Buccleuch which is in the Royal Archives (c.71/92).

Bernard Mallet's rather scrappy diary, which largely consists of lists of dinner-parties in London and accounts of family holidays, has enabled me to fill in a few gaps during Marie's days in waiting; his descriptions of occasions when he was summoned to the Court and dined with the Queen are of considerable interest.

I am greatly indebted to Mr R. C. Mackworth-Young, C.V.O.,

the Librarian at Windsor Castle, and to Mrs Aurea Morshead for their help in tracing correspondence and personalities; also to Mrs G. Bolton and Mrs C. G. Bell for secretarial assistance; and to Mrs Katharine West for her editorial assistance.

I wish to thank Miss Mary Lutyens and Rupert Hart-Davis Ltd for permission to quote from her book *Lady Lytton's Court Diary* (1961) and to copy one of her family trees; Mr Christopher Hibbert and Longmans, Green & Co. Ltd for permission to quote from *The Court at Windsor*; and the executors of Arthur Ponsonby and Macmillan & Co. Ltd for permission to quote from *Henry Ponsonby: Queen Victoria's Private Secretary*.

V. M.

INTRODUCTION

This book is concerned with two very different families. The first the greatest in the land, that of Queen Victoria and her very numerous and widespread descendants and relatives; the second, that of a middle-class, moderately well-to-do civil servant. During the last thirteen years of the old Queen's reign the only link between the two was my mother, Marie Mallet; though *her* mother had for a time served the Queen, and her uncle was still at Court. Hence the book throws some light on life as it was lived both in great and in humbler circumstances at a time that must seem strange and remote to present-day readers, since it was the end of a long period of peace and middle-class prosperity.

But while the late Victorian age was one of wealth and low taxation, it was also one of shocking poverty, of class distinctions, much snobbery and much servility. In compensation, life was less of a rush, leaving more time for thoughtfulness and kindness, for quiet enjoyment of simple things in nature and the arts. The Queen and her rather dowdy Court set the example for virtuous lives. Routine was eternal: change almost unthinkable. There is a feeling today that the Royal Family ought to move with the times; but they have already evolved immeasurably since the days recorded in Marie Mallet's letters. Queen Victoria never, for instance, set foot in her Indian Empire or in any of her vast Dominions and Colonial Empire. Whereas already Queen Elizabeth II has, in her short reign, been everywhere.

As one of the numerous godsons of the Queen, all of whom were christened Victor Alexander, I feel rather shy at the rapturous accounts by my devoted parents of my early appearances at Court. Surely I *must* have dropped a few bricks in those long romps in the corridors at Windsor? I can remember being carefully groomed for my audiences of my godmother, reminded how to bow and kiss her hand, and not to speak until spoken to. Then came the awful day when, in pursuit of the Battenberg children at hide-and-seek, I suddenly found myself in the Presence. There was the Queen, seemingly a vast figure swathed in black (though really she was very small), being read to by Princess Beatrice, the mother of my playmates. The Queen asked me all sorts of questions, and smiled and seemed less and less alarming; so that when it was all over it turned out that my behaviour had received the Royal approval. The other main impression I retain of my Windsor visits was that, in my bedroom, there was a china box full of biscuits called 'Marie' (surely after my mother?) and 'Osborne' (for more obvious reasons). This was indeed royal hospitality.

The fact of my presence at Windsor is a proof of the Queen's unfailing thoughtfulness. She knew that my mother hated the long separations from her children entailed by the periods of waiting. My father, too, Bernard Mallet, still a junior Treasury official, and for a time Private Secretary to Mr Balfour, was quite often invited to Windsor or Osborne to be with his wife. When there, he was treated as if he were a Duke or a Cabinet Minister, and honoured by dining at the Royal table. There was indeed quite a fuss one Christmas when somehow the intended invitation had miscarried and last-minute telegrams flew from Osborne to London. Yet to other matters affecting Marie's comfort the Queen was apparently blind. It seems never to have occurred to Her Majesty that her devoted lady, who suffered from a bad circulation, found the drives at Balmoral in deep winter and in an open carriage a terrible trial; or that she bewailed the all-day uncertainty as to when one would be wanted, involving hours of hanging about in the Palace which might have been more happily employed.

The picture of the Queen which I should like these letters to convey is one of deep sensibility and human understanding, and a keen sense of the ridiculous. She had her strong likes and dislikes —Disraeli and Gladstone are glaring examples—and a very feminine outspokenness. Her sense of honour was outstanding, and she was never mean. She had a definite sense of fun, but her sense of humour was limited, as Alick Yorke was to learn only too well from the much-quoted 'We are not amused,' after he had—against his will, and under Royal Command—given one of his mimicry performances. Another niece of Alick's, Lady Susan Birch, often related a different version of this story as given her by Alick himself. During a dinner party at Windsor Alick was sitting next to a German to whom he told a slightly risqué story. The German guffawed so loudly that the Queen asked Alick to tell her what had caused such mirth. Alick thereupon repeated the story and received the classic snub.

The other picture I would like to draw is of the author of most of these letters, my mother Marie Mallet. She was born in 1862 and lived most of the first eight years of her life at Babraham near Cambridge, where her father Henry Adeane was the squire and local M.P. She describes him as 'a very tall handsome man with fair hair and bright blue eyes and most beautiful hands, a good artist and loved pictures and sculpture'. In 1860 he married Lady Elizabeth Yorke, daughter of the 4th Earl of Hardwicke, and in the next five years three children were born—Marie, Charles and Maud. By 1865 their father had begun to lose his health and had started on a phase of extravagance. He added a ballroom and other improvements to the house, which he filled with pictures (mostly indifferent), furniture and china—egged on by unscrupulous dealers. He developed a form of creeping paralysis attributed to earlier attacks of scarlet and rheumatic fever, and died in 1870, leaving the Babraham estate so impoverished that it had to be let until after Charles came of age. His widow, by way of rest and change, took the children over to France to stay with a family friend, Claire, Lady Ashburton, and very nearly got involved in the siege of Paris by the Prussians. Lady Ashburton had a daughter Marie, who had married the Duke of Grafton and who became Marie Adeane's godmother. She fulfilled that function in a magnificent manner by giving her goddaughter a fine set of emeralds on her appointment to Court, 'so that she should have something to wear'.

On their return from Paris the Adeanes settled in London in Rutland Gate, alongside several Yorke relations; and here the children underwent a serious and well-balanced education, much attention being paid to the French language. Lady Elizabeth became a Woman of the Bedchamber of the Queen in 1873; but she resigned in 1877, when she married Mr Michael Biddulph, M.P. for Herefordshire, and went to live at Ledbury. She seems to have kept up with her friends at Court and was a particular friend of the Duchess of Teck. Queen Mary once told me that she believed my grandmother was in the room when she was born: 'she was a formidable old lady,' was Queen Mary's verdict, and in this I agree. I remember her as being phenomenally fat, but handsome. She had been a tall, blonde beauty when young. In later life she was sternly religious and a strong teetotaller, and a good speaker for that cause. Can it be that Harry Adeane's early death was hastened by drink? Never a word was breathed of this, but it may have been the origin of her fervour for the temperance movement, which she passed on to Marie. She had, however, one form of indulgence, rare with ladies of those days: she always puffed a cigarette after meals.

Marie's own account describes how she came to be appointed a Maid of Honour in 1887 when she was nearly twenty-six. Her letters to her mother speak for themselves. All went well until she fell in love in 1891 with Mr Bernard Mallet. She was then twenty-nine and well old enough to know her own mind; but all kinds of difficulties arose. Bernard, though not of the aristocracy, was of good middle-class, civil-service stock, and doing well at the Treasury; but he had hardly any private means, and the impoverished Adeanes and ruined Yorkes could do little to help. Wimpole, Lady Elizabeth's old home, had gone with the wind or extravagance and betting which beat upon 'Champagne Charlie'

Hardwicke—the 'glossy peer' who was for a time an ornament of the Prince of Wales's set. But lack of money was not the only trouble for Marie. The Queen took great umbrage that her Maid, to whom she had taken a great liking, should think of deserting her to get married. There were some anxious moments before all was settled to Marie's satisfaction, and the Queen weighed in with a handsome wedding-present.

Marie was indeed old enough. She had been seriously brought up, and life in Rutland Gate had not been too full of frivolities. She had, however, enjoyed the usual gaieties of the season, and had developed a love of music which she kept all her life. She was ahead of her time in her appreciation of Brahms and Wagner. Above all, she enjoyed Bach, who at that time ran a bad second to Handel in public estimation. Her love of water-colour painting, in which she was highly proficient particularly in her 'sketches' (as she always called them) of gardens and flowers, was a great asset with the various Princesses—who were also keen amateur artists, and often called her in to help and advise them. She never really took to oil painting. Her knowledge of art was, however, profound; and her taste, which did not advance to post-impressionism, was very sound on all the old masters.

Marie was tall, with fair hair and greyish eyes. She had a 'presence' in middle and later life which combined well with her wit and keen sense of humour. She had a stern sense of duty, inherited from her mother, and also a strong, rather puritanical religious faith. Her deeply affectionate nature was manifested in her love for her husband and children; and there is no doubt that the Queen understood and appreciated this quality, which Marie also showed so fully to her Royal mistress. She was a good house-keeper, though inclined to be parsimonious; and in their younger days my parents entertained a good deal in a modest way, and went out frequently to dinner-parties. They had a wide circle of interesting and intelligent friends, both political and artistic. There is no doubt that while in waiting she brought a lot of gaiety and fun to an elderly group of courtiers, and helped them greatly in looking after the innumerable visitors, both royal and political. In this she was encouraged most of all by her uncle Alick Yorke, or 'Nunks'.

Alick Yorke would from his appearance be described nowadays as an elderly pansy, though he seems to have been the kindest and most virtuous of men, and no breath of scandal ever passed his way. He had sparkling eyes, an inquisitive nose, and brown hair neatly brushed and oiled. His figure was short and rotund. He was talkative and witty, and a great amateur actor who organized the Queen's theatricals—a feature of Court life for the younger members of the Royal Family. He dressed in an extravagant manner, with huge buttonholes, jewelled rings and tiepins. I can remember the whiff of scent that accompanied his entrance into a room. As a small boy I always looked forward to this godfather's visits; and when ogres were my ruling passion he would growl and act the ogre till my brother and I were in fits of laughter. In an old newspaper cutting I find him described as 'a great personal favourite of the Queen's and the organizer of all the Court theatricals and tableaux vivants. A first-rate amateur actor, he has an enormous acquaintance among interesting people of all ranks, tells excellent anecdotes and gives charming bachelor dinners. In appearance he is very like the Duke of Portland.' His death in 1911 was a great blow to our family.

The background of these letters is a happy family life in London with holiday visits to relations and friends, especially at Christmas. Home was first at Alexander Square near the Brompton Oratory and later at 38 Rutland Gate, with Yorkes in the same square and my grandmother Lady Elizabeth Biddulph round the corner in Ennismore Gardens. Considering the smallness of their income, the Mallets lived in what would nowadays seem affluence, with four or five servants and, of course, our devoted Nannie, Frances Taylor, who carried much responsibility while Marie was at Court for four months' waiting every year. Marie had times of depression during these long partings, but her sense of duty to the Queen convinced her that she was doing a useful job. Moreover,

Lady Elizabeth Biddulph

The Hon. Alick Yorke, 1888

the small salary helped to keep up the standard of life in London and added something to the meagre civil-service pay which Bernard earned. In editing Marie's letters I have of course cut out masses of purely domestic matters and affectionate passages of only personal interest. What remains is a picture of Court life painted with a lively brush, but inevitably very discreet—too much so for the gossip columnist. In a newspaper of about 1900 I find repeated a story which, years before, had actually been a true story about Marie herself. 'A young lady who had just been appointed a Maid of Honour was receiving congratulations at a party, and her host said to her, "What an interesting journal you can keep!" The girl told him that journal-keeping was forbidden, and the answer was, "But I think I should keep one all the same." "Then," said the girl, "whatever you were you would not be a Maid of Honour." '

Little did Marie know that her admired and respected cousin, Edith Lytton, was keeping a diary one day to be published. Strangely enough, Marie seems seldom to have shared the same waitings with her. So the diary and letters complement the period picture rather than overlap. I feel sure that publication so long after the events described would not have shocked my mother; and if any excuse is needed for adding yet another to the books about the Queen, it must be that this was written by one who was really devoted to that great but formidable old lady, and who was, in return, rewarded with remarkable personal kindness.

The Court scene is set in three places, Windsor, Osborne and Balmoral. The Queen hardly ever slept at Buckingham Palace, which was used only for such big events as weddings, Jubilees and an occasional 'Drawing-room' for the presentation of debutantes. Windsor was naturally the most popular residence, as the senior officials had their homes in various towers of the castle, and the Ladies could enjoy (mostly at week-ends) visits from their family and friends. Thus Bernard often appeared there incognito,

as well as sometimes by Royal invitation. Marie's stepsister Violet
Biddulph often came down for the day and was shown the sights.
Other members of the family came and went, though most of
their time was spent in Marie's sitting-room in case she should be
summoned to duty.

Life at Osborne was much less attractive. There were no great
works of art or famous libraries—only the Italianate villa architecture in the taste of Prince Albert, with the Queen's Indian
marquee on the lawn, where she worked at her desk with the
Munshi behind her to blot her signatures. There was, it is true,
lawn tennis for the younger royalties, and also golf, which
Bernard played with Lord Lorne and Sir Arthur Bigge when he
went there for Christmas. There must have been some sailing, too,
though little is said of it. The house and garden had been largely
designed by the Prince Consort and built between 1845 and 1851
on land between Cowes and Ryde looking across the Solent. It
was thus a place of memories where the widowed Queen spent
much of her time indulging in those sentimental orgies of grief
which called forth so much public criticism up to the Golden
Jubilee—after which she became increasingly popular till the very
end. There was at Osborne little accommodation for the Court;
and the gentlemen were lodged in rather pokey quarters in the
grounds, which cannot have been at all pleasant in mid-winter.
Marie enjoyed occasional visits from her aunt by marriage,
Annie Yorke (*née* Rothschild) who owned a comfortable steam
yacht, the *Garland*, on the Hamble river, and brought with her
other friends and relations to liven up the tedium of waiting.
With no motor-cars and no telephone, Osborne was still rather
isolated from the London world.

Balmoral was undoubtedly the least popular residence with the
courtiers, though the Queen was never happier than when there.
She had made it her own in Albert's days, and later shared its
pleasures with her subjects by publishing her famous *Leaves from
the Journal of Our Life in the Highlands*. It was there that she felt
freer and more at home than anywhere. It was there that she had

the faithful John Brown to escort her on her drives and picnics. The castle had been built by the Queen and Prince Albert in the Scottish baronial style complete with turrets and pepperpots, and decorated within with tartans on the walls and on the chairs. It was too small for the whole staff, some of whom found themselves boarded out at neighbouring houses, especially when there was, as quite often, an invasion of foreign royalties. It was a bitterly cold house, and fires were few and far between. The Queen hated warm houses, for her circulation was remarkably good. She would drive out in an open carriage in a snowstorm, her wretched ladies in attendance shivering beside her. Sir Henry Ponsonby describes a conversation between the Queen and Princess Beatrice as to whether, if condemned to the choice, you would select residence at the Equator or the North Pole. The Princess was all for the Equator, but the Queen fierce for the North Pole: 'All doctors say that heat is unwholesome but cold wholesome.' Ponsonby also wrote: 'Every private house strikes me as so comfortable after the severe dreariness of our palatial rooms here.'[1] Yet there was none of the freedom of living in a large hotel; it had, rather, a curious resemblance to a school. But it was unique in one respect. In what other known establishment do persons in the same building communicate with one another by letter? It might be thought that at Balmoral there would have been some relaxation of formality, some 'Petit Trianon' atmosphere. Not at all: discipline was as strict as ever, and nobody could go out of doors until the Queen had done so. In her earlier waitings Marie went now and then for adventurous bicycle-rides; in later waitings she seems to have walked a little. But she always felt the restriction; and above all she suffered from never seeing Bernard or the children, who were 600 miles away.

One of the few diversions at Court was the periodic appearance of well-known musicians to give concerts for the Queen. Marie

[1] *Henry Ponsonby: Queen Victoria's Private Secretary*, by Arthur Ponsonby (Macmillan, 1942).

mentions the young Kreisler as a pupil of Joachim. Miss Phipps in
a letter to Marie of August 5, 1899, refers to Señor Pablo Casals:
'His cello playing is *quite* delightful.' It still is so, nearly seventy
years later!

Albani, Clara Butt, Kennerly Rumford, Plunket Greene, and
the temperamental Madame Janotha all duly appear, 'produced'
almost invariably by the Neapolitan composer Tosti, who managed to set himself up as a sort of 'Master of the Revels', and who
was often tiresome to deal with. Hardly a concert passed without
some of his songs being sung. Grieg, the famous Norwegian
composer, appeared as a pianist and explained his Scottish origin.
The Carl Rosa company came to Balmoral and performed *The
Daughter of the Regiment*. At Windsor the Queen's string band
played selections from *Carmen*, a Norwegian Rhapsody and 'a
lovely gavotte by Gillet' in an icy room where 'our teeth chattered
audibly'. Sometimes Marie wished that the programme had been
more classical, less second-rate; and she found solace at Windsor
in the Chapel music under the direction of Sir Walter Parratt.

Marie herself has left good descriptions of her work and fellow-
workers; but it may help readers to have some background
knowledge about the chief Court personalities. Marie was a Maid
of Honour (1887 to 1891) during the era of Sir Henry Ponsonby,
a great Private Secretary whose life is so well described in his
son's book. He must have been a pleasant influence at dreary
Balmoral—a place he disliked as much as the other courtiers.
Even on Sundays he could not call his soul his own: 'The Queen
must ask that both Sir Henry and Major Edwards should *not* be
out . . . at the same time. Not five minutes after the service in the
chapel was over she sent to say she wished to see Sir Henry in a $\frac{1}{4}$
of an hour but was told he was gone to church. She then sent for
Major Edwards and was then told he was out too! this is extremely
inconvenient. . . .

'Sir Henry can send the Queen questions about anything

through Miss Phipps who is very clear quick and discreet and is quite able to do what Lady Ely and Miss Stopford do.' What a missive for an elderly and very senior official to receive! It seems a bit much even for the servants' hall. Yet he never seems to have lost his sense of humour. A nice example is his story of the Minister of the Scottish Kirk who preached on the devil. Afterwards he asked Princess Louise whether the Queen had liked his sermon. 'She said she had not heard, but that she should think not, as the Queen did not altogether believe in the devil. MacGregor, the Minister, looked with a pitying eye and only said "puir body".'

Ponsonby really wore himself out in the Queen's service. By the time Marie returned to Court in 1895 Sir Arthur Bigge was installed in his place. He became a great friend of the Mallets for the rest of their lives, and his daughter Victoria married an Adeane cousin of Marie's and became the mother of Sir Michael Adeane, the present Queen's Private Secretary. Bigge, who was later to be known as Lord Stamfordham, King George V's Private Secretary, had his troubles with the ladies at Court. It must have been irritating to be by-passed as he often was owing to the Queen's habit of dealing through her lady secretaries such as Marie—particularly when the messages so passed dealt with military matters. There was occasional friction, though Sir Arthur was most tactful and discreet—so discreet, indeed, that he earned the nickname of 'Better NOT'.

Another character whom I vaguely remember was Sir James Reid, the resident physician, a shrewd and witty Scotsman of middle-class origin, who, by his personal charm became the first doctor to be admitted to the intimacy of the 'Household' dining circle. Marie was very fond of him and consulted him a good deal about her own and her children's health. Sir James could get away with most things with the Queen, even to the extent of marrying one of her Maids of Honour, Susan Baring, daughter of Lord Revelstoke and niece of Lady Ponsonby. The Queen sulked for three days but finally laughed when Sir James promised her never to do it again. His influence extended beyond purely medical matters and he was consulted on subjects of social and political significance.

Sir Fleetwood Edwards became Keeper of the Privy Purse in 1895 and seems to have been constantly in attendance. He made some attempt to economize on the waste that was caused in the Royal Palaces. In 1896 Bernard records that Mr Balfour was horrified by it: 'Class III expenses of the Household nearly £20,000 p.a. This does not include wages or salaries.'

Lord Edward Clinton, Master of the Household from 1894 to 1901, was another permanently harassed official and a good-tempered one, even when the servants plotted against him, and the Munshi intrigued.

The Munshi has been very well described by Miss Lutyens.[1] Brought to Balmoral in 1887 as a kind of footman, he soon claimed that he was not of the servant class and that his father was a Surgeon-General in the Indian Army at Agra. This was proved in 1894 by Frederick Ponsonby to be untrue: the father was merely an apothecary at the jail. Before this, the Queen had appointed him 'the Queen's Munshi' as teacher of Hindustani, from whom she learned how to address a few words in their own language to the Indian soldiers who came over for the Diamond Jubilee. The Queen trusted him absolutely and showed him secret despatches from India. Leakages were suspected, and, at last, in 1895, the Secretary of State for India managed to stop this, but only by the extraordinary threat that he would otherwise be unable to send Her Majesty confidential documents. The Queen got her own back by decorating the Munshi with a C.I.E. and designating him her 'Official Indian Secretary, Hafiz Abdul Karim'. It was feared that the favour extended to this Moslem subject might arouse jealousy among the Queen's Hindu subjects. Mr Pope-Hennessy in his *Life of Queen Mary* describes the loathing felt by the Household for this unctuous oriental. They more or less went on strike when the Queen wanted to take him with them to France in 1899, and said they would refuse to eat with him. Miss

[1] *Lady Lytton's Court Diary* (Hart-Davis, 1961), pp. 38–42.

Phipps had an awkward audience during which the Queen became so enraged that she swept all the objects from her writing-table on to the floor. Finally Lord Salisbury was appealed to: he suggested that the French, being 'such odd people', might laugh at the Queen about the Munshi. This had its effect. After the Queen's death King Edward had all the Munshi's papers destroyed, so perhaps we shall never know whether he was treasonable or not. Certainly he was distrusted by all except the Queen, who, perhaps for that very reason, stood up for him so staunchly.

Marie herself describes some of her women colleagues, but a few words can be added about Miss Harriet Phipps. She was a kind of headmistress or lay abbess, to whom the other ladies took their troubles for advice. She had a strict code of honour and always insisted on complete obedience to the Queen's wishes. 'We are,' she said, 'sheets of paper on which H.M. writes with words as less trouble than using her pen and we have to convey her words *as a letter* would do. What you would feel free to do with a letter you are free to do with her words—no more.'

As the Queen grew older she relied more on her Ladies than on her Gentlemen. The chain of command seems to have passed mainly through Princess Beatrice or, in her absence, Princess Christian, to whichever of the three Ladies (Miss Phipps, Mrs Grant or Marie) happened to be in waiting. Sir Arthur Bigge was, as we have seen, too often side-tracked, and at times became touchy about it. There was trouble in 1895 and again in 1900, when Miss Phipps wrote at some length to Marie to advise her, and restore her ruffled feelings when Bigge had spoken sharply to her. In this 'dear Harriet' was entirely successful. She was also very clever at arranging the dates of waitings to suit the different Ladies; but she could never do more than make suggestions to the Queen, who had her own very definite views on the dates. So I find an endless correspondence on these dates, even when Miss Phipps was out of waiting and living in her Grace and Favour house at Kensington Palace. The envelopes have a huge embossed facsimile of her autograph 'Harriet' on the back.

When the Court was at Balmoral there was almost always a Cabinet Minister in attendance. We get a glimpse of many of these in Marie's letters. They brought into the closed circle a breath of outside air, though some of them seem to have been boring enough, and most of them must have been bored by their duties there. It is odd that there is no mention of their being sent out shooting or fishing; nor indeed do the courtiers ever seem to have indulged in such sports for which Balmoral is now famous. Even the Czar during his visit in 1896 never succeeded in getting a stag in spite of several attempts, though he seems to have bagged a brace of grouse!

The Ministers disliked the long journeys and the formal discomfort of the Castle; but the Queen was adamant in keeping to her usual dates for her highland visits. Even the faithful Disraeli had once complained: 'Carrying on the government of a country 600 miles from the metropolis doubles the labour.' It is strange that the Queen, who was in many ways considerate to her servants, should have been so utterly selfish when it came to matters of convenience affecting the great Ministers of State. It may well be that the Queen, who adored life at Balmoral, was unable to realize that a visit to her Highland home, far as it was from London, could be anything but a delight to her guests.

CHAPTER I

MAID OF HONOUR

Marie has left her own description of the daily life of a Maid of Honour, which will serve as an introduction to the letters.

In 1627 Orders appeared that the Maydes of Honour are not to go out of the Court without leave of the Lord Chamberlain and Her Majesty. It is also the duty of the mother of the Maydes to see all orders duly observed and that any refractoriness be reported to the Lord Chamberlain.

In 1681 the Officers of 'The Board of Green Cloth' make the following entry:

> 'Order this day June 12th given that the Maydes of Honour should have Cherry Tarts instead of Gooseberry Tarts, being valued at 3d. per lb.'

Queen Victoria had eight Maids of Honour, they were divided into 'pairs' and were on duty a month at a time so that each Maid was on duty for three months during the year.

A printed Rota was provided and issued on the 1st January. This was subject to occasional alterations, such as visits to Balmoral or the annual journeys abroad which the Queen planned herself each Spring, but on the whole it could be relied on. The Maids of Honour were in the charge of the Mistress of the Robes and all official orders came through her, but as she changed with the Government the real power lay with the Woman of the Bedchamber, who acted as the Queen's Private Secretary (Lady) and she conveyed the Queen's commands and made the various changes in the Waiting necessary from time to time. When I was appointed in 1887 Maid of Honour, the Lady Secretary was the Honourable Horatia Stopford who possessed Her Majesty's entire confidence and affection but her sight and health were failing and she felt it her duty to resign her post and give up the work she loved so well, much to the regret of the entire Court. She was succeeded by the Honourable Harriet Phipps. Miss Phipps was my first 'pair', almost twice my age, she looked about thirty-five with her golden hair and trim figure, dressed in what I should call the English style with many trimmings and ribbons and bristling with jewelry of little intrinsic value, mostly Royal gifts. She wore dozens of bangles which rattled as she walked and which at times worried her Royal Mistress. Attached to these were many minute lockets containing the hair of her numerous relatives past and present. Brought up at Court from her earliest years (her father, Sir Charles Phipps, was a Gentleman on the Prince Consort's staff) she was the embodiment of early Victorian traditions, discreet almost to a fault, full of little mysteries and traditions, inspiring a certain amount of awe of the great Queen and conveying Her Majesty's wishes, commands and reprimands to the other Ladies in a tactful but somewhat awe-inspiring manner. On the other hand she could be gay and excellent company and always warm-hearted. To me she was first a kind mentor and after a loving and devoted friend. She devoted her whole life to her Royal Mistress and never married, her only interests being the Court and her own immediate family who were, unfortunately, not worthy of her. The repository of so many secrets, it became difficult at last to discuss affairs or politics with her, and she never gossiped or openly criticized her colleagues although she had her likes and dislikes. Loyalty to her Royal Mistress and her own family was the ruling passion of her life. She was trusted by all classes and never betrayed a secret.

Miss Phipps left instructions in her Will that all her papers and even the signed photos of all the Royalties she had known and loved, should be destroyed. The Queen gave her an Apartment in Kensington Palace of which her sister, Mrs Chane, was titular housekeeper and there she lived to a good old age, feeding on the past but occasionally interested in the present which included the Great War, but still mysterious if anyone alluded to old days.

During the War her small pension proved quite insufficient even for her modest requirements and her health often needed the services of a trained nurse but she refused any help. At last, I most secretly went to Queen Mary and informed her of the facts; needless to say she was most sympathetic and it ended by the King sending Harriet £100 as a Christmas present, which gift continued till her death. I was inwardly amused when she told me of this favour, and thankful that I should have had the courage to plead her cause.

My next 'pair' was the Honourable Rosa Hood, about eight years my senior. It was the custom to pair off the newcomers with veterans and this prevented their getting into mischief. She was the daughter of the Duke of Bronte, ever lively and affectionate but not clever. She married Mr Evans of Forde Abbey to save her father from bankruptcy; he was a neighbour in the country, very rich and a cultivated man, fond of Rome and Italy and a good judge of pictures. Rosa never cared for him but he offered to make a home for her father whom she adored and after some months of hesitation she decided to sacrifice herself. The marriage was a failure. After some years Mr Evans left Forde Abbey, giving them a month's warning, as well as the servants, and retired to Rome.

This brutal conduct caused poor Rosa to go out of her mind: she eventually recovered but had occasional relapses and died on her brother's estate at Maniace[1] in Sicily. He had become Duke of Bronte and inherited the Sicilian Estates, but not the English title.

[1] Maniace was the estate that the King of Naples had given to Nelson when he created him Duke of Bronte. On Nelson's death it was left to his brother, William, 1st Earl Nelson. William's daughter Charlotte succeeded her father as Duchess of Bronte, and in 1810 married Samuel Hood, Baron Bridport. It was their son, Alexander Nelson Hood, who became Viscount Bridport; and in 1897 Queen Victoria granted him Royal Lodge, Windsor. His daughter, the Hon. Rosa Hood, was Maid of Honour to Queen Victoria from 1886 until her marriage in 1894.

The present Viscount still lives at Maniace and is known locally as Duke of Bronte.

The Queen showed her sympathy by giving Lord Bridport a Royal Lodge in Windsor Park and a pension.

When I was offered the appointment of Maid of Honour I had to reply to the following questions:

1. Could I speak, read and write French and German?
2. Play the piano and read easily at sight in order to play duets with Princess Beatrice?
3. Ride?
4. Was I engaged or likely to be engaged to be married?

To the first three I could answer in the affirmative, and I was able to assure Her Majesty that I was at present 'heart-free'.

The Court had never gone out of mourning since the death of the Prince Consort. The Ladies-in-Waiting always wore black but the Maids-of-Honour with regard to their youth, were permitted white, grey, mauve and purple, except when one of the numerous Court Mournings occurred, when all the Ladies wore unrelieved black with jet jewelry.

The Court continued the traditions of the 17th and 18th centuries and was set on much the same lines. Her position as Queen Regnant entitled her to more Ladies-in-Waiting than a Queen Consort and her Household was formed in a generous scale in which the eight Maids-of-Honour played no small part. Today [*this seems to have been written in 1933—V.M.*] the exigencies of the times and the need for economy and restriction of State ceremonies and entertainments have reduced Queen Mary's Household to a Mistress of the Robes, seven Ladies-in-Waiting and one Maid-of-Honour. These ladies are not resident when the Court is at Buckingham Palace. Queen Victoria's Household was always resident but this was only natural as very few days in the year were spent in Buckingham Palace; on very special occasions such as Drawing Rooms, annual Garden Parties and occasional functions, Reviews in Hyde Park, the opening of the Imperial Institute, the laying of the Foundation Stone of the Victoria and Albert Museum.

I remember being taken to see this ceremony and watch my mother driving with the Queen. As far as I remember there was a large marquee over the Foundation Stone and the Queen sat in her Carriage and tapped the Stone, and there were Escorts of Horse Guards and a Band which I thoroughly enjoyed.

The dates of the rota at Windsor, Osborne and Balmoral seldom varied and the Queen's trip abroad to which she looked forward with immense delight, was invariably timed to include Easter and to last exactly six weeks. Visits to Balmoral took place from about the end of April until after Ascot Week. I was always chosen to accompany Her Majesty in the Spring and also had to go there for the last three or four weeks in the Autumn when the cold was intense and the days short and gloomy. Snow was not unusual in May and I can safely say I never remember a warm congenial day in the Highlands during the many months I spent there.

A certain monotony ruled our days wherever we were. Breakfast 9.30, lunch at 2, tea 5.30, dinner 8.30. The Queen's dinner was supposed to be 8.45 but it was often 9.15 before she sat down to her simple meal of soup, fish, cold sirloin of beef, sweet and dessert. Her favourite fruits were oranges and pears and monster indigestible apples which would have daunted most people half her age but she enjoyed them, sometimes sharing a mammoth specimen with Princess Beatrice, but more often coping with it alone. Oranges were treated in a very convenient manner; a hole cut in the top and the juice scooped out with a spoon. The Queen's dinner was timed to last exactly half an hour. The service was so rapid that a slow eater such as myself or Mr Gladstone never had time to finish even a most moderate helping. Pecking like a bird I usually managed to satisfy my hunger but could not enjoy the excellent fare handed so expeditiously. Campbell, the Queen's Piper in kilt, etc. dispensed the Claret or Sherry, Champagne was poured out by the butlers, while the Indian servants handed the Sweets in a cat-like manner, never forgetting which particular kind of chocolate or biscuit each guest preferred, so twisting the dish in order that it could be taken with apparent ease.

During the evening one or more of the Ladies-in-Waiting might be called upon to contribute some piano music or sing. Her Majesty was a very cultivated musician and a first-rate critic. On one occasion a lady of rank was a guest of the Queen and was accompanied by her daughter, a young lady who had just been appointed a Maid-of-Honour. The Queen asked the young lady to sing which she proceeded to do with fear and trembling. Her Majesty who knew the song well seemed much pleased but noticed the omission of a 'shake' written in the music. Turning to the older lady she said, 'Does not your daughter shake?' to which the mother replied, 'Yes, Ma'am, she is shaking all over.'

We nearly always dined in the Octagon Room panelled in white with oil portraits let into the panels, the Princess of Wales, etc., very rarely in the State Dining Room unless the numbers were large. The Household dined there as a rule and were able to feast their eyes on the monstrous silver Punch Bowl said to have been designed by Flaxman for George IV, and for which all the priceless silver tea and dinner services were melted down. The design is of clam shells and rocks festooned with sea-weed, the upper part Venus rises from the grapes and garlands of flowers.

Marie's essay ends here, but I add a story which I well remember her recounting, of a Duchess who was Mistress of the Robes, I forget which one, at the time when bustles were an adornment of ladies' costumes. They consisted, I believe, of a sort of horse-hair stuffed cushion, perched above a lady's behind under her skirt to give a kind of sham crinoline effect.

On the occasion in question the Ladies were all standing round in the Queen's Drawing Room after dinner, the Queen sitting in the middle when a Page, in modern language a footman, appeared with a large silver tray and on it a horse-hair bustle looking like a large sausage. He advanced to the Duchess respectfully and said, 'We found this on the floor, I believe it belongs to Your Grace.' The Duchess blushed furiously and said, 'Certainly not, nothing to do with me, take it away!' A few minutes later the Page re-appeared with the same object and in a loud voice said, 'Your Grace's maid says that it does belong to Your Grace.' The Queen thereupon burst into fits of laughter; the Duchess's remarks have not survived.

Marie describes how she came to be appointed a Maid of Honour at the end of 1887.

In September, 1887, the year of Queen Victoria's first Jubilee, I was about to set out with my brother, Charlie Adeane for my first visit to Italy when, a few days before starting from London, my mother received a letter from my Uncle Alick Yorke, from Balmoral (where he was acting as Groom in Waiting to Her Majesty), saying that he had been commanded by the Queen to sound my mother and me as to the possibility of my accepting the post of Maid of Honour. The Queen had been much put out because having recently appointed the Hon. Louisa Brownlow for her first Waiting and she had promptly announced that she was engaged to be married. This conduct was not very tactful. Miss Brownlow had only accepted the post about a couple of months before. She knew perfectly well what it entailed and that her engagement would cause considerable difficulty and flutter. The Queen had always been accustomed to have members of my family in her Household. My grandfather, Lord Hardwicke, had been a Lord in Waiting: my grandmother's brother, the Hon. Augustus Liddell, had, for many years, been one of her Equerries: my Uncle Eliot Yorke had been Equerry to the Duke of Edinburgh: my Uncle Alick, Equerry to Prince Leopold until his death, and afterwards Groom in Waiting to her Majesty. My mother, for a short period before her second marriage, was a Woman of the Bedchamber, which post she had to resign on her marriage. But the Queen had never seen me except at a Drawing Room when she could not have realised me at all. All she knew of me was from my uncle and one or two friends.

The conditions of service were four months (resident) Waiting in the year, proficiency in French and German, both reading and writing, good execution on the piano and facility in reading at sight, as one of my duties would be to play duets with Princess Beatrice in the evenings after dinner. The Maids of Honour were expected to ride in order to accompany the Princess when she went out. Above all there must be no shadow of any prospective engagement or incipient love affair.

This letter came as a perfect bombshell. Such an idea had never entered my brain. It was the last thing I wished or desired. I had never had any connection with the Court: I did not feel equal to cope with its difficulties and intrigues. Moreover my uncle intimated that the Queen would like my mother to bring me at once to Balmoral in order that she might see whether I was likely to suit her. Not an unreasonable request. Of course this would mean putting off my journey to Italy, and my brother declared that he would not wait for me even for a week, while I declared that nothing in the whole world would induce me to give up the pleasure which I had looked forward to all my life. My mother was extremely angry with me and frankly in despair. I was then 25 years of age, the eldest of a family of seven,[1] all of whom were at home and unmarried, and she thought this a most excellent and unique opportunity of spreading my wings and seeing something of life. But I was adamant. Nothing, in my opinion, could compensate for the loss of a journey with my beloved brother to the country of my dreams. After 24 hours of storming and weeping I persuaded my mother to write to my uncle explaining the situation, and I wrote to him myself putting my case frankly and fairly and saying that I felt sure he could persuade the Queen to understand my point of view,—that I did not for one moment under-rate the honour that was being bestowed upon me, but that I could not relinquish the dream of my life. The result far exceeded my wildest hopes. A telegram arrived saying the visit could be put off and Her Majesty would see me when she returned

[1] The seven were three Adeanes and four Biddulphs.

H.R.H. Princess Beatrice as Queen Elizabeth;
Osborne tableaux, 1888

Carmen tableau, Osborne 1888

L. to r.: Maj. Arthur Bigge, Hon. Minnie Cochrane, Prince Henry
of Battenberg, Hon. Harriet Phipps, Hon. Marie Adeane

to Windsor in November. My triumph was complete: my brother and I started on the appointed day, each armed with what we considered suitable literature. Mine was John Addington Symonds, Browning, Dante and 'Romola'. He despised this form of literature and armed himself with Murray's Guide and Boswell's 'Life of Johnson'! We started with a visit to a friend in Cadenabbia where we spent a blissful week, basking in sunshine and rowing on the lake, and then we proceeded to Milan. There I found a budget of letters including one from the Duchess of Buccleuch, Mistress of the Robes, formally offering me, from Her Majesty, the post of Maid of Honour. She said Her Majesty had come to the conclusion, from all that she had heard, that I should suit her, that she quite understood my feelings regarding my journey with my brother, and that she felt there was no reason for hesitating any longer about my appointment. The Duchess added, 'Please send me your reply as soon as possible, and in terms which can be submitted to Her Majesty.'

This was another awful bombshell—even worse than the last. I had no one but my brother to consult, and on the whole I felt rather inclined to shirk the responsibility, but we both agreed that my mother would be furious if I declined, and also that it would be exceedingly ungrateful to my uncle who had done so much for me. We at once set to work, in the hotel sitting-room, to compose a suitable document, and at first we drew largely on the style of Dr. Johnson, and composed a most pompous epistle, redolent of the 18th century and absolutely unsuitable to the occasion! After tearing up dozens of these effusions I eventually fell back upon a less stilted style and decided to treat the Duchess of Buccleuch as if she was my grandmother, but not until after two sleepless nights was the fateful missive despatched, and after writing to my family we decided to banish all thoughts of the future and to enjoy the beauties of Italy.

Marie's letter to the Duchess of Buccleuch survives in the Royal
c

Archives at Windsor.

HOTEL DE LA VILLE, MILAN. *September 22nd 1887*

Dear Duchess of Buccleuch

In acknowledgement of your letter which reached me this morning I can only say that I am most sensible of the honour Her Majesty has conferred upon me, in offering me the appointment of Maid of Honour, which I accept with a deep sense of gratitude. I do not know in what way it would be proper for me to convey my thanks to Her Majesty for the kindness she has so graciously bestowed upon me; but, I would say, that I will do all that lies in my power to serve with love and respect, one who has conferred such favours upon me.

Believe me dear Duchess
Yours ever truly
Marie C. Adeane.

RA. C71/92

Shortly afterwards Marie's mother received the following letter from the Queen.

September 30th 1887

Dear Lady Elizabeth,

I have to thank you for a kind letter and seize this opportunity of expressing my satisfaction at the prospect of having your daughter in my Household. It is a pleasure to have a grand daughter and niece of those whom I have known so long and for whom I had so sincere a regard in my service and I have besides a charming account of Marie. When I return south I hope you will bring her to Windsor for me to make her acquaintance. We are pleased to have your brother Alick, who is always pleasant and very useful here.

Believe me always
Yours
affectly
V.R.I.

Marie's account continues:

November came, and with it the expected summons to Windsor, but I was not to go on probation. Everything was settled: nothing remained but that my appointment should be gazetted. My mother provided a very smart new dress—I think it was white—and we proceeded by an afternoon train to Windsor where we were to dine and sleep. The Lady in Waiting was Lady Waterpark—fortunately a friend of my mother's. Lady Ely, the Queen's favourite Lady in Waiting, and Miss Ethel Cadogan, Maid of Honour, were the only members of the Household with whom we were at all acquainted. Being of a very nervous temperament, by the time the summons to dinner arrived, I was shaking in every limb. Dinner was nominally at a quarter to nine, but before that time my mother and I were waiting in the corridor with the other guests for the Queen to appear. She walked in from her private apartments and I hardly had time to realize what was happening before she beckoned to Lady Ely to bring me forward, and, as I curtsied to the ground, she gave me her hand to kiss, then kissed me most affectionately on my cheek, and pinned the Maid of Honour badge—a miniature of herself in her early days, surrounded by diamonds and mounted on a ribbon bow, the same texture and colour as the ribbon of the Order of the Bath—on my left shoulder.

CHAPTER II

OSBORNE THEATRICALS

First and Second Waitings

To Lady Elizabeth Biddulph

OSBORNE. *December 22nd 1887*

I made a very good journey though a slow one for the London train was three-quarters of an hour late, and of course the boat had to wait for it. A huge royal footman met me at the Cowes pier and looked straight over my humble head till I meekly suggested that I was Miss Adeane, whereupon he seized my bag and whisked me off to a royal Brougham which speedily deposited me here, the Housekeeper in black kid gloves greeted me most kindly and showed me my room, and very soon Miss Phipps appeared and carried me off to tea, and she and Lady Churchill[1] were most kind and I am sure I shall soon feel quite at home with them. I dine with the Queen tonight and perhaps wear my white garment. I hope the meal won't be quite as formidable as the one at Windsor, but I feel lost without you to look to.

OSBORNE. *December 27th 1887*

I had a very 'mauvais moment' last night; Harriet and I dined with the Household and worn out with standing around the inevitable Christmas tree for hours after tea we were toasting our toes after dinner and chaffing Mrs. Moreton,[2] thinking we were quite safe for the evening, when suddenly Prince Henry[3] appeared and after announcing that the ladies were to go to the Drawing

[1] Jane, wife of 2nd Baron Churchill; a Lady of the Bedchamber. Born 1826.

[2] Mrs Janie Moreton, *née* Ralli, wife of Hon. R. Moreton. Lady of the Bedchamber to the Duchess of Albany.

[3] Prince Henry of Battenberg, husband of Princess Beatrice, the Queen's youngest daughter.

Room the Prince came up to me and said: 'You are to sing.' I turned pea-green and stammered: 'I really can't, Sir', and with much confusion explained that I was prepared to play but that my voice was feeble and that I never sang in public; it was alarming but I think I was right for without any one to accompany and shaking with fright I should have broken down to a certainty; so he told the Queen and I was let off; however, I had to read a horrid duet with Princess Beatrice, the Queen sitting close by; I believe I got through it pretty well but I could hardly see the notes and simply prayed for the end. I suppose these horrible sensations will wear off in time and of course, being ordered to do a thing is far better than being asked. We were dismissed about eleven and then the Duchess of Albany called me back and said I really must fetch my music and sing to her as she was quite alone with Mrs. Moreton; she was such a dear and so un-stiff, that I did not feel quite so nervous and got through 'The Better Land' and the 'Chanson de Florian' without a breakdown, and she was so pleased that she begged me to get all my songs and sing to her as often as possible. . . .

I have just returned from driving in the open coach or charabanc in which Prince Henry drives his team. I sat behind the Prince and Princess with Lord Lorne,[1] who is most kind and talked the whole of the time but the cold was bitter, wind north-east, and freezing hard. We shall have skating tomorrow.

To her step-sister, Edith Biddulph

OSBORNE. *January 1st 1888*

The most annoying part of this life is that mere nothings are shrouded in deep mystery, and one never knows what is going to happen till a few minutes before it comes off; I suppose one gets accustomed to it in time, but at first it is most tiresome. We had rather a gay evening yesterday. The Maharajah of Kuch Behar dined with the Queen and a very good band came from

---

[1] John, Marquess of Lorne, heir to the Duke of Argyll, and husband of Princess Louise, fourth daughter of the Queen. Later 9th Duke of Argyll.

Portsmouth to enliven the feast. I dined with the household, but at ten we all marched into the drawing room and were stared at as usual till ¼ to 11, when the Queen having been safely seen upstairs, we adjourned to the council room and danced on a carpet! to the sound of a piano mecanique turned alternately by the Duchess of Albany and Col. Carington.[1] It really was very comical, Prince Henry [*of Battenberg*] got tremendously excited and pranced about all over the place, he nearly whirled me off my legs, for he dances in the German fashion and plunges horribly. At 5 minutes to 12 we all adjourned to an anteroom where we were supposed to partake of punch of an extremely potent character, I hid myself behind Lady Churchill and aided by Canon Duckworth[2] a staunch teetotaller I procured some lemonade, in spite however of my precautions Prince Henry espied me and enquired why I had no punch in my glass, I smirked and said I didn't like it, and so got out of my difficulty; after these potations we all became very merry and someone proposed ' consequences'; no sooner said than done, a quire of paper and fifteen pencils appeared as if by magic and we sat down round a huge table and were bidden to write whatever came into our heads, the results read out by Canon Duckworth were perfectly killing; needless to say we all came in for our share, the junior Maid of Honour not escaping and hiding her blushes behind a certain grey feather fan. I wish you had been there! At last about 1 o'clock breathless with laughter we retired to rest, having quite enjoyed ourselves, a somewhat rare event in these regions. . . .

We had early service in the house at 8.30 this morning. It was such a comfort and pleasure, but there was a good deal of mystery about it, as the Queen does not approve of people taking the Communion more than two or three times a year; she hardly ever does so herself. We had an apology for a service at 11—no lessons,

[1] Lt. Col. Hon. William Carington, Grenadier Guards. Equerry 1882–1901. Later Sir William.
[2] Rev. Robinson Duckworth, Canon of Westminster. Chaplain in Ordinary to the Queen.

psalms or prayers, only litany and hymns and a sermon from Canon Duckworth.

To Lady Elizabeth Biddulph

OSBORNE. *January 3rd 1888*

'Nunk' [*Alick Yorke*] got here at tea-time yesterday. He looks remarkably well and seems in remarkably good spirits but he does not relish being alone at Barton, a farmhouse where the Equerries and Grooms reside in lonely grandeur and live in mortal fear of rats and ghosts besides having to go some distance to their meals. Last evening I was summoned to warble duets with Prince Henry, fearfully difficult selections from Gounod's operas, which *he* knew *perfectly well* and which I was expected to sing at sight. I enacted the role of Juliet, Mireille, and I do not know what else while he shouted violent sentiments such as 'ange adorable'! at me and at one moment it was so comic that I nearly laughed outright; he has a good voice but cannot manage it and sings with very little expression. Princess Beatrice accompanied us and smiled benignly. We had Sir Robert Morier and the Duke of Norfolk at lunch today, the former seemed very cheery but has aged a good bit since I last saw him. The latter looks like the most insignificant of mechanics; of course he would not let out much about the Pope but he says Rome is so thronged that the streets are hardly passable.

OSBORNE. *January 6th 1888*

I feel more at home since Uncle Alick's arrival, and we are very busy getting up the 'tableau' which comes off tonight and will I hope be very successful. We had a full dress-rehearsal yesterday after tea and it all went well. The Princess looked so handsome as Queen Elizabeth and quite like a Holbein. You shall have a programme tomorrow which will give you all the details. I figure first as a Spanish Dancing Girl in 'Carmen' with very short petticoats and then as an Attendant Lady on Queen Elizabeth in flowing robes of a bright sky-blue, well bedizened with pearls! We are all to be photographed tomorrow by Byrne of Richmond so I shall have an interesting record of the Royal Revels on Twelfth Day, 1888.

'Nunks' is quite in his element and is a marvellous manager, thinking of everything and never getting into a fuss.

The programme of the Tableaux reveals that Tableau I represented 'the Queen of Sheba' with Princess Beatrice in the name part and Sir Henry Ponsonby as Solomon.

Tableau II—'Carmen' with Miss Minnie Cochrane, Lady in Waiting to Princess Beatrice, in the name part, Prince Henry of Battenberg as Toreador, Major Bigge (afterwards Lord Stamfordham) as Don José, and the Hon. Marie Adeane as Paquita, the Hon. Harriet Phipps as Mercedes.

The Tableau representing 'Queen Elizabeth and Raleigh' was performed by Princess Beatrice and her husband, Prince Henry, with the Hon. Alick Yorke as the Earl of Leicester.

OSBORNE. *January 11th 1888*

We have been enveloped in dense fog for four days and got no letters yesterday, as the steamers won't run in such dangerous weather. We have to go out just as usual but it is odious and even the Queen complains of the damp.

OSBORNE. *January 16th 1888*

I have just come in quite frozen from a one and a half hour drive with the Queen, the wind north-east and freezing hard and we went in at 5 p.m. Her Majesty was in excellent spirits and full of talk, she is never tired of asking questions about all of you and wanted to know if *you* were active and can still walk well. . . .

The Spanish Ambassador[1] and Mr Matthews, Home Secretary, were at lunch today; the latter has the face of an actor and a very ugly one too! He looks sharp but flighty. The Spanish Ambassador has a most grubby appearance and spat with complete sang-froid

[1] Don Cipriano del Mazo y Gheradi.

in the corridor to the horror of Sir John Cowell,[1] who was con-
ducting him to the Queen's Presence.

Soon after this Marie seems to have gone home and her next letter is
dated April 28th 1888 from Windsor Castle.

The Queen arrived here last night at half past eight looking as
fresh as a daisy and not a bit the worse for her long journey. A
few minutes later we were all summoned to dine with her,
imagine the despair of Lady Churchill and Harriet who had not
even a sponge unpacked and had just arranged to dine quietly in
their rooms being dead with fatigue; however there was no help
for it and they had to appear just as they were in their travelling
dresses and Princess Beatrice did likewise. Her Majesty was most
cheery at dinner and has fully enjoyed her trip abroad. She talked
and laughed incessantly and was full of all the interesting people
she had seen; she remarked that Bismarck was most gracious.
Meanwhile I can see that they have all resigned themselves to the
poor Emperor's[2] doom. Lady Churchill says that death was
clearly written on his face and it can only be a matter of a few
weeks, the Empress wept terribly at parting with the Queen, they
say she sees no-one and longs for sympathy which she has no
chance of finding in Germany where every hand is against her,
her sorrow must be too terrible!

WINDSOR CASTLE. *May 2nd 1888*
Lady Southampton[3] is most kind but her dullness is beyond
description, she never originates a remark. The gentlemen are
cheery but we never see them except in the evening when I am
usually required to play whist. It is such a blessing that I know the

[1] Major-General Sir John Cowell, Master of the Household, 1866–94, when
he died at Osborne.
[2] The Emperor Frederick of Germany was dying of cancer in the throat. The
Empress was the Queen's eldest child.
[3] Ismania Katherine, Dowager Baroness Southampton, daughter of W. Nugent.
Lady of the Bedchamber, 1878–1901.

important elements of that game . . . so many of the ladies do not play. . . .

The library is a great resource, I found my way there yesterday and looked at all sorts of admirable books. I hope to spend this afternoon looking at the drawings with Mr Holmes.[1] I want Violet[2] to come as she ought to see the Vandykes and the wonderful sketches of Raphael and Leonardo da Vinci. She may never get such another chance for they are not open to the public. . . .

The Queen comes to London on Tuesday for the performance at the Albert Hall and I suppose we shall stay till Thursday when I hope to get home straight from Buckingham Palace. I find I shall have to wear black feathers at the Drawing Room and black lappetts so that I shall present a hearse-like appearance. Can you lend me some black plumes for the occasion, if not I must write and order some? I have seen nothing of the Queen lately, I believe one never does here.

WINDSOR CASTLE. *May 11th 1888*

We had two hours work taking the Prince and Princess of Wales round the library and State Apartments this afternoon and at 7 p.m. we are to conduct them to the Kitchens. They are very nice and so easy to get on with, they took such an interest in everything, for they have hardly ever stayed here before except for a function. I dined with the Queen last night, a small 'hen' dinner but fairly cheery.

[1] Created Sir Richard Holmes on his retirement from being Librarian at Windsor.
[2] Violet was Marie's step-sister, daughter of Mr Michael Biddulph, M.P., by his first marriage to Miss Adelaide Peel. A good amateur artist, she never married, but was a great help and a devoted step-daughter to Lady Elizabeth.

CHAPTER III

ROYAL GUESTS

Third Waiting

OSBORNE. *August 7th 1888*

I hope to get down to Cowes for the first time this evening and may have the luck of seeing the yachts come in. I believe the place is very full, but I have not seen a soul. As to the Empress,[1] we never set eyes on her and I doubt if I shall ever have a chance of speaking to her or giving her your message. . . .

I have been playing lawn tennis this morning with Princess Alex and her Lady in Waiting; they can neither of them get a ball over the net so the game was not exhilarating, and the sun poured down on my head till I felt quite silly; the German Baron causes me some amusement, his English is extremely limited and peculiar but he insists upon speaking nothing else, and last night discoursed upon the merits of cows without 'corns', I suppose he meant 'horns'. He also talks of 'tennis robes' and evidently thinks me very vulgar for liking gooseberries.

OSBORNE. *August 12th 1888*

Lord Salisbury[2] arrived yesterday to present the new Italian Ambassador, Count Robillant who simply looks like a corpse, I never have seen such an object, not a vestige of colour anywhere, white hair and eyebrows and a greenish face, long attenuated

---

[1] The Empress Eugénie –*née* Countess of Montijo– was the widow of Napoleon III, Emperor of the French.

[2] Third Marquess of Salisbury, Prime Minister and Foreign Secretary. His second son, Lord Robert Cecil, became a distinguished M.P. and Cabinet Minister in World War I, and the great protagonist of the League of Nations. He *did* marry Lord Durham's sister. In later life he was created Viscount Cecil of Chelwood.

body and only one arm, he lost the other in 1849 at the Battle of Novara.

Dr Reid was fascinated by his appearance and said in all his experience he had never seen a living man so nearly resemble a dead one. I do not think he can live long yet he appears fairly strong. I dined with the Queen last night after driving with her in the afternoon, and sat between Count Robillant and Captain Lambton,[1] a brother of Lord Durham's, who commands the *Osborne*. He was most amusing and made me laugh rather *too* much. He did not seem very pleased at his sister's engagement to Lord Robert Cecil, and said Lord Salisbury is anxious to put off the marriage for a year, rather absurd as they are not too young and won't be any richer than they are now. The Queen leaves for Glasgow on the 21st so I shall be free.

Marie to Violet Biddulph, her step-sister

OSBORNE. *August 16th 1888*

At lunch yesterday I found myself seated opposite to the magnificent form of your Uncle Burnet [*a family name for Sir Robert Morier, the eminent diplomat.*] He was tucking in at lobster salad and looked quite at home: I believe he came here to interview the Queen and petition for more leave, and pleaded as an excuse his anxiety about Victor, which is *not* quite imaginary; a week ago he had tidings that the *Phoenix* had (as he expressed it) gone to the Devil! i.e. had been wrecked in the Yenisee not very far from Yenisusk (I can't spell these awful words) and that he had been obliged forthwith to raise £1,400, buy a new ship and despatch her to Wiggin's rescue; that intrepid tar is now at Varnoe in the north of Norway, and was thus able providentially to hear of the loss of the *Phoenix* and wait there for the new vessel; of course all this will delay the expedition at least a month, and meanwhile the danger from floating ice increases daily. Your Uncle was on the point of tears when he reached this part of his

---

[1] Captain The Hon. Hedworth Lambton; later became Admiral the Hon. Sir Hedworth Meux, having inherited a fortune and name from Lady Meux.

narrative, and was about to draw out his pocket-handkerchief when the Queen sent for him, and he at once assumed a jovial appearance, and I heard no more. . . .

I was summoned to play duets with the Princess, and had to go on board the *Alberta* with the Queen at 4.30. We went a very solemn little cruise to the Needles and got back at 7.30. The Empress came with us, she talked to me a little and made great enquiries after Mama, and has invited me to tea on Friday. You will be proud to hear that I have become a species of house-painter and decorator in ordinary to Her Majesty; she has bagged my chef-d'œuvre of daisies and poppies and I am now busily engaged in painting a bunch of heather by royal command; it is odiously difficult thing to tackle and I feel so nervous that I can hardly wield my hogshair! I have also been ordered to paint one of those horrid earthen pots for Prince Ernest of Hesse, I have no time at all to myself and have an awful pile of letters to answer.

Sir Robert Morier was at that time Ambassador at St Petersburg. It is an indication of how personal Her Majesty's Ambassadors were in those days that Morier should think of having to get the Queen's permission to extend his leave. There were, however, at that date only about eight Ambassadors, Ministers being accredited to all except the most important countries. Victor Morier returned all right from the Yenisei, but later died when quite young on a journey to South Africa.

OSBORNE. *August 17th 1888*
I have just come in (7.15 p.m.) from playing violent lawn tennis with Prince Ernest, so please excuse a shaky hand for I must scribble hard to catch the post.

I dined with the Empress [*Eugénie*] last night, Acting Lady in Waiting to Princess Beatrice and enjoyed myself very much. I was taken in by the Prince de Poix, son of the Duchesse de Mouchy, and Captain Fullerton sat the other side of me so I had a very pleasant dinner and plenty of chat. The Empress told me to give you a series of messages from her and said she should so like to see you again some day, and Madame Le Bréton did nothing but talk of you and said you were 'si charmante' and 'si intelligente' and that she quite longed for a glimpse of you so I really think you must try and see them all again some day. The Empress reminded me of the old days at Cowes and asked after Charlie and 'la petite Maud', who I informed her was 'petite' no longer. She is certainly a most fascinating woman so wonderfully graceful and those beautiful features will be the same to the end, but I so wish she would not paint her eyes and eyebrows. I went out walking with the Queen this morning, which is always a great pleasure as one can talk much more comfortably. She always asks for news of poor Aunt Mary[1] and Princess Beatrice thinks the Cravens behave abominably to you and to their poor mother.

I have been hard at work painting for everybody. Tosti has been here for three days giving lessons to Princess Beatrice and Princess Louise and he admired my flowers so much that he has promised to write a song specially for me and give me the manuscript if I will paint him a bunch; this is too good an offer to be refused and I must set to work as soon as possible.

F. Paolo Tosti, a Neapolitan composer of ballads and songs, was a familiar figure at Court, having during one of his early visits to London had the luck to sing before the Prince of Wales and attract his favourable attention. He settled in London for the last 30 years of his life and was constantly patronised by the Queen and later by Edward VII who made him an honorary K.C.V.O. His most famous song 'Goodbye' was sung in every fashionable drawing-room. There were also 'Te souviens-tu?' 'Si tu voulais', 'Napoli' and suchlike, which appear in the programmes of several of the Queen's private concerts referred to in Marie's letters. He became a kind of impresario for these concerts and gave himself great airs. He died during the first war.

[1] Mary, Countess Craven, was the sister of Lady Elizabeth Biddulph. A raving beauty, and scandalously promiscuous, she ended in great misery completely declassée and mad.

Marie appears to have gone on a holiday to Spain during the summer, but was back in waiting at Balmoral by the beginning of November.

BALMORAL. *November 2nd 1888*
I am to remain In Waiting till the end of this month and possibly even a little longer. The Empress Victoria is coming over and I suppose they want a few young people to entertain the Princesses.

I have been out walking with the Queen this morning relating all my Spanish experiences. She thinks you were most wise to let me go and advised me to travel as much as possible while I was young, but remarked that you must be wishing to have me at home now, which I confessed was the case.

BALMORAL. *November 3rd 1888*

Mr Biddulph had through Marie sent some of his Herefordshire apples to Balmoral.

I must send you a line to tell you that I dined with the Queen last night and beheld her peel and eat a Ledbury apple with evident relish and many expressions of admiration as to size, beauty and flavour. Her Majesty wished me to tell you how very much pleased she is with the fruit and I had to answer many questions on apple growing, etc. Presently the Queen said: 'I have never tasted Perry and only Cider once or twice in my life; do you think your mama will send me some?' Of course I replied in the affirmative and have written to Edith [*Marie's step-sister*] to ask her father to send some, just a bottle or two of each.

We leave for Windsor on the 15th but I think if it could be managed it would be better to send it here, and I expect the Queen would prefer it not too dry. I daresay you will send Mr. Biddulph a line to explain it all.

The weather is more dismal than ever and I drove with the Queen this afternoon in a pea-soup fog. . . .

I am very well and my cold is disappearing. The dear Queen

makes me wear a shawl all the evening as well as tulle over my shoulders and takes such care of me as you would.

BALMORAL. *November 6th 1888*

The weather is deplorable, it pours every day and we have some ado to get a little exercise between showers. I managed a walk yesterday with the 'Nunk' and we mean to try for another this morning. We went a chilly drive to the Garawalt yesterday, a fine waterfall which no doubt looks lovely on a fine hot day but which quite gave me the creeps in the gloom of semi-darkness of the pine forest. It is almost dark by four and yet that is about the hour we are able to go out and imitate the bats. Lord Knutsford[1] is here and is one of the most charming men I have ever met, so young for his age, so full of humour and possessed of such perfect and easy manners. The Queen evidently delights in him and talks to him a great deal. We did some 'willing' last night after dinner and after Uncle Alick had experimented on Ethel [*Cadogan*] the Queen wished me to try. I naturally shook with fright for as you know I have done nothing of the sort for ages; however I stoutly shut my eyes, made my mind as blank as possible and resigned myself. Fortunately it was a perfect success. I flew over all the company straight to Lord Knutsford and promptly unpinned his Jubilee Medal, which was exactly what I had been willed to do. The Queen was much impressed and also slightly mystified I think.

BALMORAL. *November 8th 1888*

The 'Nunk' is in great form. He shines tremendously when In Waiting and makes things so pleasant for all the Household suggesting walks and rides and always including the Ladies. Lord Knutsford has taken a great fancy to him and is full of his cleverness and good judgment. It did my heart good to hear him so much appreciated by a really clever man. As for the Queen, she

[1] Sir Henry Holland, Secretary of State for the Colonies, 1887-92. Created Viscount Knutsford.

Queen Victoria at Cimiez, 1890

The Household Staff, 1889 (?)

Standing l. to r.: ?, Harriet Phipps, Minnie Cochrane, ?, ?. *Sitting:* Dr J. Reid,
Sir Henry Ponsonby, Marie Adeane. *Foreground:* Alick Yorke, Maj. Arthur Bigge

invariably sends for him after dinner and we have comic songs, etc. Last night he did 'The Pigs', 'Sleepy Song' and most of his imitations, the evenings are really quite cheery and I am sure it does the Queen good to laugh. I exhibited my sketches and photos the evening before last and explained the Bull Fight at some length illustrating it with these little coloured pictures. I think Her Majesty thought me rather faint-hearted to have taken fright so soon and not to have seen the slaughter of one bull. We are just off to the Glasalt Shiel (12 o'clock) an easterly gale is blowing and I feel convinced it will be snow long before our return. I do not suppose we shall be home before dark.

BALMORAL. *November 11th 1888*

The Cider and Perry arrived yesterday and the Queen partook of both for lunch and thought them quite delicious but she preferred the Perry. Lord Knutsford left this morning much to everyone's regret. The Queen gave him the print of Angeli's picture and wrote him a charming letter; he is in high favour and well deserves to be so.

BALMORAL. *November 14th 1888*

The Queen has just given me a Balmoral Tartan Shawl and a very superior Cairn-gorm to fasten it with. I think I shall sport it at Ledbury and astonish the neighbours.

Marie Adeane to her step-sister Violet Biddulph

WINDSOR CASTLE. *November 16th 1888*

Your distinguished relative has safely passed through the manifold perils and luxuries of a Royal journey. She confesses that she felt thankful more than once that she does not belong to the more larky but eminently unsafe court of Russia, especially when the train gave a more violent lurch than usual.

My dear, I can't tell you how much food we were provided with. There were three large hampers stuffed with every kind of cold meat stuffed rolls, grouse, and enough cake and biscuits to

D

set up a baker's shop, then we had bottles of hot tea, cream, claret, sherry, seltzer water and finally champagne! But this was not evidently deemed sufficient to support life, so we had a hearty tea at Aberdeen, where royal footmen rushed about wildly with tea-kettles gazed at by a large crowd, and a huge dinner at Perth, with six courses, the table was beautifully decorated with orchids, which were pressed into our hands at parting, and at 11.30 p.m. on our arrival at Carlisle, we partook of tea and juicy muffins . . . I send you a paper of the train. Our names were painted on tin and hung on the doors of the carriages to prevent mistakes.

The Emperor Frederick of Germany, the Queen's son-in-law, had recently died after a reign of only a few weeks—ninety-nine days. The Empress came to visit her mother.

WINDSOR CASTLE. *November 19th 1888*

I came up in time to receive the poor Empress—it was too sad for words. She came with the Queen and the Princess of Wales and walked into the Hall quite listlessly and draped in crêpe and her face quite invisible, but I could see her trembling with grief. She shook hands with all of us and kissed Ethel and Lady Ely but never spoke a word. Then she pulled herself together and shook hands with each of the gentlemen before going upstairs. It must have been an awful effort for her! Poor thing. Her cup of sorrow is terribly full and this place must be so full of happy memories now all turned to pain.

CHAPTER IV

A ROYAL WEDDING

Fourth to Sixth Waitings

WINDSOR CASTLE. *May 26th 1889*
I sent my little picture in to the Queen last night and after dinner when we repaired to the corridor she was most kind and thanked me and seemed quite pleased with it. I gave her your messages and she enquired a great deal after Maud, Charlie and Madeline [*Marie's brother, Charles Adeane, had married Madeline, second daughter of the Hon. Percy Wyndham*]. Her Majesty then presented me to the Duchess of Edinburgh who also made many enquiries after the young couple and said she understood they were both charming. The Duke of Edinburgh[1] is better but has to be careful of the cold and dines at 7.30 with Princess Louise, who is also 'souffrante' with neuralgia.

Princess Beatrice is marvellously flourishing and the baby[2] very pretty with lots of soft brown hair and large blue eyes.

WINDSOR CASTLE. *Undated*
Today we have been pretty active welcoming and speeding parting Royal guests. The Princess Clementine,[3] an old cat with a gigantic ear trumpet, the Duc and Duchesse de Montpensier, the Duc and Duchesse de Chartres[4] and their daughter. They brought as suite a Spanish lady and gentleman, both bores of the

---

[1] The Duke of Edinburgh was the Queen's second son, Alfred (1844–1900), who later became Duke of Saxe-Coburg-Gotha; married to Grand Duchess Marie of Russia, daughter of Alexander II.

[2] Leopold, second son of Prince Henry and Princess Beatrice.

[3] Princess Clementine of Saxe-Coburg Gotha, wife of Prince Augustus.

[4] Robert, Duc de Chartres, son of the Duc de Joinville, and his wife Duchess Françoise.

first water, they lunched with us and I had to make French conversation with the man for over two mortal hours, my throat is still quite sore from the effort, mercifully I was able to recount my Spanish travels and hope to meet with a warm reception if ever I return to Seville. . . .

Antoine, Duc de Montpensier, was the youngest son of Louis-Philippe, King of the French. In 1846 he married the Infanta Maria Luisa, sister of Queen Isabella II of Spain. His eldest son may be the one mentioned here. His son, Don Antonio, married the Infanta Eulalia, daughter of Queen Isabella of Spain. Their eldest son Infante Don Alfonso of Bourbon-Orleans married Princess Beatrice, youngest daughter of Alfred Duke of Edinburgh in 1909. This delightful and talented Princess died in 1966 at the age of 82. Don Alfonso still leads an active life on the Montpensier estate at Sanlucar de Barrameda near Jerez, having been the first Spaniard to obtain a pilot's certificate. After King Alfonso's abdication the Infante, as 'Mr Orleans' worked for years with the Ford motor company. He returned to take an active part in aviation during the Spanish civil war.

WINDSOR. *July 17th 1889*

We had a delightful concert about an hour this afternoon the performers being Albani[1] and the two De Reskes. They sang Lohengrin, Faust, Carmen and at the special desire of the dear Queen 'Parigi, O Caro' which I can still remember dear Grannie humming to herself. I have heard no finer singing and they modulated their voices so wonderfully but they were not a bit too loud for the Drawing Room though they had wished to sing in St. George's Chapel. There was no audience beyond the Household. . . .

[1] Madame Albani was a celebrated singer of opera and oratorio. She was in great favour at Court. Married Mr Gye, a director of Covent Garden Opera. Their son, Ernest Gye, was a diplomat and for a time Consul-General at Tangier.

Jean de Reske was the most celebrated operatic tenor of his day. His brother was rather less well known.

This letter describes the Earl of Fife's wedding to Princess Louise, eldest daughter of the Prince of Wales. He was created Duke of Fife on his marriage, which took place in the chapel of Buckingham Palace.

OSBORNE. *July 28th 1889*

We did not get home from the Opera on Friday night till 12.30 and my rest was somewhat disturbed by reminiscences of Lord Randolph's speech on the Royal Grants and all the most thrilling scenes from Die Meistersinger until at last I distinctly heard Jean de Reske chanting an Ode on the Civil List instead of the Wagnerian 'Prize Song'. At this juncture I woke in a rage and found it was 9 a.m. and as gloomy as November. I jumped out of bed and flew to the glass, I grant you it was vain but was I not to prance in my first procession and be photographed by rival artists and be criticised by rival Ladies in Waiting, and even approved or disapproved of by my Royal Mistress? Well, whether it was the atmosphere or the pleasure of seeing you or the effects of the 'Music of the Future' I must confess I did not look my best, however I pinned my faith on breakfast and my new gown and clothing myself hurried down to breakfast. Downstairs there was a general atmosphere of red cloth and 'lilium auratum' and we were bidden not to linger over our meal as the room must be aired and decorated for the Procession to pass through. After a peep at the Chapel where Princess Beatrice was putting the finishing touches to the decoration we hurried off to dress, which terrible process occupied a whole hour at the end of which time Caroline was quite triumphant and I think even your critical eye would have been satisfied. My hair was curled and crinkled and rolled up in the newest style and adorned with gold braid to match my white and gold dress which fitted perfectly and looked very smart, my precious emeralds were as usual most useful and I sailed down fairly satisfied with my appearance and simply longing for one of my own people to give me an approving nod. The Household assembled in the room adjoining the Bow Room so we had a good look on the Royalties while we were all waiting and Princess Mary[1] plunged forward and embraced me, which was kind but so embarrassing. She looked very handsome but rather like a large purple plush pincushion. Princess Louise was lovely and Princess Frederica[2] in a sort of mediaeval costume towered above them all.

The dear Queen looked so well and her costume was not too mournful, black and silver brocade with a good deal of white about it and a diamond and pearl crown on her head, she seemed quite to enjoy the bustle and excitement. The Princess of Wales looked as usual much younger than the Bride but rather tired. About 12 the Procession was formed and we all started off at a slow and solemn pace through several rooms in one of which were about eighty privileged spectators, I noticed Ethel Cadogan, Rachel Gurney and Margot Tennant[3] in the front row, at last we reached the Chapel which really looked better than one had expected, the little pillars were wreathed and festooned with ivy and white roses, and huge palms sprouted from the alabaster pulpit which not being available for any other purpose was used as a gigantic 'cache pot' by the Prince of Wales' express desire. The congregation were all provided with seats but mine was taken from me for the Prince of Wales so during prayers I had to fall down upon both knees to the imminent risk of my new gown and the intense amusement of my friends. However the ceremony was not lengthy, both the Bride and Bridegroom's responses seemed inaudible and the latter lost his way in the 'Have and to hold' sentence so the Archbishop had to repeat it, there was also a good deal of fumbling with the ring but there were no tears and very little agitation. I thought the bridesmaid's dresses quite hideous and most unbecoming, even Princess May did not look as pretty as usual, and the bouquets were very small and not the least artistic.

[1] Princess Mary Adelaide, Duchess of Teck. Mother of the future Queen Mary, who is referred to below as Princess May.

[2] Princess Frederica of Hanover. Married Baron von Pawel Rammingen.

[3] Daughter of Sir Charles Tennant. m. H. H. Asquith, the future Prime Minister, who later became Earl of Oxford and Asquith.

Princess Louise looked her very best and her gown was lovely very simple and graceful, her manner so charming too. After signing the Register she shook hands with everyone and simply beamed with joy. Miss Knollys says there never was anyone more in love and it is quite a romance. I must say Lord Fife looks a nice man and he behaved very well, his manner to the Queen being particularly good. He provided a splendid coach with gorgeous footmen in green and silver livery and carried off his bride in great style. I went down to the door and saw the very last of them, the cheering so tremendous I could still hear it a quarter of an hour after their departure.

I think the only amusing incident was due as usual to Mrs. Gladstone. She lay in wait for the Bride and drawing her very seriously aside said, 'I have Lord Fife's permission, ma'am,' and embraced her to the surprise of those standing near. You will be glad to hear that the old sapphire-blue did not appear and Mrs. G. was resplendent in maroon satin trimmed with gold, her wedding veil adorned her head and many were the touching allusions to which she treated her friends.

I never sat down from 11.30 a.m. till 3 p.m., when I tore off my wedding garments and put on morning dress for Marlborough House, where I rushed with Evelyn Paget in the hope of seeing the presents, however the crowd was so great that we found it impossible so we contented ourselves with exchanging a few words with some of our friends and returned to the Palace in time to start on our return journey [*to Osborne*] at 3.50 p.m.

The weather cleared up and we had a lovely passage, all the ships fired salutes as we passed along the line and it was every bit as good as the Review will be on Saturday. . . .

BALMORAL. *October 24th 1889*

We had a great treat last night, Madame Janotha who was appearing in the neighbourhood came and played to the Queen after dinner. I wished her programme had been a little more classical but the Queen is fond of rather second-rate pieces and we only had one piece of Schumann, Scherzo and Berceuse of Chopin, the two latter were marvellously played. . . .

I am in despair about my clothes, no sooner have I rigged myself out with good tweeds than we are plunged into the deepest mourning for the King of Portugal [*Louis I*], jet ornaments for six weeks! And he was only a first cousin once removed. So I only possess one warm black dress; the Sunday one is far from thick, it is a lesson *never, never* to buy anything but black!

Natalia Janotha, born 1856 in Warsaw, died in the Hague 1932, of German origin and her father was Paderewski's teacher. She started as a child prodigy and completed her education as a pianist under Clara Schumann. She became one of the foremost pianists of her generation, played before three successive German Emperors, and for Queen Victoria and Edward VII. She specialized in Chopin and wrote a book about him. Being a German Court pianist she was expelled from England in 1916 and lived the rest of her life at The Hague. She composed a few minor works.

BALMORAL. *October 25th 1889*

There has been much commotion in the House for the Queen heard yesterday of Freddie Fitzroy's[1] engagement to Mr. Crutchley and does not relish the idea of losing one of her favourite Maids of Honour. I believe the stereotyped phrase is '*most* unnecessary'. There have been rumours of this romance for many years but it tarried so long that at last no-one believed in it so it has fallen as rather a blow. I have just come in from a long walk with the Queen, which I always enjoy; one can talk so much more easily and we conversed on many topics, Father Damien and Bradlaugh amongst others.

BALMORAL. *October 28th 1889*

The grapes have not yet turned up but perhaps they will come by second post today. I told Sir Henry about them and I am sure

1 Hon. Frederica Fitzroy, d. of 3rd Lord Southampton. m. Percy Crutchley, 1890.

the Queen will enjoy them. They grow them at Windsor so entirely for quantity and not quality that one never sees a decent looking bunch at table.

My cold is better but this climate which combines damp and cold is deadly for anyone with a circulation like mine and I am never really warm except in bed.

Lady Downe[1] has also got a cold and the poor old Duke of Rutland[2] an ordinary chill so we are quite like a hospital and the dear Queen is in rather a fright about the Zanzibar Envoys one of whom is sixty-three and the other seventy-five and fears they may catch chills too! I think she is at last beginning to realize that we are all mortal and not utterly impervious to cold.

BALMORAL. *October 30th 1889*

The Zanzibar Envoys were very funny yesterday, they talked Arabic and presented the Queen with a gigantic letter sealed with a Golden Seal the size one usually sees in a pantomime. They told us they enjoyed the sights of London especially the Fire Brigade which they say is a sign of good Government. They ate their curry very awkwardly. I could see they were dying to fling aside the knives and forks and use their brown fingers. They brought no presents with them which was a disappointment.

The grapes have never turned up.

BALMORAL. *November 1st 1889*

The grapes arrived safely and in first-rate condition yesterday and were beautifully arranged on a golden platter and duly presented to the Queen at lunch. Her Majesty ordered the bunch to be weighed before she touched it. The weight was 5 lbs. at which there was great astonishment and when I dined with the Queen and they re-appeared praise was simply lavished on them and I was told to thank you and Mr. Biddulph for so kindly thinking of sending them, etc. In fact no present could have been more

---

[1] Lady of the Bedchamber, 1889–1901. Succeeded Lady Ely.
[2] 7th Duke. Chancellor of the Duchy of Lancaster, 1886–92.

appreciated, and no-one likes little attentions better than the Queen, so you may be more than satisfied. . . .

BALMORAL. November 7th 1889

I have very little to tell you except that Mr. Ritchie[1] is here and that I do not take a fancy to him. He may be clever but he is very vulgar and unrefined in all his ways, in short he has not the manners of a gentleman and I wonder how the Queen tolerates him. He lifts up his loud voice at dinner and shouts under her very nose and last night I heard him deliver a lecture on Socialism to Her Majesty which I could easily perceive was not relished. I think it will be rather a relief when he takes his departure on Monday. . . .

Prince Henry is off tomorrow on a four-month yachting trip to Corfu and next to Albania where he expects to get plenty of sport, woodcock, wild boar, etc. He is in the highest spirits just like a boy going home for the holidays but poor Princess Beatrice daily appears with red and swollen eyes and we all dread tomorrow, I think she will dissolve when she finally bids him 'Goodbye'. I am so sorry for her, she will be lonely and her children are not much to her as yet. I am sure she sometimes longs for liberty. I went on a huge drive with the Queen yesterday, thirty-four miles to the Linn of Dee. It was dull and we got quite chilly sitting so long bolt upright in one position but the Queen was wonderful, not a bit tired and as brisk as a bee all the evening, I wish I might think I shall be like her at 70. . . .

BALMORAL. November 8th 1889

We trotted behind the Queen's chair to the Prince Consort's Cairn this morning, a tremendous climb, I feel rather limp in consequence but the view was splendid! The Queen asked particularly after Charlie and Madeline and wished to know the baby's name. When I said Pamela she said, 'Of course, because of

---

[1] Later the 1st Lord Ritchie of Dundee. He was President of the Local Government Board and finally Chancellor of the Exchequer in Mr Balfour's Government.

Lady Edward Fitzgerald', and then said she well remembered seeing her, for of course Lady E.F. was then quite old and no longer beautiful. Is it not wonderful she should have such a memory and take such an interest in all one's belongings? She asked after Uncle Johnnie, Aunt Edie and Aunt G. B. the other day and frequently refers to Aunt Nety[1] and every few days she asks of the news I have of you. It sounds trivial but these are the little things that make one love the Queen. Her interest is *real* and not the least put on.

BALMORAL. *November 11th 1889*
I went for a long walk with the Queen this morning and felt very tired after it. It is no'joke trotting up these mountains after a chair drawn by the most stalwart of ponies at the rate of at least 4 miles per hour! We were out from 11.20 to 1.10. Mr. Ritchie has left, I got to like him better, he is a very rough diamond but most kind-hearted and ready to do anything to benefit the poor.

BALMORAL. *November 19th 1889*
The Queen gave me some beautiful lace yesterday. I think it is Irish hand-made and a good pattern, there are several yards of it, plenty to garnish an elegant evening dress. Her Majesty was so pleased to hear that Uncle Alick was so near on his way home. I think she thought him a little faint-hearted not to have had a little glimpse of Colombo and India. . . .
The Queen has this moment sent me a tiny photo of herself framed with the message that I can always keep it on my table. Isn't it sweet of her?

WINDSOR CASTLE. *February 1890*
I have just heard that you and Mr. Biddulph are invited to dine and sleep on Tuesday. Remind him he must wear tights. . . .
Sunday.
I drove with the Queen this afternoon and Her Majesty spoke

[1] They were all sisters and brothers of Marie's mother.

of Mr. Biddulph being possibly prevented from coming on Tuesday and said of course he could not miss a Division. Her Majesty wished me to say that if the Division was likely to take place late he might still dine and go back to London by the 10.38 p.m. train which reaches Waterloo at 11.46 p.m. She says it has often been done before and successfully. However I hope he has found a pair. We have just been hearing some music in St. George's Chapel by Herr Kreisler one of Joachim's best pupils who has been playing the violin accompanied by Mr. Parratt[1] on the organ, Handel's 'Largo', the 'Romance' of Beethoven, a Concerto by Bach, etc. Last night we had an evening party and the Queen's private band played a delightful Suite by Grieg, Wagner's Rienzi, etc., quite a modern programme.

WINDSOR CASTLE. *March 2nd 1890*

We have gone back to mid-winter, snow and bitter north-east wind; the Queen goes out in an open carriage just the same and does not seem to mind it. I drove with Her Majesty yesterday morning in a Victoria, it snowed hard the whole time. . . .

BALMORAL. *May 26th 1890*

Uncle Alick and I both feel very low and we think it must be the East wind and sudden change from July to December which took place yesterday. We drove this afternoon or rather evening, for we never get our orders before 4.30, to the Gelder Shiel where we had tea and got as far as we could. It was a Household party and therefore rather cheery but all our wonderful wraps could not keep out the biting wind and your astrakhan collarette was much envied. Prince Henry is off tomorrow to join his beloved *Sheila* for a cruise to the Scillies I see so that the party will be more reduced and duller than ever. The seven children take up every spare corner and we have no possibility of any piano. The oil paints to which I am driven as my sole occupation make my bedroom stuffy not to say smelly.

[1] Later Sir Walter Parratt, Master of the Queen's Musick.

The Ladies in Waiting on Princess Henry of Prussia are very dull and by no means easy to get on with. I air my German to them for it is the only thing that makes them laugh. They are no addition to the party!

I have had no duty of any sort to do except the answering of sundry epistles congratulating the Queen on her birthday. Her Majesty gave me a new photo of herself taken at Aix and a pair of little German glasses in remembrance of the day. She is looking very well and young and has adopted a much more becoming cap for evening wear.

BALMORAL. *June 12th 1890*

Putting grumbling aside the life here is utterly dull, we see nothing of the Queen except at dinner on alternate nights, we have *no* duties to perform to occupy our minds and the weather is horribly cold and wet. At the same time it is impossible to settle to anything on account of interruptions. We just exist from meal to meal and do our best to kill time.

The Queen is very sad about poor Lady Ely though she quite realised how near the end was and how undesirable it would have been to have lingered on, yet the final telegram was a shock and she cried bitterly.

We had a ladies' dinner last night and the Queen wore jet and hardly uttered. She was a little more cheerful this morning and asked a great deal after you and all the sisters. We journey south about the 20th. I believe the Duke of Connaught arrives on the 22nd.

BALMORAL. *June 14th 1890*

First painting for the Princess (she begins things and gets me to finish them off) but do not repeat this; then trotting for an hour beside the Queen, who to my intense astonishment ascended a huge ladder in order to mount a horse twenty-six years old, which pranced along quite gaily, only conceive what energy at seventy-one! Then at 3 p.m. more painting and 4.30 a drive of at least twenty-four miles with the Queen. We were not in till 8, and the wind was so cold my face turned first blue and then crimson and by dinner-time I looked as if I had been drinking hard for a week. All these last days the talk has run continually on Kensal Green 'worms and epitaphs' and most meals have been funereal, of course this is quite natural for the Queen was devoted to poor Lady Ely. Her Majesty says that if she had been at Windsor she would have gone to the funeral.

CHAPTER V

ENGAGEMENT TO BERNARD MALLET

Seventh Waiting

The following letter contains the first mention of my father. He had followed Marie and her mother to Venice in the autumn of 1890, and had been most attentive. 'He was perfectly charming,' she wrote to her step-sister, 'and spent all his time with us.'

OSBORNE. *January 18th 1891*

I made as good a journey yesterday as I could expect under the circumstances for the cold was vile and I had no less than five changes! However I was by no means dull, we were a large and cheery party up to Swindon and Mr. Mallet was most kind afterwards and made himself so agreeable that the time passed very quickly. He took such care of my luggage that he managed to lose most of his own and he was put down at Micheldever Station in possession of one small bag containing a shooting suit and a pair of evening shoes, one collar and his Sunday hat! He is not afflicted with a large share of personal vanity but I think he felt somewhat depressed at the idea of appearing at a large and fashionable dinner[1] in the chocolate tweed attire in which he had travelled all day. . . .

The House is as full as possible for the Christians are here 'en masse' and Aribert[2] the youthful lover is being shown to his new relatives. He really is extremely good looking even for a Prince, tall and slim with a sufficiency of chin in spite of the libel in last

---

[1] At Stratton, Lord Northbrook's house in Hampshire.
[2] This prince married Princess Marie-Louise, daughter of 'the Christians' and turned out a thorough bad hat. The marriage was annulled. *My Memories of Six Reigns* (Evans, 1956), by Princess Marie-Louise gives the full story.

week's 'Illustrated London News' and they seem very happy and are to be married in July. . . .

The dear Queen is looking so well, she kissed me last night and asked after you and all at home, I always feel more loyal every time I see her. The House is fairly warm but the Drawing Room so 'Siberian' and I came to bed chilled to the bone and generally depressed.

OSBORNE. *January 24th 1891*

Existence here just now is very deadly, the weather is so awful we cannot even go out. The place is swarming with Relatives and so we have no duties whatever to perform. . . .

We relapsed into jet today for the poor young Count [*of Hanover?*] and I am rather hard up for attire having only one deep black garment with me.

Princess Louise has just arrived, she is fascinating but oh, so ill-natured I positively dread talking to her, not a soul escapes.

Some time between January and March 1891 my mother became engaged to my father. Bernard Mallet was then a civil servant working in the Treasury. He had little money beyond his official salary and as Marie was also not well off she had to contend with a certain amount of questioning from her mother. It was considered in those days that £1,200 per annum (which would nowadays, I suppose, be equivalent to £4,000) was not very much for a young couple to start on. The Mallets were descended from Mallet du Pan, the famous journalist from Geneva who did much to form moderate opinion during the French Revolution and whose advocacy of a limited form of monarchy for France on the English pattern got him into such trouble with the Jacobins that eventually he had to flee to England. His son, John Louis Mallet, was eventually given a job in the Audit Office. His grandson, who became Sir Louis Mallet was a most distinguished civil servant who helped, when Permanent Under-Secretary at the Board of Trade, to negotiate the 'Cobden' Treaty, and afterwards became Under-Secretary of State for India. Sir Louis married Frances Pellew, a great-grand-daughter of Lord Exmouth

Bernard Mallet, about 1890

Marie, April 1891, engaged to Bernard Mallet

who had been one of Nelson's great frigate captains and in 1816 com-
manded the Mediterranean Fleet which bombarded and captured Algiers
and finally destroyed the power of the Barbary pirates, who had for
centuries plagued the Mediterranean. My father, Bernard Mallet, after a
successful career at Balliol under Jowett, passed into the Foreign Office,
but when his younger brother, Louis, also did the same, Bernard decided
to move across to the Treasury.

There was a good deal of trepidation as to how the Queen would take
Marie's engagement as she was known to consider the marriages of her
Maids of Honour as a form of desertion. In March, 1891, the Queen and
her small Court embarked in the Royal Yacht to cross the Channel and
proceed by train to the South of France, where they arrived on March 25th
and settled down in the Grand Hotel at Grasse. The following letters to
her mother describe Marie's stay there.

To Lady Elizabeth Biddulph

CHERBOURG. *March 23rd 1891*
We have had a splendid passage, both sea and sky more like
the Mediterranean than the English Channel. I sat on the bridge
nearly the whole of the time and enjoyed myself as much as was
consistent with a headache and a bad attack of homesickness! . . .

Harriet told the Queen last night that I hope to be married
about the end of the Season and Her Majesty was most kind and
said she should speak to me herself later on. The Empress
[*Frederick*] was perfectly charming this morning, she kissed me
twice and wished me every sort of happiness. She said she should
so like to see you for a few minutes during her stay in London.

I have already been for a long tramp through Cherbourg with
Princess Beatrice and her spouse and written eight telegrams for
the Queen and now I must change my dress for dinner.

GRAND HOTEL, GRASSE. *March 26th 1891*
We arrived safely yesterday after a most luxurious journey. I
need hardly tell you the Queen was less tired than any of us,
looked as fresh as a daisy and beamed upon all the Grasse officials

who met her at the Station. They gave her a most cordial reception, we drove about half an hour at a foot-pace up to this Hotel, along streets lined with people clapping their hands and shouting 'Vive la Reine d'Angleterre' with the greatest enthusiasm. The view from my window is quite ideal, the lovely old town lies straight before me with a background of blue hills and the still bluer sea in the far distance. There are, however, two 'contretemps' more or less tiresome if not serious; first there is smallpox in the town, though solely in the slummy part of it, and Dr. Reid insists upon vaccinating everyone he can lay his hands upon. I am to fall a victim this evening and it is a horrid bore. . . . Secondly Prince Henry, after being very seedy all through the journey, has developed the measles! Though if it were one of us we should be banished to the local hospital, infection in his case is utterly ignored and Princess Beatrice refuses to hang up a carbolic sheet because she declares it will make a horrid smell! Lady Churchill and I live on the same floor and in the same corridor as the invalid and I run every chance of again falling a victim to my favourite disease. No precautions have been taken and the whole thing is treated as a joke.

GRAND HOTEL, GRASSE. *Good Friday, 1891*

The Queen has been so dear about my marriage, she could not have been any kinder if I had been her own daughter. She said, 'I am so sorry for your mother!' I must tell you some day of the delightful things she says about our family. . . . The mistral is raging today and the hotel positively rocks with the violence of the gale. Nevertheless we drove for two hours with the Queen along a dusty road and returned as white as millers! . . .

I cannot help longing to go my own way and scramble among the olive trees and pick the wild flowers instead of trotting demurely in attendance behind the Queen's chair. I have a certain amount of writing to do and have just composed an account of our arrival for the Queen's Memorandum Book. I hope and trust it will pass muster. Poor Prince Henry is really quite ill and I do not expect he will be fit to leave his room for a fortnight. I rather hope he won't for it would be a horrid bore if he were to sow the measles about. I was badgered into being vaccinated last night, I believe it is a very unnecessary precaution and if I have a bad arm I shall be in a pretty fix for there is no possibility of resting a single moment. We went to church this morning, such a pretty little building only finished three weeks ago, and as the natives say, quite 'le style anglais' . . .

GRAND HOTEL, GRASSE. *April 2nd 1891*

I really have not one instant to myself and am for ever dawdling about waiting to be sent for. Even if I try to sketch or write or read, every ten minutes there is a knock at my door. I spend most of my time now sitting with Princess Beatrice while she paints, handing her brushes and colours and making myself generally useful. At three the old Emperor of Brazil arrived to pay his respects to the Queen and we were in attendance. That hideous Comtesse d'Eu came with him, also a grandson, Pierre de Saxe-Coburg. The Emperor is a most extraordinary looking old man with a piercing voice, very squeaky and quite cracked, an intelligent face entirely spoilt by the most appalling 'râtelier' I have ever seen. I expected every moment to see his teeth upon the floor. His Suite consisted of a middle-aged Comtesse and two men exactly like monkeys. The Brazilians must indeed be an ugly people.

The letters at this time constantly refer to illnesses. The measles apparently did not spread, but various courtiers and servants became ill and one of the messengers developed diphtheria. On top of this one of the Queen's house-maids died.

GRASSE. *April 10th 1891*

The poor house-maid has just breathed her last, it is all very sad and there is a gloom over us all. The Queen went to see her last night and again this afternoon about an hour before she died.

GRASSE. *April 10th 1891*

It is very curious to see how the Queen takes the keenest interest in death and all its horrors, our whole talk has been of coffins and winding sheets. We had a sort of funeral service last night in the Dining Room, the coffin in our midst not even screwed down, everyone in evening dress, the servants sobbing; it was too dreadful and got upon my nerves to such an extent that I never slept all night. The Queen was very grieved and placed a wreath on the coffin rather tremblingly; and then the body was removed to the little English church close by and this afternoon we had to visit it again with the Queen. The final funeral is tomorrow and after that we may hope for a little peace. Of course I admire the Queen for taking such a lively interest in her servants, but it is overdone in this sort of way and it is very trying for the Household. . . .

We went over the largest Perfumery with the Queen this morning and it was very interesting and I did my best to pick up bits of useful information. The work is light and the factory airy and extremely clean, they work ten hours a day and the women get 1 fr. 25 centimes a day and the men just double. Such a shame!

GRASSE. *April 23rd 1891*

I have had rather a bother with the Queen; I told Princess Beatrice to say that I hoped to be married early in July and this raised such a storm! The Queen wrote me a letter and accused me of inconsistency, etc., and told Lady Churchill she was terribly vexed; she expected me to stay on quite indefinitely and said *you* had promised I should, that I was so useful and just suited her and that she hated my leaving. All this is extremely flattering but somewhat inconvenient, and I spent rather a miserable time yesterday, but I do really love the Queen so much and it pains me to vex her but short of breaking off my engagement nothing would please her. So I must resign myself. I answered the Queen's letter at some length and explained the change of plans, saying you had now given your full consent to the wedding taking place earlier and indeed were anxious that it should do so and that in the first instance I had merely obeyed your wish that the time of the marriage should not be definitely fixed. Lady Churchill also calmed her down and this morning I got a most affectionate note saying all was now clearly understood and that Her Majesty often hoped to see me in the future. The Queen is really very reasonable when you can get at her but the odious practice of doing everything through a third person makes endless difficulties and misunderstandings. However, my mind is now at ease and I can only feel flattered that I shall be so much missed.

These are the Queen's letters:

GRASSE. *April 21st 1891*

Dear Marie,

Beatrice gave me your message that your mother now wishes your marriage to take place early in July. I cannot help saying how much this has surprised me, though Henrietta did tell me before we left that you thought your marriage would be earlier than *I* had hoped it would be; and when you wrote to me in February you said you *hoped* you would have 'many more Waitings', and now this will be the last!

You will easily understand that *this* has disappointed me *very much*. Of course nothing can be said and I fear I am less reconciled than ever to the prospect, and owe Mr. Mallet quite a grudge for carrying you off. However I can only repeat my sincere wishes for your happiness and I trust I may still sometimes see you.

Ever
Yours
Affectionately,
V.R.I.

GRASSE. *April 23rd 1891*

Dear Marie,

Many thanks for your two letters, I quite understand *now* the change in your plans and only regret that your means will for a time not be as good as they should be. I hope that we shall often see you and *not* 'at a distance', as you will be living in London so much and that your future husband will I trust not object to your coming to see us.

Ever
Yours
Affectionately,
V.R.I.

Marie's letters written to Bernard Mallet during the same period of Waiting complement the story of the visit to Grasse.

CHERBOURG. ROYAL YACHT. *March 23rd 1891*

The Empress Frederick was so kind to me last night and so full of sympathy, I wish you could have heard her speak of your father; she seemed so entirely to have appreciated his talents and said she was proud to have had him as a friend; she is now deep in your book[1] and has read about half, it interests her deeply and she seemed to find it quite easy to understand. How clever she is and how fascinating! Her faults are all on the surface and one entirely forgets them when in her presence. I wish you knew her, she so regrets not having met you at Venice. . . .

We left Windsor in a blizzard, amid gloomy prophecies and visions of trains snowed up, fogs at sea and many other horrors; to find on our arrival at Portsmouth brilliant sunshine, blue sea and calm weather. The Queen beamed with satisfaction and looked quite good in a black lace bonnet garnished with edelweiss. It took nearly half an hour to unload the train and stow away the innumerable retainers both black and white, who follow in our wake. The luggage seemed unequally divided, the whites having tons while the blacks carried all their worldly goods neatly tied up in a couple of pocket handkerchiefs. The cold was intense at first so we put on all our wraps and ate as much lunch as possible, then sat on deck under cover till 6, when we made this port and

---

[1] Probably *John Lewis Mallet* written by Bernard's father, Sir Louis Mallet and printed for private circulation in 1890 after his death. No doubt edited by Bernard.

moored close to the place from which the train starts tomorrow at 6.30.

Lady Churchill and I walked for an hour with Princess Beatrice and Prince Henry and explored some of the big slums of Cherbourg, then I wrote eight telegrams for the Queen. At 8.30 I dined with the Queen to the strains of the Marine Infantry Band who ended their programme with Mendelssohn's 'Wedding March', an endless source of chaff to my fellow servants who declared it was arranged in my honour and after sitting for an hour with the Queen we were released and told to rest well and rise early for the long journey. We begin at 9.50 tomorrow.

March 25th 1891

I spent about two hours alone with the Queen writing, reading to her and then talking. She was more wonderfully dear and kind than it would be possible to imagine. So anxious I should be thoroughly happy and have no worries, so keen to know all about you and your family, taking the liveliest interest about all I could tell her of your father, mother and brothers, even Mallet du Pan. She too alluded to your book and said the Empress had told her of it. In fact the Queen could not have been kinder or more affectionate had I been her own child and this great sympathy is what endears her to all who come within its scope for it is thoroughly genuine.

GRASSE. *March 28th 1891*

We drove to the Pont du Loup with the Queen yesterday afternoon, a glorious road with enchanting views on either side, but we were literally blinded by the dust and I still feel gritty all over. The wild flowers were lovely, I longed to stop the carriage and pick armfuls, one mossy hill was yellow with primroses and the orange trees looked so beautiful. The Queen was delighted, she enjoys everything as if she were 17 instead of 72. Last night she was laughing heartily at the extremely comic account of our arrival in the local newspaper. The English papers are nearly as bad for they describe Mrs. McDonald, the Queen's Dresser, as the Hon. Flora McDonald, and the head detective as Colonel Fraser. I figure in the French accounts as Lady Adeane.

GRASSE. *March 30th 1891*

At 9 a.m. I sallied forth with the Princess to walk along a dusty road for an hour; at 11 a.m. I pranced forth again to trot behind the Queen's donkey chair (thank goodness the beast is lazy and obstinate and refuses to be hurried!).

GRASSE. *March 31st 1891*

I cannot conceive why the Queen never catches cold, she is tremendously strong and will outlive us all. Old Duleep Singh drove here from Nice this afternoon to beg the Queen's forgiveness for all his misdeeds. The Queen said he was quite calm at first then wept bitterly imploring forgiveness and finally when she stroked his hand recovered his equanimity. No wonder! I believe he is a monster of the deepest dye and is treated far better than he deserves. . . .

I have to write an account of the 'bataille de fleurs' for the Queen, the Duchess of Rutland has already done one, but it is pronounced 'rather extraordinary'. She goes in for being poetical and talks of 'the fishless sea'.

Prince Duleep Singh (1837–98), a Sikh, became Maharajah of Lahore under the Regency of his mother but was deposed after two anti-British risings in 1849, taken into custody and deported to England, where he lived on a Government pension for the rest of his life and became a Christian. He was a famous game shot, as were his two sons, Prince Victor and Prince 'Freddie'. The former was a godson of the Queen and married a daughter of the 9th Earl of Coventry. The latter was a friend of my uncle Jack Cator and used to shoot with him at Woodbastwick, where I remember a rather portly, somewhat dusky, jovial sportsman. Duleep Singh was 'advised' by the Governor-General at the time of his deposition to present the famous Koh-i-noor diamond to the Queen: so he may be said to have earned his pension! I cannot imagine what 'misdeeds' Marie is referring to here, as he must have been long ago forgiven for the events of his childhood. Miss Lutyens ('Lady Lytton's Court Diary', p. 172), from whom I have gathered most of the above facts, does not mention misdeeds.

GRASSE. *April 1st 1891*

Our daily drives are beautiful as far as scenery goes but absolutely wanting in interest or incident, and yet I am expected to supply *both* in my descriptions, and messages arrive from the Queen, 'Why do you not mention the old woman on a mule or the brown goat with the tuft on its head', and I rack my poor brains in vain and feel desperate.

GRASSE. *April 3rd 1891*

Princess Beatrice is very anxious to be at our wedding and hopes it may take place before she leaves Windsor on the 17th July. I suppose we shall have to ask diverse Royalty to the ceremony. What a bore! Shall we follow the example of the Duke of Cambridge and be secretly married at St. Giles, Cripplegate?

GRASSE. *April 4th 1891*

I could quite imagine life here being very pleasant if one could wander through the streets and avenues and poke about quietly and bask in the sun like a lizard with a charming book or a pleasant companion, but Grasse à la Royale is not a toothsome dish! Some ancient Austrian Royalties have been here today, an Archduchess with grey frizzled hair and a face like a good-natured bull-dog, and an Archduke exactly like an undertaker! You say you are Republican, so am I except as regards the Queen whom I really *love* and respect. You know how the Frenchman (I am not sure it was not La Rochefoucauld) described the three phases of Court life:

1. éblouissement

2. republicanisme
3. enfin philosophe

I sometimes think I am on the verge of No. 3, at least I hope so.

GRASSE. *April 5th 1891*

I went for a walk with Princess Louise and some of the gentle-men, she skipped like a goat up some of the steepest mountain paths and left us all behind. She was amiable enough but never have I come across a more dangerous woman, to gain her end she would stick at nothing. One would have given her a wide berth in the sixteenth century, happily she is powerless in the nineteenth.

GRASSE. *April 13th 1891*

Today being bitterly cold the Queen elected to drive to Cannes cemetery and visit the tombs of various friends. We started soon after 3.30 and were not home till ten to seven! The gentlemen went in a separate carriage full to overflowing with wreaths for the favoured tombs; when we arrived we formed a doleful little procession headed by a blowsy woman, the wife of the Guardian, and slowly proceeded from grave to grave.

Marie then described a tomb with the name of Mallet on it, which was indeed that of a young cousin of Bernard's who had died at Cannes.

GRASSE. *April 14th 1891*

Lord Lytton[1] and Mr. Austin Lee dined here last night. I plucked up courage and talked about you and felt happier than I have done since I left England. Lord Lytton spoke so nicely of your father, you would have been pleased had you heard all he said. What enormous personal charm your father must have possessed quite apart from his other talents. This always strikes me when people talk of him. Their faces light up at once as if at some

---

[1] He was then Ambassador in Paris and died that autumn. Mr Austin Lee was for many years on the Embassy Staff in Paris.

very pleasant memory. I regret more and more that I never even saw him.

Next day Lord Lytton came to lunch and Princess Louise took him to see the Fragonards, I danced attendance, so saw them too at last. They are splendid, I had no idea he could do anything as bold, the finish is exquisite yet only produced by a few touches, the colour very thin, mostly glaze. The old proprietor began by being rather crusty but the Princess soon mollified him, he is however a good Republican and kept his hat on the whole time besides sitting down ostentatiously whenever he thought the Princess had her eye on him. The room is a curious mixture of squalor and magnificence, the very finest Louis XV furniture covered with priceless tapestry, the walls adorned with the still more priceless Fragonards, a splendid ormolu 'garniture de cheminée', also Louis XV, a fine Aubusson carpet full of holes, dust thick on everything, several common chairs, an appalling table with black and gold legs and the vulgarest antimacassars scattered broadcast and spoiling the whole room. The rest of the afternoon was absorbed in a drive and a four-mile walk and we did not get home till nearly seven; then a mild form of birthday banquet (for Princess Beatrice) and finally some very good fireworks in the garden which the Queen enjoyed like a child.

GRASSE. *April 15th 1891*

I have been painting roses for the Queen and she is delighted with my efforts and very complimentary, but the result is a large bough of quince blossom to form a 'pendant' which is more than I bargained for. I have no oil paints here and have to work in water colour which I don't understand. The Archduchess Stephanie[1] has been here today, I acted housekeeper as usual and received her at the door. She is tall and handsome, golden hair and a brilliant complexion, but does not look the least interesting. She

---

[1] The Archduchess Stephanie was a daughter of Leopold II of Belgium, who married in 1881 Crown Prince Rudolph of Austria who shot himself at Mayerling in 1889. It had been an unhappy marriage.

is only 27. She steadily refused to wear mourning for her husband (no wonder) so there is a great coolness between her and the Empress of Austria. The secret marriage of the Grand Duke Michael [*to Countess Torby*] has created great excitement in Cannes. The shock killed his poor mother who had heart disease and all are agreed that the Tzar is a terrible tyrant. It is quite true that the Duchess of Sparta[1] is about to be received into the Greek Church, her brother, the Emperor, is furious and vows she will never set foot in Germany again and that he has seen her for the last time. Another fine specimen of the domestic tyrant!

GRASSE. *April 21st 1891*

We went to another funeral this afternoon, a military one this time. One of the officers of the Chasseurs des Alpes died yesterday of consumption and as the Queen really enjoys these melancholy entertainments she determined to see the procession and poor Major Bigge, much to his disgust, was ordered to put on full uniform and attend the ceremony which lasted nearly three hours. . . .

Princess Beatrice is really very fond of me and very friendly though you would never think so from her manner, and I am very fond of her. I recognise her many good qualities and appreciate her good sense and liberal mindedness. They are all very much bored at the Emperor of Germany's visit and are dreading what he will say and do. The more I hear of him the more I dislike him, he must be such a despot and so terribly vain. However, poor man, he has a most insipid and boring wife whom he does not care for and from whom he escapes by prancing to the four corners of the world. . . .

GRASSE. *April 24th 1891*

The old Duke of Saxe-Coburg Gotha has been here to day with

[1] Sister of Kaiser Wilhelm II, she married the heir to the Greek throne, who afterwards became King Constantine I, who was notoriously pro-German in the First World War.

his wife. He is the Prince Consort's only brother and an awful looking man, the Queen dislikes him particularly. He is always writing anonymous pamphlets against the Queen and the Empress Frederick, which naturally creates a deal of annoyance in the family.

This evening twenty-one officers of the Regiment stationed here were received by the Queen and afterwards had supper in the large Dining Room. The entertainment was quite a success and will make a good impression.

There has been an amusing row with 'The Times' correspondent, a sharp little man who wears pince-nez and is positively ubiquitous. The Queen is furious with the reports on her day in the papers and ordered Sir Henry to publish a paragraph saying they were all unauthorised and inexact; whereupon there comes such a letter from the outraged correspondent who says 'The Times' pays £50 per week for its information. He challenges us to discover any inexactness in his reports and finally reports that the Court Circular is meagre, uninteresting and most incorrect. This makes matters worse as the Queen always corrects the Court Circular with her own hand. However as a matter of policy the fiery little man has been propitiated and peace may reign for a few days. Meanwhile his rival of the 'New York Herald', the fattest man I have ever seen, will also demand an interview and we expect more fun tomorrow.

GRASSE. *April 25th 1891*

The Queen is very angry about the paragraphs which appeared in the St. James Gazette, saying that Grasse was unhealthy and that if she had escaped, her entourage had greatly suffered. Telegrams have been sent flying in all directions to try and discover the author and his authority. Sir W. Jenner is furious because it reflects on him as the Queen's Medical Adviser and in fact there is a tremendous row. It is a shame to say the hotel is unsanitary for the drainage is first-rate and to my mind there is nothing to blame but the climate which does not suit the majority of English people. Everyone is well now just as we are going away.

GRASSE. *April 26th 1891*

The 'Times' correspondent has been interviewed today and ordered to write an article refuting the St. James Gazette paragraph which originally came from 'The Lancet'. He says 'The Lancet' always abuses the Riviera and cracks up Bournemouth and Torquay, and no doubt got its information from Cannes where envy reigns supreme owing to the Queen's preference for humble Grasse. . . .

We all feel better, but the gentlemen complain bitterly of the dullness of the place and indeed it is too dull for words!

The Royal party seems to have returned to England just after this, and Marie went out of waiting to prepare for her wedding on July 11, 1891. Before that she records two further interviews with the Queen.

WINDSOR CASTLE. *Sunday*

I dined with the Queen last night and Her Majesty talked to me afterwards for sometime but never as much as alluded to my marriage. I can see it is still a sore point: she asked a great deal after you and was sorry to hear of you being so unwell. . . .

Her Majesty looks wonderfully well, really better than ever and seems quite to enjoy the prospect of the wedding tomorrow. We are all to go up by special train and return at 6.30, having tea at Lady Cochrane's en route.

WINDSOR CASTLE. *June 26th 1891*

I have just had an interview with the Queen, almost the fare-well one, and it is far worse having to say 'Goodbye' than even I had expected. I did my best not to break down but all 'in vain,' and the kinder the Queen was the more I cried, it is really dreadful to think I shall never see her in the same way again. I told her how good you were and how I loved you and she said I was quite right to have had the courage to make up my mind to leave all for you, I love her all the more for her kind words and sympathy.

H.M.'s presents are a diamond brooch, a cheque for £1000, an Indian shawl and several photos.

CHAPTER VI

THE RETURN TO COURT

For the first years after marriage there are no letters, but in 1895 we have the following account of Marie's Audience of the Queen to present Victor, aged 1 year and 11 months to Her Majesty, his godmother.

March 4th 1895

This morning soon after 8, I received a telegram from Windsor telling me the Queen would receive me and Victor at Buckingham Palace at 3 o'clock. The day was sunny but about 10 it snowed heavily, however I struggled out to see my mother and tell her the news and also to secure the loan of a carriage. At 2.30 we were ready to start, taking the nurse Frances Taylor with us—and a little box containing Victor's best frock to be put on when we reached the Palace—by 10 minutes to 3 we found ourselves at the Equerry's Entrance and knowing the Palace well I dispensed with the services of the red coated footmen and conducted my little party safely to Miss McNeill's room—in the corridor we met the Duchess of Roxburghe and Victor took her for the Queen and began to cry, however we hurried on and soon he was quite happy, gloating over his smart brown velvet blouse and his picturesque pleated muslin collar and ruffles and talking away as if at home. We did not have long to wait, the summons came about 10 minutes past 3 and then with a beating heart I took his little hand and followed the page down the long dark passage leading to the Queen's apartments. Victor danced by my side shouting 'Go to Queen, Go to Queen' to the intense amusement of the maids and pages.

The Queen received us in the Prince Consort's dressing room, seated on a writing chair, a table behind her covered with flowers, miniatures, photographs and writing materials. I noticed two enamels of the Czar and Czarina framed together in red enamel and the Queen wore as usual the portrait of the Prince Consort set in blue enamel and pearls hanging from a chain round her neck. I curtsied and kissed the Queen's hand and H.M. kissed me and then I said to Victor 'What do you say? this is the Queen', he promptly kissed her hand and answered clearly 'Good morning Queen'—charmed at once by the Queen's beaming smile and great gentleness of voice and manner—then half turning H.M. said 'I have got a present for him' and there on a little low table was a miniature landau drawn by a pair of grey horses, gaily painted and lined with blue satin—Victor's eyes grew large and murmuring 'Gee-gees' he ran to the table while the Queen admired his golden hair, said his eyes were like his Father's, that he was splendid for his age and that she wished her grandchildren had brown eyes and were half as well behaved.

For a quarter of an hour H.M. talked about my concerns and my relations—asking 1st. after Bernard, how he was, remembering how ill he had been from influenza the first year of our marriage, then after my dear mother, Maud, Edith and Violet, not forgetting the one was delicate the other handsome, in fact making me feel not only at my ease, but as if I were still in her service and had been with her last month instead of last year! Of Edith and Violet the Queen used the expression 'Your stepsisters who you love so much'—then H.M. said 'Poor Sir Henry (Ponsonby) it is 8 weeks today since he was stricken down and there has been *no* progress; (her eyes filled with tears) it is too terrible for us all—now, he has bronchitis and is so restless he cannot keep on even the bed clothes.' At this moment Victor whose eyes had been roving round the room suddenly pointed to a picture by Landseer of the Prince Consort's favorite greyhound, a beast with curling tail guarding a top hat and a pair of kid gloves, and murmured 'Bootiful dog'—the Queen was enchanted, no courtier could have spoken better.

After more talk about the Morier's and poor Victor M's sad death and career, which it would not be discreet to record here, the Queen touched her electric bell and the audience was at an end; then I said to Victor 'What do you say for the beautiful present'. 'Thank-oo kind Queen' was the immediate reply and then H.M. said 'Remember I am your Godmother' he kissed hands, the Queen kissed me *most* affectionately saying 'Have him painted and send me a photograph, he is a beautiful child, the Empress Frederick and the Princess ought to see him', and then Mrs. Macdonald (the Queen's head dresser) entered the room with a little white spitz dog and with much difficulty I persuaded master Victor to leave the room—so happy and at home had he become. We saw Princess Beatrice for a few minutes and left the Palace soon after 4—feeling happy and satisfied.

Not long after this audience Marie was asked by the Queen to return to Court as an 'Extra Woman of the Bedchamber', in fact a kind of Lady in Waiting. She was also to act as a private secretary to help the Queen with correspondence some of it of a confidential nature. Although this entailed separation from her family for at least three months in the year, Marie's sense of duty and devotion to the Queen decided her to accept: there was also a financial inducement, even though it seemed un-likely to exceed £200 a year, that was not to be sneezed at. The Queen then wrote in her own hand the following letter from Osborne to Marie, who was yachting with Mrs Yorke in the Garland *off Hamble:*

August 8th 1895

Dear Marie,

Your kind letter gives me much pleasure and I need not say how truly I rejoice at the prospect of having you again about me.

I trust you will not find the duties of your new office too onerous. Harriet Phipps will be able to tell you all about them.

Ever,

Yours

affly

V.R.I.

Miss Phipps indeed took the matter in hand at once. I quote from one of a long series of letters which passed between her and Marie over the next few years. Harriet was mainly responsible for the tricky task of arranging the rota of waitings, which had both to satisfy the Queen and keep the Ladies from too lengthy periods of waiting in the same place. There was always some reluctance to be picked for the Balmoral team and a good deal of bargaining went on with Harriet, who exercised her power with much tact and kindness.

Harriet's letter of August 5th 1895 asks where Marie will be next week.

I hope as soon as Princess Beatrice returns she may write you all the details of your new post and future arrangemei ts. I feel there are several points you ought to have mentioned to you—for instance your salary. I know that you and Mrs Grant are to divide what 'the Duchess' received but I don't know what that was, and I cannot very well ask what my colleague's salary was! Then Mrs Grant being in India has a little delayed—not her acceptance which has been received but a letter as to when she will be available. If you are pressed for time as regards your husband's holyday how would it be if you wrote me a line I *could show* saying he was arranging his leave and could I tell you if you were likely to be required at Balmoral so that you could fit in Mr Mallet's holyday with The Queen's wishes regarding yourself. It don't seem to me as if The Queen had quite made up her mind as to our dates at present but that *might* bring the matter to a decision. I have for the last few years usually left Balmoral between the 20th and 31st October—last year I left on the 31st. It may be different in the future. Pss Beatrice is due here [*Osborne*] on the 13th and has a bazaar at Carisbrooke I think on the 14th. I have told The Queen that no particulars have been definitely made known to you and I think The Queen had not previously realised how little had been communicated but took it as a matter of course that you knew. It would seem best therefore I think to leave it till Pss B. arrives as she spoke to your Uncle. I should be so glad to be helpful to you, dearest Marie but I think you will agree this is best.

Harriet Phipps was often helpful thereafter, particularly in matters of dress which, owing to frequent Court Mournings of different duration and blackness according to the esteem in which Her Majesty held the deceased, often needed guidance. Though it dates from January 1st 1897 the following letter seems relevant at this stage:

I think we three [*Miss Phipps, Mrs Grant and Marie*] have always been supposed to cling to more sober tints than the Maids of Honour, and *mauve* has of late been forbidden to them in its fashionable pink tints, but I am sorry this edict has been issued as it makes it all more inconvenient. My only *grey* evening dress is a grey brocade given me by *The Queen* herself ! ! ! ! It was a length of those beautiful specimen English silks shown at Stafford House. I shall struggle to wear that for some years to come! As a matter of fact I do mostly wear black as being so much on duty I can't afford to constantly change whites and greys. It is curious an order for deeper mourning should come out now again—but many years ago the original permission for grey, lilac &c was only given to Maids of Honour. You will kindly let Victoria know I suppose dear as The Queen gave you the order. I have lately bought myself a toque with lavender ! ! ! At all events black gowns will be economical. I am sorry for you if H.M. is giving you a share of certain 'coloured' worries—but the longer you are at Court dearest the more you will learn what all the real worries and difficulties are.

The duties of a Woman of the Bedchamber in the reign of Queen Anne are described in 'The Court at Windsor' by Christopher Hibbert. 'The Queen spent a great deal of time at her toilet, an operation performed with all due ceremony the clothes being handed by the bedchamber woman to a Lady of the Bedchamber who helped the Queen put them on.

"When the Queen washed her hands the page of the back stairs brought and set down upon a side-table the basin and ewer", according to Mrs Masham. "Then the bedchamber woman set it before the

Queen and knelt on the other side of the table over against the Queen,
the bedchamber lady only looking on. The bedchamber woman poured
the water out of the ewer upon the Queen's hands. The bedchamber
woman pulled on the Queen's gloves. The page of the back stairs was
called in to put on the Queen's shoes." [1]

These menial offices had long since fallen into disuse before Queen
Victoria's reign, and Marie and her colleagues' duties were social and
secretarial.

On October 16 Marie duly arrived at Balmoral for her first waiting
in her new rank. It was characteristically snowing on the way from the
station.

To B. M.

BALMORAL. *October 17th 1895*

The Queen sent for me directly after lunch yesterday and
greeted me so warmly and in such an affectionate manner that I
had the tears in my eyes. She said, 'I am so very glad to have you
back, dear Marie, you will remember how very angry I was when
you married!' and added that she knew how perfectly she could
trust me and that I could not fail to please her. In vain I suggested
that I might make mistakes and feel very diffident. She would not
hear of such a thing. Of course this is highly flattering but it
makes me more nervous than ever instead of more self-confident.
However I really believe that there is less to do than I have
always imagined and that my principal business is to listen
attentively and then hold my tongue.

Last night while dressing to dine with the Queen Princess
Beatrice knocked at my door and invested me there and then in
petticoat and dressing jacket with the Order of Victoria and
Albert, Third Class! It is quite lovely, just like Mama's, so I
need not describe it further. It made me look very smart and
I swelled visibly with pride when I appeared in the Drawing
Room. The Queen asked countless questions about you and

---

[1] *The Court at Windsor*, by Christopher Hibbert (Longmans, 1964), p. 94.

Victor, and of almost all of my family. She takes such an interest in our little angel, waxes quite grandmotherly whenever she speaks of him and thinks it such a good plan that your mother should guard him during my absence.

BALMORAL. *October 18th 1895*

The weather is cold and frosty but very fine, brilliant sunshine and the most glorious colouring. I walked yesterday with the Queen and she was much pleased to find I could trot along as well as ever, in the afternoon I drove with Lord James[1] and Uncle Alick over the moors, ending with a visit to the Empress [*Eugénie*] at Abergeldie, where by some mistake I was announced as Lady Lytton, so the Empress sailed up to me in a dignified manner and began pretty speeches, 'Nunks' hurriedly explained who I really was, when she flung her arms round me and kissed me on both cheeks, amused and delighted to see me again, and asking greatly after Mama and 'la chère petite Maud', whom she could hardly believe married and done for! She was too amusing for words full of fun and clever conversation. I hope to see her pretty often.

BALMORAL. *October 20th 1895*

I began my new duties last night by reading to the Queen till past 12, but the interest and excitement kept me wide awake and mercifully I had no inclination to yawn. Harriet gave me a message from the Queen to the effect that she intends increasing my salary and Mrs Grant's, £50 per year, from her own Privy Purse, so I shall have £200 after all.

BALMORAL. *October 22nd 1895*

Seven inches of snow. . . . All the gentlemen go cycling here most vigorously, except 'Nunks', who steadily resists and declares that the more it is urged upon him the less he feels inclined

---

[1] Lord James of Hereford, Minister in attendance.

to venture. The Queen drove to Braemar yesterday in a blinding snowstorm. . . .

BALMORAL. *October 26th 1895*

There was a very deep fall of snow last night and we shall not be able to walk for we have all forgotten to bring our snow-boots and the sledges of which I believe there are 30 are all at Osborne, so means of locomotion are not easy and we might be at the North Pole and members of the Peary Expedition. You ask me about my rooms; I am very well lodged on the sunny side of the house and have a cosy little sitting-room next to my bedroom which contains a sofa, writing table with drawers, two other tables and a fairly comfortable armchair, I am also entitled to one dwarf palm in a pot, and 'The Times', 'Morning Post' and the 'Scotsman' daily. I study all these papers with a view to reading tit-bits to the Queen in the evening but as she has all the telegrams at once and does not care for controversy it is not always easy to pick out what may interest her. I drove with Her Majesty yesterday and she was most talkative and amusing, indeed Mary Hughes and I had much ado to keep from immoderate laughter. The acting which is to take place next week (a State secret, mind!) was fully discussed followed by reminiscences of the Queen's 'Mary's' and the solitary Marie! Then other family matters and finally we met a company of gypsies and the Queen insisted on speaking to several of them and gave them money.

BALMORAL. *October 28th 1895*

After the heaviest fall of snow I have ever seen we had 14° of frost last night and there are 4° now at midday. . . . The Empress dined last night and comes to take leave of the Queen this afternoon. She goes South tomorrow—lucky woman. The Queen has asked a great deal after Victor and tells everyone he is 'such a beautiful child, with such lovely eyes', so he is becoming celebrated and the Household are quite anxious I should bring him in Waiting with me, Ethel Cadogan brings a dog and they say why should I not bring a baby? The Queen spoke so nicely of your father, as he had to do with India it interests her. If only you were in the India Office we should be even more in favour.

BALMORAL. *October 29th 1895*

The announcement of Princess Maud of Wales' engagement caused much excitement here yesterday and has been the cause of endless telegraphing. I was quite busy last night. The Queen is delighted and healths were drunk at dinner. The Danish Prince [*he afterwards became King Haakon of Norway*] is three years younger than his fiancée but clever and good-looking. He is in the Navy and just off for a five months' cruise to the West Indies, so the marriage will not be for some time.

BALMORAL. *October 31st 1895*

We had a Ladies' Dinner last night which I always think very pleasant as the Queen talks much more freely and gives her opinion in a most decided and amusing manner, but after the meal was over Mary Hughes and I were requested to seat ourselves at the piano and rattle off various duets which we had never seen before. What made us have the cold shivers all the more was that we had *never* played together before in our lives and had no idea how our four hands would trot together; however it was a great success and the Queen praised us and was very pleased and said to me later in the evening, 'It is really wonderful, Marie, how well you have kept up everything', so I simply burst with pride and lifted my head on high. I do not quite know how I managed it for I was so nervous I could hardly see the notes. . . .

Last night a dog of sorts took to wandering outside my door and much disturbed my slumbers; however that is better than poor Lady Ampthill's adventure here sometime ago, one night during the visit of Prince Ferdinand of Bulgaria she heard snorting and snarling outside her bedroom door and after shaking with terror for sometime, visions of burglars, anarchists, etc. passing through her brain, she rose, lit the candle, and cautiously opened her door; on the wool mat outside she beheld a gigantic Bulgarian covered with pistols and daggers in full national costume. You can imagine how she banged the door and double-locked it! This formidable creature turned out to be Prince Ferdinand's body-servant, who finding his master's door-mat somewhat hard had moved on to a softer one.

BALMORAL. *November 2nd 1895*
The dress rehearsal of the theatricals last evening was a great success and the Queen was delighted. The poudré piece is very pretty but to my mind insipid and the actors too good for their parts, the second is first-rate, the only blot being that there is no part for Uncle Alick who always convulses everybody whenever he puts even his head on to the stage. Mary Hughes as an intriguing elderly widow and Fritz Ponsonby as a penniless Baronet of twenty-five, are quite inimitable. Lord Wolseley has just arrived but I have not seen him yet. . . .

BALMORAL. *November 4th 1895*
You asked me to describe my day, so here it is. Breakfast at a quarter to ten, then general conversation till about eleven, when we repair to our respective dens and do what writing we have for the Messenger (this morning I have only had two letters to answer and two telegrams to send). When the Queen goes out about twelve, we all emerge and walk for an hour weather permitting which it has *not* done lately; at one we write again or read, I sometimes play duets with Princess Beatrice or read aloud to her and occasionally I see the Queen and take messages to Sir A. Bigge or 'Nunks', at two we have a sociable meal and have coffee afterwards in the Billiard Room where we gossip and wait for driving orders, by 3.30 to a quarter to four we all drive out or on our own; tea at 5.30, more talk, then to our rooms again or we pay each other friendly visits, finally dinner at nine (if with the Queen), quarter to nine if with the Household.
At eleven the Queen leaves the Drawing Room and I wait in

my bedroom till I am summoned at twenty or a quarter to twelve and go to the Queen in her Sitting-room where I talk and read and take orders till about 12.30, then 'Good-night' and I fly to my bed and hot-water bottle! I do not keep up my maid. This routine never varies by a hair's breadth, as soon a revolution as to drive in the morning and walk after lunch, and boiled beef on Thursday and 'mehlspeise mit ananas' on Friday recur with unfailing regularity. Now you see my letter is gone and nothing related but petty details while I had so much to tell you about Lord Wolseley. I am simply grovelling at his feet enchanted with his cleverness, his versatility, his charming manners, his quick sympathy. I talked to him of your father and he told me much about him and how they had long talks about you and Loulou.[1] How your father used to say he thought you would both get on, that you were clever and good and ought to make your way in the world. He asked me kindly after your mother and after you and seemed immensely interested in our marriage and prospects. I hope we may see him occasionally now that he has five years of London life before him.

BALMORAL. *November 6th 1895*

I was very lucky and sat next to Lord Wolseley at nearly every meal while he was here and became more and more fascinated by him every hour. He talked of Marlborough and his researches at Blenheim and of his intense overpowering admiration of Cromwell. What struck him almost most in both these great Generals was their genuine religious belief in the supreme power of God, and he declares in neither case was it cant in any sense of the word. Marlborough's letters to his wife which were never intended for any other eye abound in expressions of genuine faith and reliance on the Almighty Arm able to save and give the

---

[1] Louis Mallet, Bernard's brother, at that time in the Foreign Office. He later became Private Secretary to Lord Lansdowne and to Sir Edward Grey, and became the last ambassador to the Sublime Porte at Constantinople in 1913, a Privy Councillor and G.C.M.G.

victory; the naughty Duchess on the contrary was a free thinker and a perfect materialist and by her awful temper and appalling arrogance finally ruined both herself and her husband.

Lord Wolseley most cordially invited me to call on Lady Wolseley when they were settled in Grosvenor Gardens and even offered to take me over the Tower some day. Lord George Hamilton, our present Minister, is I think good, worthy and dull! Most kind and friendly but no genius, perhaps he may improve as time goes by.

BALMORAL. *November 7th 1895*

I can hardly decipher your writing and I tremble for your reputation as Private Secretary. Can you send me a 'Swan' Quill pen, I hear they are only supplied to Cabinet Ministers so I thought you might 'prig' one from A. J. B. especially as it will be O.H.M.S., for none of my pens write black or thick enough to please the Queen and I want to make experiments.

The weather is lovely today, showery but just like July. We are all rejoicing but rather trembling too, lest the Queen should postpone her journey South. Lord Pembroke arrives tomorrow to prepare for the King of Portugal and some of our gentlemen have to turn out and take up their abode in a tin cottage nearby to make room for the Portuguese suite. We have been suddenly ordered to throw off our crêpe during the Royal Visit, which is most inconvenient as we have no coloured garments with us.

BALMORAL. *November 8th 1895*

At a Ladies' Dinner last night the Queen was so amusing. We discussed 'The Souls' but do not breathe this, and H. M. said they really ought to be told *not* to be so silly! and made most sensible and delightful comments on them. Then golf came on the 'tapis' and I ventured to remark on A. J. B.'s passion for it. 'I cannot understand it at all'.

The Souls were a group of young aristocrats whose membership was confined to a circle of 'personages distinguished for their beauty, breeding, delicacy and discrimination of mind' (St James's Gazette). Its female members—all of whom had to be married—included Tennants, Wynd-hams, Balfours, Custs, Lytteltons etc, and were mostly related to the male members. They dined together in London or met at country house parties to talk of literature and the arts, act charades, write verses or plays which they performed for their own amusement. Curzon was a familiar figure with his amusing imitation of Tennyson reciting 'Tears, idle tears' (see 'Curzon', by Leonard Mosley).

The King of Portugal arrived this morning looking fat and pink just like a prize pig, his Suite visibly suggested decayed monkeys, newly escaped from barrel organs, not an attractive lot by any means. The King eats enormously and they say he takes a good deal of exercise but the more he takes the more he eats and I should fear apoplexy at 40, he is but 32 now!

After a heavy lunch the 'Portugeese' as we call them were taken for a chilly drive in our wagonette which they insisted on calling a 'charabanc', and then scaled a neighbouring hill carrying torches with all of Her Majesty's Highland retainers, a huge bonfire was lighted at the top, whisky dispensed with a generous hand, and then followed Reels outside the front door beautifully danced by some of the Pipers of the Black Watch. I have seldom seen anything more graceful than the way one man danced the most intricate steps waving his flaming torch, now high, now low and hooting all the time.

BALMORAL. *November 11th 1895*

The King of Portugal takes his departure this morning at cock crow accompanied by his monkeys. The impression left on my mind is that of a King in a comic opera. He is so fat that he bounds rather than walks and his greediness is quite appalling. The gentlemen call him the Champion Liar but as he never addressed a single word to any of us ladies I cannot say we had an opportunity of judging. I however heard him last night describing the capture of a salmon so large that it must have been a whale, but we were all rather disappointed that he did not draw the long bow more in our hearing. The Suite kissed and pressed our hands at least four times a day and scattered Portuguese compliments on every possible occasion, but do not be alarmed; they were all married men and most unattractive.

We had a great banquet on Saturday night and the band of the Black Watch played all the evening. After drinking the health of Dom Carlos and the Queen, which I did as usual in water, nine pipers marched round the table and nearly blew our heads off, however they looked magnificent in their kilts and huge feather bonnets. . . .

I have ended up quite liking Lord George Hamilton; he is so really kind-hearted.

The unfortunate King Carlos and his eldest son were murdered in Lisbon some years later.

The Court returned to Windsor soon after this and I find the first invitation to Bernard Mallet to dinner at Windsor Castle on Saturday, 23rd November, and to remain until the following Monday.

WINDSOR CASTLE. *November 20th 1895*

We had a most interesting ceremony this afternoon, i.e. the reception of the African Chiefs and I was present with the Queen as well as the Lady-in-Waiting, the first time I have ever had such an honour. To begin the story we had a State Lunch, the Gentlemen in levée dress and I had Lord Selborne on my right and Chief Bathoeu on my left; he seemed the least attractive of the blacks but enjoyed his food thoroughly and ate in a very civilised manner. Indeed their manners were excellent quite a lesson to many Britons! They are all tee-totallers and drink nothing but lemonade but Khama is the finest of them and wins golden opinions wherever he goes. Lord Selborne says he is a better Christian than anyone he knows and a very intelligent man to boot, a great hero. I must say he looks it and and I was so struck with his face and slim upright figure. The Queen received the Chiefs in the White Drawing Room seated on a Throne like a chair, and the Chiefs advanced through a long line of Life Guards with drawn swords, stationed in the two large Drawing Rooms. The Queen welcomed them and they presented their gifts, three Karosses or rugs of leopard skins of doubtful smell but intrinsic worth. Then the Queen spoke saying she was glad to have them under her rule and protection and felt very strongly the necessity of preventing strong drink from entering their lands. This was duly interpreted and they replied each in turn. Then the Queen gave them a New Testament in their tongue with her own hands and huge framed photos, and an Indian Shawl was handed to each of them by Lord Clarendon, and with grateful grunts they retired backwards leaving us much impressed by their quiet dignity and wonderful self-possession. I could see they were immensely impressed but they tried not to show their feelings and succeeded admirably. I had a nice chat with Lord Selborne, he adores Joe [*Chamberlain*], who looked very proud and pleased but quite hideous in official garb and bereft of his orchid.

WINDSOR CASTLE. *November 21st 1895*

The Queen held a Council and sent for me just before it to comment on the order about Princess Maud's marriage so that with much trembling I had to convey this State Paper to Sir Charles Pellew and the Duke of Devonshire and found myself in the Corridor the only woman in the midst of twenty men, very nervous and uncomfortable. Do not mention this for I think the gentlemen do not like the idea of a woman having to meddle in their affairs. We had another State Lunch and I sat between the Peruvian Ambassador and Sir Richard Paget, who had just been made a Privy Counsellor. They were more than amiable and the Peruvian who was a sort of co-operative Ambassador and works Rome, Paris and London turn and turn about begged me to come to the former place in order that he might do all in his power to please me.

WINDSOR CASTLE. *November 26th 1895*

Frances[1] will have told you of Victor's angelic behaviour, he kissed the Queen's hand twice in the most courtier-like manner and answered all her questions quite promptly telling Her Majesty you were at your office and that you rode a 'flying machine'. The Queen said, 'I suppose you mean a bicycle, dear', upon which he answered in shrill tones, 'Nanny says it is a flying machine' which made her laugh heartily. Then Her Majesty said, 'Do you know who I am?' 'Keenie' replied he quite loud and decided. The Queen thought him prettier than ever and more like me and admired his white satin frock so much. So did the dear Duchess of Albany who came to my room to play with him for over twenty minutes. The Royal Nurses gave a glowing account of his manners to Princess Beatrice so I think we may surely congratulate ourselves upon his bringing-up as far as it goes.

To B. M.

Undated: 1895

Prince Henry is going to Ashantee, poor Princess Beatrice is inconsolable but so patient and unselfish and declares she is glad he should do some real work and that *she* will never stop him in any sort of way. I admire her more than I can say, never should I have the courage to pack you off, my darling, on such an expedition but then I am an arrant coward. Do not mention this till you see it in the newspapers. I have been talking to the poor Princess and comforting her as best I can. Of course he is bursting with excitement, it is the climate I fear, *not* the enemy.

The following letters to Lady Elizabeth cover the same period.

BALMORAL. *October 17th 1895*

My welcome here was even warmer than I had expected and the extraordinary thing is that everything is so exactly the same as when I left five years ago that I feel as if I had not even been away

[1] Frances Taylor, our very dear Nanny.

at all! The same chairs in the same places, the same plum cake, even the number of biscuits on the plate and their variety, absolutely identical, the same things said the same done, only some of the old faces gone and a selection of new dogs follow the pony chair.

BALMORAL. *October 20th 1895*

The Concert on Friday was a great success and Albani stayed the night here and was most graciously received by the Queen. Her voice, alas, is well on the wane. She can no longer 'filer' a note and screeches horribly now and then, while Miss Butt[1] who really has the finest voice in existence knows no more how to sing than a pussy cat. I am writing to the Empress.

WINDSOR. *November 20th 1895*

I was rather knocked up by the journey which was not very agreeable for the sad accident to Princess Beatrice's favourite Collie on the way to the Station and the delay of three quarters of an hour owing to a breakdown on the line just in front of us rather unhinged our nerves. The Queen and Princess were dreadfully upset by the dog's death and poor little Prince Drino is crying still. I had to get into the Queen's carriage at Perth and read aloud for nearly three hours which tired me a good deal and then on arriving here my maid was ill and sick and so could do nothing for me.

WINDSOR. *November 23rd 1895*

Imagine the beloved Queen's kindness! At a tiny Ladies' Dinner of six last night I was in the seat just opposite H.M. when she leant across the table and said, 'So *he* is coming'. I grew red to the roots and murmured, 'Who? when? where?', truly surprised and wondering what she meant. It then transpired that she had invited Bernard here from Saturday to Monday as a pleasant

[1] Later Dame Clara Butt, the celebrated vocalist married to Kennerly Rumford, a well-known tenor.

surprise for me! Conceive my delight and gratitude and the intense pleasure it will give not only to me but to his mother and family and I know will to you too. It is so wonderful that the Queen thinks of everyone from the highest to the lowest and although she is quite absorbed in grief for the loss of the best and wisest of all her servants and working all day long to do everything in her power for poor Lady Ponsonby she still finds time to think of what would give me intense pleasure.

WINDSOR. *November 27th 1895*

Bernard's visit here was a great success, he dined with the Queen on Saturday and looked very distinguished in his new breeches and black silk stockings. He was very nervous but hardly showed it at all and talked to the Queen for over five minutes with perfect self-possession. I always feel so sure of him doing and saying the right thing quietly that I did not tremble, but *it was* an ordeal. Princess Beatrice also talked to him and the dear Duchess of Albany was as charming as she invariably is and treated us both as old friends. Victor came down on Monday and won all hearts, the Queen saw him and admired him immensely in his white satin frock. He showed her his 'evergreen heart' and when she said, 'Who gave you that?' he replied, 'Grand-mama Elizabeth' without the slightest hesitation. Then H.M. said, 'Do you know who I am?' and he answered 'Keenie' in a moment.

CHAPTER VII

POLITICS AT BALMORAL

Second Waiting as Extra Woman
of the Bedchamber

To Bernard Mallet (now Private Secretary to A. J. Balfour)

WINDSOR. *May 17th 1896*

The gloom is very great [*Prince Henry had just died in Ashanti*]. We had a Ladies' Dinner last night and the Queen hardly uttered, the poor Princess did her very best to be cheerful and made gallant attempts at conversation but I kept thinking of how different it all was when I was here so short a time ago and how all the brightness is gone, I quite fear *for ever*. . . . The Queen sent for me before dinner and talked a long time holding my hand and crying most bitterly, still she found time to ask after you and Victor and how I felt, and was as usual more than kind and thoughtful; then I went to Princess Beatrice and we both sat and sobbed for half an hour while she told me the whole tragic story. Prince Henry knew he was dying and sent long messages to her and all his friends by the Doctor and a chaplain with whom he had made great friends. He felt the fact of dying so far away and alone very much and this makes the poor Princess very miserable but her grief is perfectly natural and she is extraordinarily brave and unselfish.

WINDSOR. *May 18th 1896*

I have discovered that dear old Watts[1] *is not* to be made a Privy

[1] G. F. Watts, the celebrated painter and sculptor, whose pictures, mainly allegorical, used to fill a room at the Tate Gallery, and whose 'Physical Energy' statue dominates part of Kensington Gardens. He had been offered a Baronetcy in 1886 at the same time that Millais accepted one. He was made a member of the Order of Merit by Edward VII, so honour was suitably satisfied at last.

Councillor. The Queen will not hear of it because she says an artist sells his pictures and is not the equal of a man of science like Huxley who did get it or of Max Müller who will. Of course she knows nothing of the case or its merits. Lord Salisbury proposed it but gave no special reasons for wishing it, there remains of course a K.C.B. Can't you get A. J. B. to press this on Lord Salisbury? I dare say there might be a good chance of getting that for him and it does seem a shame that his great services to the nation and generous gift to the Portrait Gallery should be ignored completely. I have made it clear why he would never take either a Baronetcy or Peerage, the reasons were great news here where the world is so shut out and somehow he and Lady Millais were bracketed together. I begin to think a little wholesome gossip should be encouraged. Pray use this knowledge warily but do what you can for the dear old man who is and will always be one of the grandest figures of the Victorian era. . . . With my views on art I cannot conceive why a poet should rank higher than a painter. Tennyson would never have denied that he lived on his brains! I find the Queen considers a Privy Councillor nearly the equal of a Peerage, so you see your father was very highly honoured, the only drawback is that it is soon forgotten while a Baronetage lasts for generations.

WINDSOR. *May 19th 1896*
The Chamberlains came last night and I sat by him at dinner, a great pleasure, he talked incessantly and was most agreeable, I did not dare discuss the burning topic but he talked a little on the subject and said the 'Reform Leaders' richly deserve punishment and imprisonment and that we had shut up plenty of Irishmen for less. I am sure he has no sympathy with Jameson & Company and not much with Rhodes, but of course this is completely conjecture on my part, so do not repeat it. We talked about gardening and orchids and about the 'Spectator' and St. Loe.[1] Chamberlain's

---

[1] J. St Loe Strachey, editor of the *Spectator* after Hutton. He was a great friend of Bernard's from Oxford days. *(footnote continued overleaf)*

admiration for the former knows no bounds and he thinks the latter admirably trained. He remembers Hutton as a dark consumptive youth seated in front of him at a Unitarian Chapel in the City of which Hutton's father was Minister, and says from that time he has been much interested in him.

BALMORAL. *May 27th 1896*

Just as the train was off from Windsor station the Queen sent for me and I had to remain in her august presence squatting on a bright blue moiré silk camp stool for nearly three hours reading the papers and making conversation. Can you imagine a more awkward predicament; dressers and pages tumbling in and out opening and shutting windows, changing capes and caps, the unfortunate 'lectrice' trying to make the incidents of the coronation intelligible above the babel! It was hot too and that in spite of a huge foot-bath full of ice placed in one corner of the saloon into which I very nearly took a header! Tea and muffins at Leamington restored exhausted nature and I was left in peace for the remainder of the journey. . . .

We had a most sumptuous breakfast at Perth this morning all the delicacies of Scotland and the season, trout and salmon and scones, strawberries and peaches and best of all a huge bunch of lilies-of-the-valley for each lady. The heat has been intense all day and we reached this house at 4 p.m. and after a wash and some tea I was ordered to drive with the Queen alone and am only just in 8 p.m. . . .

I had a talk with the Bishop of Ripon about Mr Lang.[1] He thinks Lang has made a *very* great mistake about his being fit for the post he undertakes. He apparently has no parochial experience and is very young and the Bishop adds 'much spoilt', he also

---

Spoken word of Strachey, shall it
Fail to raise a smile in Mallet?
(*Masque of Balliol*, by Cecil Spring-Rice.)

[1] Cosmo Gordon Lang, later Archbishop of Canterbury, was at Balliol with Bernard. He had just been appointed Rector of Portsea.

thinks him narrow in his views, high church. I cannot say I agree in this for the addresses I heard in Holy Week were quite broad enough to please anyone.

BALMORAL. *May 28th 1896*
We had a small Ladies' Dinner last night and no-one spoke but unfortunate me. Conversation is more impossible than ever since the crêpe pall descended on this luckless house and dear Lady Erroll, whose chats invariably run on the end of the world and kindred subjects is not much help. I tried to crack up Sir A. Milner but Princess Christian was rather snubby and said, 'He may be charming but *I know* he invented the death duties and therefore he cannot be nice.'

BALMORAL. *June 1st 1896*
Dr Cameron Lees preached very well but it was an unfortunate sermon and rather upsetting. The Queen cried a great deal and I thought it tactless of Dr Lees until I discovered that both prayer and sermon were 'by command'. The New Testament Lesson was a mysterious choice being the story of a woman who had seven husbands. Whether it points to Princess Beatrice's marrying her brother-in-law is a moot point but it only shows the mistakes a Scotch form of worship leads its Ministers to commit. . . .

The article in 'The Spectator' on the Queen was excellent and I read it to Her Majesty last night slightly 'bowdlerised'. She liked it extremely and said it contained some interesting facts she had not realised before, i.e. ruling over one quarter of the entire population of the known world. She said she has always *disliked* politics and does not consider them a woman's province but that the Prince Consort forced her to take an interest in them even to her disgust, and that since he died she has tried to keep up the interest for his sake. This is very touching. Then as to likes and dislikes of Premiers she remarked that she had them *very* strongly, and that Mr Gladstone had caused her more pain, anxiety and trouble than *any* of them, so often insisting upon measures which she felt and knew were mistaken and dangerous and which have turned out to be so! The Queen said, 'I like the article very much, it is sensible and loyal, but the "Spectator" has often been the reverse and at one time I never allowed it to come into my room.' She asked about the Editor so I launched into a eulogy of Hutton. 'The Spectator' is really a great power, all the men who read it are admiring and all speak of it with respect. . . .

Dear old Lady Erroll departs tomorrow, she gives us tracts about the end of the world which is certainly to come twenty years hence and her talk is ever of Abraham, Jonah and other remote prophets and she thinks us all backsliders and unregenerate.

BALMORAL. *June 2nd 1896*

The Queen talked to me about Armenia last night and I was thrilled by hearing the real truth, which is that no one single Christian Power would co-operate with us in spite of their asseverations and outward say. It is disgusting and it must be hard for Ministers, who have done their best, to be abused and blamed all over the country. . . .

My bicycle has not arrived. I will be very careful but you need not fuss for the roads are flat as teaplates and perfectly smooth and obstacles and traffic simply do not exist. Princess Christian progresses on a tricycle, a charming machine but pronounced by competent judges, far more perilous than a bike.

BALMORAL. *June 3rd 1896*

I mounted my bike yesterday for ten minutes after I came home from my drive with the Queen and sailed away to the admiration of all beholders but I felt rather nervous and toddled down a slight incline, I am quite determined to do it every day and get confidence. The accounts from Moscow are more harrowing every day and the Emperor and Empress most fearfully distressed. They sent such a touching joint telegram to the Queen but I do not expect the Russian nobles 'care a button', and they dared not put off the fetes from political reasons, though the account of rejoicing and revelry side by side with such an appalling catastrophe sounds very bad to more civilized ears. Moreover it is quite certain that this is not due to the Emperor.

The catastrophe referred to is described in 'Lady Lytton's Court Diary', Chapter III, p. 68:

'... *Four days after the Coronation, came a terrible accident on the Khodynka Field just outside Moscow [now the Moscow Airport]. During a huge Coronation fete the crowd broke through the inadequate police cordons, swarmed over the ground, which was cut up by unseen trenches, and thousands of people were suffocated or trampled to death. That evening there was to be a ball at the French Embassy which was part of the Coronation festivities and on which the French Ambassador, the Comte de Montebello, had been authorized by his Government to spend a million francs. The Tsar and Tsarina made the mistake of not only failing to cancel the ball but of going to it themselves. There is a conflict of opinion as to why they did this. Their detractors say it was lack of feeling and imagination on their part; their supporters that Alix begged Nicholas to have the ball cancelled, or at least not to attend it himself, and indeed it was his own wish not to go, but that he was overruled by his advisers who considered that for their Majesties not to attend the ball might be construed as an insult to France. There seems to be a possibility that Nicholas was not aware until much later of the gravity of the accident. It happened before he appeared on the Khodynka Field to distribute food and gifts to the people, and every effort was made by the authorities to disguise it from him. It is even said that the bodies were shovelled under the grandstand on which he stood to get them out of sight. But whether it was their fault or not they were very much criticized for going to the ball, and the chief blame for such apparent callousness fell upon Alix.'*

BALMORAL. *June 4th 1896*

The Queen was most interesting last night on the subject of racing and gambling and said she could not be pleased at the Prince of Wales' success at the Derby, though she did not wish to be unkind and she had telegraphed to him. She said it was the example she minded, not the actual fact and added, 'Il faut payer pour être Prince', then quoted what my grandfather had said the very last time she had seen him at Osborne when he was already very anxious about Uncle Charlie.[1] Much more passed which it would not be right to record in this manner showing how she and Prince Albert had always had the highest ideals of what a good ruler should be and kept this free from anything that might shed an evil influence and give a bad example. It is wonderful to see how straight the Queen's life has been and how strict herself and yet how charitable when discussing others.

BALMORAL. *June 5th 1896*

We do not mention the Derby in public and the subject will be yet more taboo if H.R.H. wins the 'Oaks', but the enthusiasm in London must have been quite picturesque. There is a deluge today and I fear no biking for me. I am so anxious to get on that I rode twice yesterday and accomplished two miles in twenty minutes up and down a gently sloping road. . . .

I find from what they say here that Lord Rosebery thought highly of Mr George Murray and one day said to Bigge, 'I sometimes think George Murray[2] ought to be Prime Minister and I his Private Secretary.'

BALMORAL. *June 6th 1896*

The weather is heavenly today and I have been four miles on my bike accompanied by Sir Arthur Bigge at the rate of seven miles per hour! Up and down slight hills without getting off, started myself and altogether progressing rapidly. Sir Arthur is

---

[1] Charles, 5th Earl of Hardwicke, was a great gambler and spendthrift and ruined the family so that eventually Wimpole had to be sold. He was an intimate of the Prince of Wales' circle and was known as 'Champagne Charlie' or 'The Glossy Peer'. He always tipped the railway porters with a golden sovereign.

[2] George Murray, a Treasury Official, who later as Sir G. Murray, G.C.B., became Head of the Treasury.

very friendly and really very kind to me and I think we understand each other very well. He won't hear of me biking when
Aline can't and offers to be my escort. I get hotter than you can
imagine and looked like a lobster fresh from the pot, but enjoyed
my spin immensely. . . .

The Italians have behaved disgracefully about the Green Book
and put the Government into a deep hole but I never felt happy
about that Egyptian situation and nothing makes me alter my
opinion. (Private) Slatin has written the Queen a letter of eight
pages in German, which I am to see some day. Her Majesty takes
the greatest possible interest in him and has read his book right
through. All here think Lord Cromer has been *most* loyal to the
Government. He has always been averse to the policy of push
which Lord Salisbury seems determined to indulge in. We are
amused at Lady Salisbury larking off to the Derby. Sir Francis
Laking[1] is a very agreeable man, he looks like an actor but from
his constant use of Latin names and technical terms one soon
discovers his profession. He is a great botanist and we fraternise
over the wild flowers which are innumerable and quite lovely,
some of them exceedingly rare. Heated arguments take place at
meals over the relative merits of Butterwort and Milkwort and
Herr Müther[2] and I nearly come to blows over the Lesser Stitch-
wort. I see a great deal of Princess Christian who is most affectionate and very amusing but pours confidences into my unwilling
ears of such a dangerous character that I tremble. She is furious
at having to stay up here so long, so are we all but there is no
help for it.

BALMORAL. *June 8th 1896*

My rheumatism is bad my temper worse for I cannot bear to
think of my bike eating its head off in the little wooden house
consecrated to its species. I got out for a walk yesterday morning

---

[1] He was one of the Queen's doctors.
[2] Maurice Müther was the German secretary in charge of the archives at
Windsor.

after another funereal sermon from the minister at Ballater, who ought to have known better, but it poured all the afternoon and I spent most of it reading to Princess Christian, she is a perfect dear and says I am a comfort to her, so I feel I am of some use and that always makes me happy. Lord Balfour of Burleigh has quite won my heart and has been so very nice to me, he says he will send for you tomorrow and tell you all about me, if he does not you are to go to him. I hope I may meet him again some day. He was very interesting about Mr Craik of whom he has an excellent opinion, but he finds him very peppery at times and he received a most violent letter from him the other day because his secretary Mr Atkinson had not been invited to the party at Dover House. Lord Balfour says he ought to have had a K.C.B. this birthday so perhaps that means he will get it next. Altogether he praised his policy much and evidently finds him useful. Lord Balfour pitched into the Treasury dreadfully and says they were all *bears* in that office. I soon traced this acrimony to the insolent letter from Bergne; so bad that Lord Balfour sent it back to Sir M. Hicks-Beech [*Chancellor of the Exchequer*] and said if he had no apology he should complain to the Cabinet. Sir M. sent an ample one but of course it only shows what harm that *brute* does to the office. Do not quote me or bruit this abroad but it will amuse you and your confidential allies at the office.

BALMORAL. *June 9th 1896*

The Queen asked for and chose a photo of Victor and I am to write his name and age on it, she says she must see him again quite soon. I hope when he does he will be prevailed upon to sing his patriotic ditties. The Queen is tremendously interested in the Sudan Campaign and hankers after telegrams. I think her spirits are a little better but there is so little up here to change her thoughts. Did I tell you that I drove to Mar Lodge and back with the Queen and Princess on Saturday to see what progress has been made with the new building; we were disappointed for there is very little to see but the drive 27 miles was lovely. Captain

Harbord[1] leaves today and we are very sorry to lose him, he is a very nice frank good-hearted man, not a bit smart and most thoroughly simple and kind. His manners are not polished but still they are good. Sir J. McNeill takes his place and will be great fun, he treats us all like children or nieces, and pats us on the back freely.

BALMORAL. *June 11th 1896*
Princess Christian has given me a most delightful and useful present, a sort of tray fitted with ink pot and writing things, a splendid blotting book forms the lid and the whole thing locks with a tiny silver padlock so letters could be left inside with perfect safety. It is most dear of her but she is affectionate beyond words and a great help in the evenings doing her best to be cheery. Aline and I on bicycles formed a body-guard yesterday afternoon to the Princess on her tricycle and we went five miles at a good round pace and came home simply dripping. I longed for our huge bath but was very careful. This morning the heat is too great for any exertion so I shall not ride until after tea. Lord Cross[2] is here in great force letting out all the Cabinet secrets in the exuberance of his joy at being here once more and meeting me! Or so he says!

BALMORAL. *June 12th 1896*
I have been busily employed copying a huge document from the Bishop of Peterborough about the Coronation,[3] first-rate in style and deeply interesting, I am amused to have detected an error in spelling very characteristically ecclesiastical, when he talks of 'cannons thundering' he gives but one 'n' (canons) so it may mean quite another thing.

---

[1] The Hon. Charles Harbord, Groom-in-waiting. Later succeeded his father as Lord Suffield.
[2] Lord Cross was Cabinet Minister in attendance. Lord Privy Seal.
[3] Presumably that of the Tsar.

BALMORAL. *June 13th 1896*

Lord Cross was quite drunk on Thursday evening after dinner and talked so loud and paid such fulsome compliments that Bigge and I could hardly keep our countenances or conceal our disgust but this is strictly 'entre nous' for he is in high favour and openly says that the Queen cannot do without him! I overhear him telling her all sorts of tales which I do not believe to be true, for I doubt whether Lord Salisbury would tell him more than he is actually obliged to. I see the Queen far more frequently now and am evidently more trusted, but it means more work and less time for home letters and other occupations; it makes me feel, however, that it is more worth the pang of separation if I can really be of use.

BALMORAL. *June 15th 1896*

It is almost too hot for riding today, quite abnormal for the Highlands and very pleasant if one could only sit out, but on these occasions the Queen spends her mornings in a little cottage in the garden and I have to remain in my room in case I am wanted, so do not get out much before six in the evening. . . . I am glad Mr Balfour is showing fight, 'Biggy' says the Opposition think him very flabby and quotes 'Dizzy's' dictum, 'A man who sits on his shoulder blades can never be a Statesman' the Government ought to show their teeth a bit now. . . . The Queen is eager about every scrap of Egyptian intelligence and blood-thirsty when she speaks of the 'Khalifa'.

BALMORAL. *June 17th 1896*

I have had a good deal of responsible work to do for the Queen in the last two days, which always makes me anxious, I try not to fuss but if anything does go wrong in these particular matters I shall be to blame. I was up till past one last night making notes and trying to put on paper the many and various comments and directions in Her Majesty's own words. However this is really what I like, so it makes me feel of use and mercifully my brain works well and quickly at night when once roused. . . .

BALMORAL. *June 18th 1896*

Of course I hear indirectly a good many things Mr Balfour includes in his letters to the Queen, and I know he considers the Opposition to be behaving as badly as possible, almost without precedent. I also feel quite sure that unless he means to drop the Bill[1] altogether he will be forced to an Autumn Session in November and I am sure the plans proposed last Monday will have to be modified although most evidently he will not wish it so. I think poor man he must be getting rather weary for 'Biggy' tells me that either yesterday or the day before he sent his daily letter to the Queen in a box labelled to *himself* so it puzzled the Pages considerably and they came to Sir Arthur for information and explanation. Please do not repeat this. 'Biggy' says it is better not to as it may only bother Mr Balfour and it really was of no consequence. I only tell you to amuse you. . . .

[*As Bernard was at that time Private Secretary to Mr Balfour at the Treasury one would have rather thought that he might have been responsible for putting the wrong label on the box.*]

Sir Arthur has just received a most interesting letter from Major Wingate dated May 31st with a plan of the Camp at Firket entirely composed after descriptions furnished by deserters and stating they meant to attack that day week, which exactly came to pass. He describes the joy of many deserters at meeting Slatin again and the horrors inflicted by the Khalifa, families of fifty entirely swept away tortured or enslaved.

The following letters refer frequently to the Education Bill, in whose fate the Queen took a passionate interest. It was introduced by Lord Salisbury's Government of which Mr Balfour was leader in the House of Commons. Its core was State aid for Voluntary Schools. These denominational schools had fallen into financial difficulties and were no longer able to keep up their standard of teaching and buildings. The rate-built Board Schools set up under Gladstone's Act of 1870 had by the 'Cowper-Temple Amendment' excluded from these schools every

[1] The Education Bill. See editorial preceding next letter.

*catechism or formulary distinctive of a denominational creed, and
severed all relations between the School Boards and the Voluntary
Schools, which were managed by the Church of England and other
religious denominations and paid for from their own funds with some
help from State grants. About half the children in England and Wales
attended such schools, which flourished mainly in agricultural areas.*

*The 1896 Bill proposed to set up a local education authority over all
National Schools in the shape of an education committee of each County
Council. This new authority would administer all State grants, including those to Voluntary Schools, on condition that in every Elementary
School separate, denominational religious instruction should be given to
children whose parents desired it. Thus the 'Cowper-Temple' arrangement, so dear to Nonconformists, would disappear. The Nonconformists
were opposed to this, and also the Church party disliked the idea of
popular control of their schools.*

*Nevertheless the Bill passed its second reading by a majority of 267
and Mr Balfour pinned the Government's credit to the Bill. However,
in Committee endless amendments were introduced from all sides and
Sir John Gorst, Minister in charge of the Bill, weakly accepted, in Mr
Balfour's absence, some which effectively killed the Bill. The Government then decided to withdraw it. Lord Salisbury was much annoyed
and the Queen furious at this treatment of a measure promised in her
Speech.*[1]

BALMORAL. *June 19th 1896*

The Queen talked of nothing but the Education Bill last night
and suddenly turning round said, 'And pray what does your
husband think?' I nearly collapsed but thought it better to tell the
truth as diplomatically as possible! These bombs fairly take me
off my legs. H.M. discussed Mr Balfour and said his letters were
most interesting far better than those she usually gets from the
Leader of the House but that I was to ask you to beg him to use
blacker ink and try to write more distinctly; my private opinion

---

[1] The above is a summary taken from *Arthur James Balfour* by Blanche E. C.
Dugdale, published by Hutchinson in 1936.

is that not only does the Queen find it impossible to decipher his epistles but that they tax the resources of the Princesses who are called upon to do so; thank goodness they never fall to my lot. It makes me nervous enough to read the plainest hand-writing to my most gracious mistress.

Another bomb has fallen, Princess Christian has this moment announced she intends lunching with us on Friday, 26th, the very day I return, a quarter to two before the Sale at the School of Art. I am writing to Aunt Nety [*Lady Agneta Montagu (née Yorke)*] and 'Nunks' to come and support us and you must arrange to come back at one and help me or I shall entirely collapse. I feel horribly flustered for heaven knows how the cook will react, however I won't terrify her too early in the day and will send directions next week.

BALMORAL. *June 20th 1896*
Forgive me for differing but I cannot help thinking you are quite in the wrong when you say so decidedly 'Drop the Education Bill'. It will be the greatest proof of weakness on the part of an exceptionally strong Government and I fear of dissension in the Cabinet. The Opposition will triumph so wildly that they will never settle down again and it will be just the beginning of the end. I really feel in despair but it just shows that in these democratic days the Prime Minister MUST be in the House of Commons. I cannot think what Mr Balfour can be about! You always said from the beginning of the Session that all three Bills were routine, so they should be too; this is one which they are obliged to pass and which if they drop entirely will be fatal to their existence. The Queen is very much interested and *excited* about it all and I get a peep behind the scenes now and then, but keep this to yourself. I long for a good wholesome talk with you and a pouring out of various interesting things that have come under my notice but in less than a week, my darling, we shall be together once more. . . .

Sir Vincent Caillard made a very good impression here, his

manner is very good and dignified and he is brimming over with information of the most interesting kind but it is a little difficult to extract it and I had to cross-question him freely in order to learn all I wanted. His account of the Sultan [*Abdul Hamid*] is most curious, he is *not* blood-thirsty and nearly always remits capital sentences but the anarchy is such that massacres occur more because he is powerless to prevent them rather than anxious to order them. His amusements seem to be very simple, giving his favourite Collie dog a daily bath, shooting tame ducks on a tiny pond and learning the bicycle. . . . The Queen sent me two books to present to him [*Caillard*] on her behalf at midnight and he had to be fetched from the Smoking Room and conducted to my apartment very much to his astonishment I should think. I hope he was not scandalized but no-one would believe the curious inconsistencies of this life unless they were of it or in it! He left at 7.30 the next morning so there was some excuse.

BALMORAL. *June 22nd 1896*

I have written to Babraham[1] for provisions, a chicken, vegetables and fresh eggs and to Mama to beg her to see our cook and consult me as to what she can produce for lunch on Friday. I am very nervous but trust it may go off alright. Can you get some hock, I think that would be nice and cool to drink with ice. Princess Christian is dying to see you and talk politics. We have all enjoyed Sir F. Grenville's visit and he tells some thrilling tales of Russia. The Russians like us personally but hate us politically. However they loathe the French still more and took every opportunity of snubbing the Montebellos at the Coronation. Montebello refused from Republican sentiments to kiss the Empress's hand, so she retaliated by refusing to take his in the State polonaise so they marched along side by side, he looking very sheepish and silly. Sir F. is wildly interested in the French Revolution so I told him of your connection with it and of your

---

[1] Babraham, near Cambridge, was the house of Marie's brother Charles Adeane.

Queen Victoria at Grasse, April 1891

The photograph of the Queen
that Marie always kept on her desk

Little Victor with his curls, see p. 162

article on Mallet du Pan. He wants me to send it to him when I get home.

BALMORAL. *June 23rd 1896*

We are all packed up and ready to start but I have just time to send you a few lines before we devour our final meal. I must confess that barring the absence from home which I never get over, I have liked my stay up here very much, the flowers are lovely and the weather better than I had expected and we have been a very happy little party quite like a family with all our private jokes and good-humoured chaff and no jars of any kind.

(Private—The Queen talked to me a great deal about the Education Bill last night, she is very cross at the way in which the Government have dropped it and cannot make out why they make such an open profession of weakness. What particularly strikes her (and indeed everyone) is the complete 'volte face' between Monday and the following Friday, if as they declared the Party meeting on Monday was unanimous how could such a revolution have been effected in four days!

The carrying of the Second Reading of 'Deceased Wife's Sister' is a source of much pleasure in the highest circles. I join in congratulations to the House of Lords.

Bernard and Marie went yachting with Mrs Elliot Yorke in the Garland *for a summer holiday. Bernard's account of a day at Kiel gives a good picture of Kaiser Wilhelm's brother, Prince Henry of Prussia.*

KIEL. *August 12th 1896*

Went up the harbour to the Naval Exhibition which is prettily arranged and well situated. In afternoon waited for Prince Henry of Prussia who had announced himself to arrive from his country place by yacht, but he did not arrive till 8.30. We had all got into comfortable clothes and the ladies out of their smart ones and there was a bustle of preparation; dinner was interrupted and

H

begun again when he came on board. He was very pleasant and talked a good deal about the Queen and her blindness. Told us about his place at Eekanfirde where he is now living. Talked about Kiel and the yachting, necessity of having—as he has—English crews. (No English yachts *this year* at the racing at Kiel.) Afterwards he took Nunks and S. Lyttelton and me on board *l'Esperance*—a fine sailing yacht he had bought from Lord Dunraven— very comfortable and good accommodation—set a bottle of champagne before us and cigars and we had a pleasant talk. He described a function at Krupp's works, where he had been to represent the Emperor (who was ill) with the Empress—a service of two hours with two sermons, receptions in 4 towns, where part of the ceremony was to drain a goblet of Rhenish wine at each place, speeches, etc. He said they were all disappointed at seeing him instead of his brother. The present Krupp is the son of the great Krupp and grandson of the founder. He is a pleasant man and good man of business but knows nothing of the actual work. Employs 40,000 men—a regular disciplined army, and never has any trouble with them. We all thought him what Minter and Marie described him—the nicest male royalty going. Has got a beard and is rather like all his cousins, Dukes of York and Hesse. He is simple, friendly and courteous. He slept on board and sailed away at 5 next morning.

CHAPTER VIII

KITCHENER AT WINDSOR
Third Waiting

BALMORAL. *23rd October 1896*

Lord Cross is here and stays till Wednesday next, pompous and silly emits ridiculous criticisms of Lord Rosebery whose shoes he is not fit to black. Louisa Antrim comes on Monday, Minnie Cochrane tomorrow night, neither Lady Erroll or Bertha Lambert are much resource to me, but luckily I have 'Nunks'. Lady Erroll considers a real good that has resulted from Prince Henry's death is the cessation of theatricals, which is ever thought the work of the devil.

BALMORAL. *October 24th 1896*

The Queen is looking better than she has done for years which is very remarkable, she is not a bit tired in the evenings but sends for me sooner about 11.30 and I therefore escape about 12.30 and find myself in bed a quarter of an hour later. I gather to my intense surprise that the Bishop of London [*Dr. F. Temple*] is to be advanced to the See of Canterbury but as it is not yet in the papers you must keep the secret. It appears to me a very suitable appointment in many ways. Bad manners and personal blindness are to say the least peculiar qualifications for such a post, but as a temperance partisan I feel he will push the cause and perhaps be able to accomplish something definite.

BALMORAL. *October 26th 1896*

Our life here is intensely monotonous and I always feel when I return to it, even after months of absence, as if I had but left the week before. If I were a Queen how differently I should act but there seems a curious charm to our beloved Sovereign in doing the same thing on the same day year after year. Our drive on Saturday to the Bridge of Dee a good 35 miles on a chilly afternoon returning home in the dark after six, could hardly be called pleasure, but the Queen enjoyed the sense of continuity as she had always done, talked the whole time and when getting out of the carriage after being wedged firmly for three and a half hours wondered why her knees were so stiff. I could hardly use mine and shudder to think of the cripple I shall be if I live to sixty. It snowed most of yesterday but I drove with my royal Mistress for an hour in the afternoon, the carriage was shut and the Queen dozed not a little. Princess Alice of Albany[1] had tea with us and amused us much with a description of her little cousin, the Queen of Holland who is now to have a year of semi-liberty and amusement, then a year of complete liberty before she takes the reins of government at 18. I said, 'Why, what would she do? Give balls and parties?' 'No,' replied Princess Alice, 'She only likes dancing by herself, twirling round on one leg or in a "valse", but when she is really Queen she means to visit her *own* Indies and she is learning the language out of lesson time.' I replied, 'The Duchess won't let her leave the country.' 'Oh, she has thought of that, she will leave her mother as Regent; Grand-mama goes abroad, why should not she?' It was amusing to see how these children confidently looked up to the Queen as an example to all Sovereigns and meant to model their conduct on her's. Uncle Alick says when he was at the Hague one of the Court ladies told him the little Queen said one day to her mother, 'When I grow up I shall not be a Queen like you but a *real* Queen like the Queen of England.'

The Queen has talked about the appointment of the new Archbishop, she wanted Winchester [*Randall Davidson*] but it has been evidently borne in that he is too young and too freshly established

---

[1] Princess Alice of Albany (b.1883) is now Princess Alice, Countess of Athlone; the Queen was Queen Wilhelmina of Holland who died recently. She came to the throne as a small child.

at Winchester and she dwells on the fact that old Temple cannot last long and is a suitable stop-gap. (This is very private.)

BALMORAL. *October 27th 1896*

I entirely agree with all you say about the Bishop of London, he is a great deal too old to begin a new career, in five years he will be a dotard and then as you say the Radicals will have their opportunity. I suspect the Queen has urged a stop-gap having been told probably that Winchester's promotion just now would raise a howl of indignation. . . .

Dear Lady Erroll's evangelistic efforts culminated in the presentation to Lord Cross of a tract on temperance! He related this last night to the Queen at dinner amid shouts of laughter. I never saw the Queen more amused; but the dear old lady is rather in disgrace especially since she begged the Queen to prevent people visiting Kew Gardens on Sunday.

BALMORAL. *October 28th 1896*

Here is an anecdote about the Bishop of London [*Dr. Frederick Temple*] at the Garden Party this year at Buckingham Palace. He said to a good looking middle-aged man with whom he had been affably chatting: 'Well, and how is your father?' 'Don't you remember, he died long ago,' was the reply. Then, 'How is your mother?' said the Bishop. 'Very well for her years' was the answer and the conversation ended. Later in the afternoon the Bishop turned to his wife, 'Now who was that charming young man I was talking to just now?' 'The Duke of Connaught.'

I paid a visit to the Byngs yesterday and inspected the Somerton baby, the image of Sydney[1] minus the revolving eye. Then went to the Carringtons where we partook of a sumptuous tea and met a contingent of the Clanwilliam party including Mr. Savage Landor, discoverer of the Hairy Ainus and not unlike one himself. Lord Carrington is most good-natured but to my mind something of a snob, he literally grovels before the meanest Royalty

[1] Sydney, Earl of Normanton.

and makes an extraordinary fuss with all of us merely because we can date our letters 'Balmoral'. Louisa Antrim is a great resource, we read together 'The Reign of Queen Anne' by Mrs. Oliphant and hope to spend many pleasant hours together in my little sitting room.

BALMORAL. *October 30th 1896*

The Queen told me yesterday that Creighton is to be promoted to London and I am delighted London should have such a vigorous Bishop to stir it up. I wish I knew him, I feel sure I should like him. The Queen is much pleased with Lord Rosebery but I cannot make out whether she thinks he is likely to be less radical, I rather think she does and will shortly be undeceived.'

BALMORAL. *November 2nd 1896*

I drove with H.M. in the afternoon and discussed Roman Catholicism and the Low Church party, the Queen said that none of her Roman Catholic relatives of whom she has several, had ever tried to convert her but that she admired the Greek Church most outside her own as being far more tolerant. For instance the Tsar and Tsarina went to Scotch Service here a thing no Roman Catholic monarch would ever do and which even private individuals would avoid. The Emperor of Russia loaded everyone here with gifts and left £1,000 for the servants, he is extremely generous.

BALMORAL. *November 4th 1896*

The Queen quite apologized yesterday for enjoying the cold weather so intensely, 'I always feel so brisk,' said she! It is more than her daughters or Ladies do! I am surprised at Mr. Carr Glyn's rise in life, I somehow don't fancy him as a Bishop.[1] How careful Lord Salisbury is to conciliate the broad Church party. Have you many livings on hand? The Queen talked about books yesterday. Said she admired Mrs. Craven's more than anyone,

[1] He became Bishop of Peterborough.

the 'Récit d'une Sœur' above all. I must write and tell Sir M. S. I told H.M. he could repeat it by heart and she was much interested, also to hear that York House was to be sold again to the Orléans family. She says it must be to the Duc d'Orléans, as he has told everyone that he means to settle in England. His bride is three or four years his senior, rather a plain lady and of a very decided character. The Queen hopes she may be able to keep him in order but I do not think it likely.

BALMORAL. *November 5th 1896*
The Queen says she must see Victor again soon. You could accustom his mind to the idea. I do not feel quite the same confidence in his conduct as I used to do. How awful it would be if he fell down flat and said, 'I am afraid of her', as he did to Mama. I have been walking with the Queen this morning and we went to the Church to wreathe the tombs of various Browns; H.M. got out of her chair and laid a bunch of fresh flowers on John Brown's grave with her own hands. The Prince Consort and the Highland tenants share this unique honour, it is really very curious, but do not mention the curious fact. H.M. is very much depressed by the knowledge that we are so actively hated by other countries. She frequently refers to the subject and says she cannot conceive why it should be so. The Germans become more odious and aggressive every day and the Kruger telegram has given the German Emperor a popularity in his own country he never would have earned in any other way. Lord James[1] is very agreeable but I do not budge an inch from my opinion formed of him last year. He amuses me but does not attract me.

I am getting a little mixed up in high politics too which is what I enjoy but by the time I am really faded in I rush off and then the thread breaks and some months later is not taken up again immediately.

I have just been to see the Munshi's wife (by Royal command). She is fat and not uncomely, a delicate shade of chocolate and

---

[1] Lord James of Hereford, Minister in attendance.

gorgeously attired, rings on her fingers, rings on her nose, a pocket mirror set in turquoises on her thumb and every feasible part of her person hung with chains and bracelets and ear-rings, a rose-pink veil on her head bordered with heavy gold and splendid silk and satin swathings round her person. She speaks English in a limited manner and declares she likes the cold. The house surrounded by a twenty foot palisade, the door opening of itself, the white figure emerging silently from a near chamber, all seemed so un-English, so essentially Oriental that we could hardly believe we were within a hundred yards of this Castle. Do not repeat this, it would not be safe, but in days to come it will be a curious bit of history.

BALMORAL. *November 7th 1896*

Drove with the Queen yesterday and we went to Birkhall and only got home after dark. At dinner came the telegram announcing the birth of twins to Princess Margaret of Hesse [*née Prussia*]. The Queen laughed very much and is rather amused at the list of her great grandchildren being added to in such a rapid manner.

BALMORAL. *November 10th 1896*

Aunt Jane[1] has sent me her book; it is delightful and the Queen has consented to receive a copy. This will please the family, especially as Her Majesty remembers the old lady perfectly well and talked to me about her with great interest. I was reading Dean Stanley's Life to Her Majesty last night, some parts about the Abbey and mentioned how curious it is that there should be no monuments to Kings and Queens after Elizabeth. The Queen was very much interested and said there *should* be one to William and Mary. This is curious as showing what she thinks of her ancestors and I am surprised for I thought she did not like the usurpers of Stuart inheritance but this is so characteristic of her, she is a real constitutional monarch and never allows private prejudice to triumph over public good.

[1] Miss Jane Adeane, an aunt of Marie's, who wrote a book about her grandmother, Maria Josepha, Lady Stanley of Alderley.

BALMORAL. *November 11th 1896*

Did I tell you of an interesting discussion with the Queen as to the rival chances of Orléans and Bonapartes, she plumps for the latter and declares in her opinion they are the only dynasty with any hold on the French imagination. It really is curious that some of the people here say the reason is that Napoleon III was the first Sovereign who treated the Prince Consort as a reigning Prince. I think it very likely, for personal matters weigh heavily with the Queen. For instance last night she showed me a small jewelled dagger in an ivory sheath studded with rubies (oriental). 'This was always on dear Lord Beaconsfield's table and when I went to Hughenden after his death Lord Rowton wished me to take it, ever since it has always been on mine. Lord Beaconsfield was always so kind to me. I can never forget it.'

Her Majesty talked about Mr. Balfour's book.[1] 'I must read some of it but they tell me it is *very* difficult. I know it is beyond *me*. Have you read it?'

'Only partly Your Majesty.'

'Well you must find some bit not too hard to read to me.'

I promised Mr. Balfour I would read it and so I must. Can you advise me for I really do not know how to pick out any passages that would be intelligible without going into the whole argument?

I read Lord Salisbury's speech, the Queen highly approved and we both laughed over his hit at women! Of course he commits himself to nothing but will not budge from Egypt or Cyprus.

BALMORAL. *November 12th 1896*

I read the Queen 'The Times' leader on Lord Salisbury's speech last night. She is so tenacious of Egypt, says it is a great mistake we ever promised to go and that we owe all this European enmity to Mr. Gladstone. I expect this means between the lines that Lord Salisbury will not give it up under any circumstances. I wonder what Lord Rosebery would say to this policy.

[1] Presumably *The Foundations of Belief*, by A. J. Balfour (1895).

BALMORAL. *November 13th 1896*

We are all much on Bridge the new game of Whist imported by Lord James, very amusing and equally gambling. However our stakes are 'Love' so we can stand the shot.

Bernard's diary

November 14th 1896

Went to Windsor and had a delightful meeting [night of Nov. 13–14] with Marie. She had had a terrible journey south. After reading 2 hours to Queen she had dinner and retired. Then came violent sickness 7 times and colic, evidently *poisoned*. Sat. she had to spend in bed and slowly recovered. Still very weak on Sunday, but we took a walk. I lunched with Bigge, after which we talked till I came away at 6. She is evidently a great success with *all*, from Queen downwards. H.M. really dependent on having someone about her who can amuse her, talk to her and interest her, and she feels Marie can do this. It is some consolation, but tells against me!

The Queen last night turned to Marie and said 'Mr. Balfour's writing is worse than ever! I cannot read it at all, it is like a spider crawling over the paper. The duplicates are very well written— I can read them quite easily. Does your husband write them?' This referred to submissions to the Queen, of which a duplicate is always sent in the box, and I write them!

Some talk with Bigge and Edwards about Civil List matters. Mr. Balfour is horrified at the waste. Class III Expenses of the Household nearly £20,000 p.a. This does not include wages or salaries. There ought to be some one officer with powers over expenditure of all departments—a Chancellor of Exchequer.

WINDSOR CASTLE. *November 16th 1896*

I have been very busy walking with the Queen this morning to visit the Mausoleum where she deposited a simple little bunch of fresh flowers tied with white ribbon upon the Prince's tomb, and this afternoon looking after poor Mrs. Benson, the Archbishop widow who arrived at five with Miss Tait and Mrs. Davidson to have an interview with the Queen. I had to give them tea and entertain them a full hour, rather trying both for Mrs. Benson and for me as we had never met.

[*The same letter goes into a long plan for Victor to be brought down to Windsor with his nurse. As the Queen may wish to see him, and as his hair has been cut too short, might it be better for him to come a little later?*]

WINDSOR. *November 17th 1896*

The life here is more solitary and less homely than at Balmoral and Osborne, and though the pastimes are many and I really like it best yet I miss Louisa Antrim more than I can say and at first the many hours in one's room alone seem to pass but slowly. The Queen did not go out this morning for some unknown reason so I did not get any air till a quarter to four when I and a huge cavalcade bicycled for an hour in the slopes. It was most exhilarating such perfect paths and such gentle inclines, I sped along very well and was pleased with my performance. 'Biggy' congratulated me on progress and I really think I may be of some use before very long. . . .

You ask about Kitchener. I dined with the Queen last night so had ample opportunity of studying him. He appears to be either a woman-hater or a boor for he would hardly utter to us ladies in spite of many and strenuous efforts at dinner, though well enough placed between Lord Breadalbane and Minnie Cochrane he barely answered their questions. To the Queen after dinner he talked much and showed some Sudanese trophies he has brought as a present to Her Majesty, chain armour probably mediæval, banners, spears and a Crusader's sword with the motto: 'Do not draw me without reason, do not sheath me without honour' in old Romanesque on the blade. This was found in an Emir's tent. My own impression of Kitchener (which may be quite wrong) is that of a resolute but *cruel* man, a fine soldier no doubt, but not of the type that tempers justice with mercy. He has a low narrow forehead, very blue eyes and a fine figure. 'Biggy' tells me that later under the influence of whisky and tobacco he thawed and gave an appalling account of the young Khedive. He says he could not possibly be more wicked, cruel and weak. He hates the French, and the Turks; the Sultan most of all, and openly asked why we do not assassinate the Sultan. He simply longs for murder and executions would be his greatest joy were he to have his own way in Cairo. The Egyptians detest him and if we left the country his reign would not be long. Kitchener says he *means* to go to Khartoum and returns this day week to begin preparations. He appears to take it for granted that the money will be found. He thinks the Caisse will lose their case. He is very proud of having made ten miles of railway for nothing. What slave-driving and sweating there must have been!

To Lady Elizabeth Biddulph

WINDSOR. *November 18th 1896*

Victor has been here today in a truly seraphic mood. The Queen kindly expressed a wish to see him and I was only too glad of the excuse so Lady Mallet and Frances brought him down and you may really be proud of your grand-son for his behaviour has been quite perfect all day, very loving and affectionate to me and delighted with the Corridor and State Apartments, and when he entered the Queen's room he made a very low bow and walked calmly up and kissed Her Majesty's hand and then her face as she told him to do so. After this he introduced the comic element by suddenly producing a small but beloved black pig which he had insisted on bringing from London and said rather loudly, 'Look at this pig, I have brought it all the way from London to see you.' The Queen laughed till she cried then gave him a picture book which he thanked for very prettily and by this time feeling quite at his ease he gazed round the room and said, 'What a dear little Grenadier Guard.' This was a picture of the Duke of Connaught when a child in uniform. This interview (a nervous one for me) being over I took Victor to the Royal Nursery where he had an excellent lunch with the two little Princes Maurice and Leopold who were most kind to him, giving him toys and other treasures and rather to my dismay on coming back from my own meal I discovered my little rascal had again been summoned to the Royal Presence and was playing with the other children in the Queen's Dining Room under her very nose as happy as possible and without a vestige of 'mauvaise honte'.

At the end of twenty minutes I was sent for to carry him off and found him seated on the floor directing the construction of a tunnel, the Royal children working like slaves and simply hanging on his words! The Queen said 'I have *never* seen so good a little boy, it is quite astonishing,' and purple in the face I bowed a deprecating and final curtsey inwardly congratulating myself that he had not rolled on the floor or screamed, as we know he can when the fit takes him.

I well remember the celebrated pig, a small black and white skin-covered animal about four inches long which, after the Royal visit was set up in a glass case with an acorn under its nose and lived in the Nursery for years with the proud inscription, 'The pig who went to see the Queen'.

WINDSOR CASTLE. *November 19th 1896*

There is always enough going on here to keep one alive though the guests this week are not particularly interesting. Lord Salisbury however was splendid, extremely amusing and cynical about the foreign Ambassadors who bore him at his weekly receptions. He and the Queen talk to each other across the Corridor so we had the benefit of a most entertaining conversation. It appears Hatzfeldt, Courcel[1] and the Italian are the most valuable of the Corps Diplomatique. They stand in the corridor and converse on geography and philosophy, in short anything but politics. I fear Lord Salisbury cannot have a long life before him, he is gigantic, his legs simply refuse to bear the weight of his body and the Queen says he eats enormously; his eyes are red and the pouches

[1] Courcel's grandson is now French Ambassador in London, 1966.

beneath them purple, if he were my father I should tremble. Lord Edward Cecil has returned none the worse for the campaigns, but out in Egypt he had fever and dysentry and was very ill.

The Rumbolds are very pleased about Vienna and in high spirits, I believe the Emperor asked for him and the Queen had to give in, though she still believes he boxed the Dutch Lord Chamberlain's ears.

WINDSOR CASTLE. *November 20th 1896*

The ambassadors enjoyed themselves last night, but poor Sir Horace [*Rumbold*] stood cheek by jowl with Colonel Clerk all the evening, his deadliest enemy who never ceases calling him a scoundrel and declares he robbed the Nizam of £60,000 and that Rumbold père was only a waiter at White's! Lady Monson is rather pretty but like most Ambassadors' wives very second-rate.

WINDSOR. *November 23rd 1896*

The Queen has a slight cold but appeared to enjoy a performance of cinematographie very badly done by Downey which has just taken place (7 p.m.) in the Red Drawing Room in honour of Prince Drino's birthday; it has given me a lot to do in the way of messages, etc., and I have been very busy. This evening I have had Mr. Howard Sturgis about some articles to appear in 'The Cornhill', diaries etc. of Sir Charles Murray which have had to pass the Queen, and I have had to read them to her and bowdlerise rather freely. They are of moderate interest and I think 'twaddly', so does the Queen, but St. Loe is dying to have them and I daresay the public will eagerly devour anything with the magic date 1837 that can appear about the Queen.

CHAPTER IX

THE DIAMOND JUBILEE

Fourth Waiting

To B.M.

WINDSOR CASTLE. *May 18th 1897*

I always feel stranded here just at first and nervous lest I should make mistakes or displease anyone, but they are all very nice to me and Sir Arthur I feel and know thoroughly trusts me, and therefore is glad to confide many things to me he would not mention to any of the Ladies or even to Uncle Alick, so this gives me confidence and makes me feel I can be useful. The dear old Duchess of Athole died this morning at the age of 83 and the Queen feels her loss *very* deeply. For forty-three years she has been in the Household and she was universally beloved. It is a comfort to hear from Fanny Drummond her near relation that she talked with great pleasure of her last Waiting at Balmoral, and said that Aline and I made her so very happy. The Queen is so fully occupied with a hundred questions of the utmost importance that I hope she may not dwell so much on this fresh grief. The Princess of Wales came down last night in an awful stew about Greece, imploring the Queen to do something to stop the war and stay the hand of the triumphant Turks. However, the Queen has just told me the Emperor of Russia *is* stopping it in spite of Germany. Of course this is a secret, it seems a pity we should play second-fiddle. *We* ought to have asserted ourselves and been backed up by Russia. I have been driving with the Queen this afternoon and Her Majesty has specially put me on her dinner list, no doubt in honour of your Chief.

WINDSOR CASTLE. *May 20th 1897*

I have enjoyed a long drive in the Park with the beloved Queen who was very chatty and full of interest and amusing gossip. From time to time I was commanded to read the newspapers, for she has been so frightfully busy the last few days that we had got rather behind. We had a lively discussion as to whether the Duc d'Aumale married Madame de Clinchamp after all. The Queen says 'Certainly not', but Colonel Carrington who has just returned from representing her at the funeral declares there can be no doubt about it and imagines that the young protégé who inherits the English estates is her son. We shall know for certain for he has telegraphed to Sir E. Monson [*Ambassador at Paris*] for the exact truth.

On the way to Balmoral the Queen paid a State Visit to Sheffield to mark the Jubilee Year.

BALMORAL. *May 22nd 1897*

Words fail me to tell you how deeply the loyalty and order of the people of Sheffield impressed me yesterday, they were in the streets by tens of thousands, looking well-to-do, contented and simply bursting with enthusiasm and general love for the Queen. I never saw a single creature attempt to break the rank or even push rudely and the soldiers and police had an easy task. The streets were most beautifully decorated and on a regular plan, Venetian masts with garlands of paper flowers, red, white and blue, varied by pure white, hanging festooned across the streets, and huge crowns and flowers suspended at intervals for the carriages to pass exactly under them. Of course many triumphal arches of a more solid character here and there with some very original mottoes, 'True as Sheffield steel', etc. I have never seen a more grimy town and I believe the normal climate is fog tempered by rain, but the sun shone brilliantly yesterday and we were glad of parasols till nearly seven. It made the whole difference to the people's pleasure and even the dirtiest little streets

The Munshi, Hafiz Abdul Karim

The Queen at work at Osborne, about 1898

looked gay. The climax of the whole thing to my mind was not the Town Hall where all the 'big-wigs' were presented in turn and any amount of Addresses handed to the Home Secretary, but Norfolk Park, a lovely piece of hilly ground, well-wooded, where the Duke of Norfolk had assembled 50,000 children with their teachers; it was both touching and most thrilling when they all began to sing in their clear, shrill and musical voices first a short hymn specially composed and then 'God Save the Queen'. The Queen stopped twice for several minutes in order that all might see her, and when she finally moved off they cheered and waved coloured flags in perfect unison, it was marvellously arranged, perfect order prevailed and the children looked beaming with happiness. The ground lent itself to such an undertaking as the hills on both sides of the road were densely packed and I should think nearly all could see more or less, but it must have required great courage on the Duke's part to embark in such a difficult enterprise. He is extraordinarily popular and was tremendously cheered, it only shows that if a man is really good religious difficulties disappear, for Sheffield seemed to me a mass of dissenting chapels and I never saw a single priest. The Queen looked extremely well and bowed vigorously, so enjoyed the whole thing, so immensely touched, and wonderful to relate not a bit tired; after this I do not dread the Jubilee Procession for her, it won't take long, we were close on two and a half hours in the carriages yesterday, and I fear the Londoners will not cheer and shout and clap half as much as the Yorkshire folk did. The noise could not possibly be greater, the intense enthusiasm brought tears to my eyes many times. It is a wonderful thing to see thousands of human beings possessed by one thought and showing their feelings quite naturally. The Life Guards created great admiration especially Mr. Ozzy Ames, mounted on a gigantic charger and looking magnificent.

[*I myself remember Captain Ames, an immensely tall officer, to whom I had been introduced somewhere and who was one of my main memories of the Jubilee Procession in London which he led on horseback.*]

I

The Home Secretary was much cheered and our Carriage came in for it too, so many recognised the Lord Chamberlain by his beard, I expect! The Duke of Norfolk presented us all with lovely baskets of flowers, roses and lilies and clove carnations and we had a dinner worthy of Voisin put into our Carriage at Preston, in fact we felt like Princesses for once in our lives and I for one shall never forget my visit to Sheffield and think myself most fortunate to have come in for it. From the time we left Windsor till past ten at night, twelve hours, we were literally never out of the sound of cheering from one end of England to the other there were people on both sides of the line patiently waiting to see the Queen's train pass and give her an 'Hurrah'. At Manchester and Derby dense crowds, I doubt if such a thing could happen in any other country.

King Leopold II of the Belgians visited the Queen at Balmoral for a day. 'Quelle voyage, cher cousin', she greeted him. 'Quelle butte!' was his reply.

BALMORAL. *May 25th 1897*

We have just been receiving the King of the Belgians in the chilly front Hall, he can only shake hands with two fingers as his nails are so long that he dares not run the risk of injuring them. He is an unctuous old monster, very wicked I believe, we imagine he thinks a visit to the Queen gives him a fresh coat of whitewash, otherwise why does he travel five hundred miles in order to partake of lunch! Tosti and de Soria are here and we had delightful music last night with the promise of more this evening. De Soria was present at the Paris fire and says the stories told of the 'jeunesse dorée' are, alas, too true, they simply behaved like brutes and several ladies who escaped are badly wounded by the blows they received from the heavy sticks. . . .

The Queen gave me a charming set of photos mounted in silver yesterday as a souvenir of her birthday.

BALMORAL. *May 28th 1897*

Feo Gleichen[1] is very nice, but we hardly see her as she is treated entirely as a Royalty and keeps very much to herself. I know she is bored by that but I suppose she cannot do otherwise; it is very funny when one knows how democratic she is at home.

BALMORAL. *May 31st 1897*

I do all I can to help poor Sir Fleetwood [*Edwards*] and that gives me more writing than usual, besides the Queen has more work owing to the Jubilee and I verily believe everybody's work increases as time goes on. I now see the Queen regularly twice a day which is an improvement as I do not have to worry her with questions in the evening and can read calmly without interruption. She is much distressed about Lady Salisbury's condition and I shrewdly suspect fully alive to Lord Salisbury's poor health, which could be a disaster for the country, but the Queen is very devoted to Lord Salisbury and has great confidence in him. She declares the Turks *are* to be kept in order and won't be allowed to occupy territory or crush the Greeks, this is reassuring but I cannot feel the same confidence in the Concert of Europe that the Queen has. The German Emperor is in bad odour everywhere and the final coup is his acceptance of six Greek guns presented by the Sultan. He ought to be kicked; my only joy is that he is simply frantic at not coming here for the Jubilee and would like to kill his poor brother for daring to accept the Queen's invitation. We had a dismal preacher yesterday, Dr. Mitchell. He discoursed on death and worms and judgement for thirty minutes and we all felt inclined to howl. I believe Lord Rowton comes soon. Lord Balfour of Burleigh is heavier than lead and I am in his bad books for suggesting he was related to A. J. B. How was I to know he came of the Bruces and had a six-hundred years pedigree?

[1] Lady Feodore Gleichen was the daughter of Prince Victor of Hohenloke-Langenburg and a very good sculptress. Her brother, Count Gleichen was later known as Lord Edward Gleichen, a keen and intelligent soldier who commanded the 37th Division during World War I. I was his A.D.C. for over a year in France.

BALMORAL. *June 1st 1897*

I enclose a very amusing letter from Sir Arthur. The Captain Ahmed referred to used to hand us plates at dinner a few short years ago. Now he poses as a Captain of Cavalry and has come over for the Jubilee at the Queen's invitation and we Ladies are expected to receive him and make a fuss of him! Do not breathe a word of this but I am sure it is just another dodge to exalt the 'Munshi'! . . .

The Queen is a marvel of health and strength. We played our duets last night after dinner and she was quite pleased. I shook and Ethel [*Cadogan*] used bad language.

BALMORAL. *June 2nd 1897*

I am very busy, my room looks like 'Rorke's Drift', a mass of letters and portfolios and Jubilee thimbles and illustrated papers. We are all at our wits end and the Queen hates being asked questions and it falls to my lot to ask her more than anybody else. I had a truly trying afternoon yesterday, four hours tête-à-tête with Ethel in a wagonette racing behind the Queen's four-in-hand to old Mar Lodge, plenty of dust and a bad headache, Ethel harangued me on her grievances without ceasing for a single moment and I told lies by the bushel. I hope I shall be forgiven, for if I told the truth there would only be a row and my duty is to keep all worry from the Queen. It will be a comfort to have 'Nunks' tomorrow, Emily Ampthill arrives Friday. The weather is lovely at last and I pine to be out sketching from morning to eve but that is impossible so I snatch half an hour when I can. . . .

I hear Lady Salisbury is really very ill, do you think Lord Salisbury will resign if she dies? The Queen thinks *not* and evidently hopes it.

The letters during this month are full of complaints of the row with Ethel Cadogan, which upset Marie considerably. It is rather a mystery what it was all about, but evidently in that small Court circle it was highly embarrassing, as Miss Cadogan had quarrelled with practically everyone there.

She was six years older than Marie and had been a Maid of Honour since 1876. It is not clear what her grievance was, but she and Miss Phipps did not get on well. Perhaps she was getting a bit old for her job, and she seems to have expected promotion, which she appears to have got in 1897 when she became a Woman of the Bedchamber. It seems that this merely left her as a substitute with no real duties and junior to Miss Phipps, Mrs Grant and Marie. Anyhow she made life very disagreeable for the others during the pre-Jubilee waiting at Balmoral. In May Marie had written to Miss Phipps, who was out of waiting. Harriet answered in two long letters from which I quote.

'I am extremely sorry for her as I know what the change and loss of self-importance will be to her. And the despair that will fall upon her family in having her at home!! but if she can be persuaded to view the appt in the light of promotion and consideration that will greatly help and she should be backed up to the world, as one does not want her to feel humiliated. It will be a great thing if The Queen is saved from worry on the subject, but I shall be surprised if there is no frantic last appeal to H.M. as you see there has already been to poor Pss B. I think it hardly possible it will be warded off entirely, but if it comes after the Jubilee it will be less bad than before it.'

Again on June 11 Harriet writes to Marie:

'I am very grieved to think there should be all this trouble going on just when all should be as quiet and restful as possible for The Queen. I too feel very much for Ethel for she makes herself so impossible. I always regretted her having this waiting at Balmoral—at Windsor would I thought have been so much better for the reason she wished to go to Balmoral was the hope of getting The Queen's decision changed. I am sure, as I wrote to you at Windsor, that the only way to keep the peace is to treat her firmly and kindly and refuse to discuss with her the question of the appt The Queen has seen fit to make. H.M. decides for herself naturally—we have only to carry out her wishes. Ethel has freely stated her case to Pss Beatrice for The Queen's consideration and as I wrote Ethel we can neither question nor discuss it. I am very sorry for* *what pain and mortification Ethel may feel. She has always been foolish enough to give out that she was greatly needed by The Queen and she minds her family realising that her vaunts are false. I am sure that when the matter is discussed with her that talking goes to her head! and she can by her own voice persuade herself of anything. She has been quite civil to me since I convinced her of the falsity of her most objectionable idea that these decisions were brought about by someone influencing The Queen, an idea I detest. One tells The Queen the truth and naturally does not presume, or wish to throw light or shadow on what H.M. may decide on the facts. I would certainly not discuss it any more if I were you. It is bad of her to listen at your door but curiosity is a strong feature of her character.'*

BALMORAL. *June 4 1897*

It is hard to exactly define or describe my work. I spend a good deal of time in the passages running to and fro for the Queen, the Princessess, Sir Fleetwood and the Wardrobe. Then I have letters to write to all sorts of people, today Princess Beatrice, yesterday Princess Louise, for the Queen, of course plenty of smaller fry who send and ask for photos and posters and tickets for every imaginable fête and procession, in short it all sounds trivial and boring and often is so, but it happens to be my work and it cannot be hurried. I expect yours is much the same but your Chief is more accessible than mine. I have seen a good deal of Countess Feo and like her immensely. We have long talks about Münthe[1] and I long more and more to see him. 'Nunks' is in excellent spirits but complains of his health. However he is always better here and I think he is very happy with us all. The Queen was very gracious to me last night and altogether she seems satisfied. Lord Balfour and Müther[2] made the ascent of Loch Na Gar yesterday and were rewarded by a magnificent view, the sky was cloudless and the sun brilliant, they found plenty of snow on the top over

---

[1] D. Axel Münthe, Swede, author of *San Michele*.

[2] Maurice Müther, the German Secretary, was in charge of the archives at Windsor.

six feet deep. I bicycled nine miles with Emily Loch up hill and down dale and felt justly proud of myself. I hope to do twenty miles before I leave.

Marie was much upset by the death of a cousin Charles Earle who fell off his bicycle on to his head. Bernard and she exchanged anxious letters about the dangers of bicycling, begging each other to be very careful.

BALMORAL. *June 10 1897*
Lord Rowton is rather what I call a 'boot-licker', he flatters one like anything, but I see through it and laugh in my sleeve, talks of me as one of the Queen's greatest props, etc. He grovels before the Royalties in rather a sickening way, and I expect he is an ideal courtier, I wish I was that a little more, but it is not in me. . . .
The Queen is very much worried about the question of precedence at Banquets, etc. and won't leave it to the Prince of Wales who always makes bothers, until he always has it all his own way. And then the horrors of Greece on the top of it all! I fear she is getting tired and I feel so sorry, by this time the whole thing should be settled for ever. The Queen ought to have a quiet week before the real fatigue begins.

BALMORAL. *June 14th 1897*
We live for nothing but the Jubilee and seem to ignore the doings of the world in general even the attack on President Faure hardly moves us and we snort at the Greek question.

The remaining letters deal with plans for witnessing the Jubilee Procession to which I went with my nurse, Frances Taylor, to Lord Rothschild's house in Piccadilly. I can just remember the Jubilee Procession. Captain Ames on his horse leading the Escort, Indian Cavalry Lancers, and the Queen in an open carriage seeming to my young eyes to be immense, although she was in fact a very small woman.
Bernard's diary notes some of the special events. He describes

. . . the Ball, at which all the foreign representatives were present and to which over 1500 were invited, the garden party at Buckingham Palace, and perhaps most interesting of all, the party to the H. of Commons at Windsor, to which I went as Mr. Balfour's secretary with Marie. The most interesting ceremony we attended was the private service on Jubilee Sunday at St. George's—Queen, Royal Family and those in waiting and hardly anyone else except Cadogans and Devonshire. Touching, simple and beautiful service. All her family embraced the Queen at the end. . . .

CHAPTER X

BERNARD'S CHRISTMAS AT OSBORNE

Fifth Waiting

Marie was not well during this waiting. My brother, Arthur, was born in the following May.

WINDSOR. *November 15th 1897*
The Queen had given me a dear little brooch in pink and grey enamel with small diamonds as a memento of the Jubilee. She is marvellously well and in excellent spirits in spite of poor Prince Maurice's death which was a painful shock. Princess Beatrice has been to White Lodge today. Lord Salisbury came yesterday fatter than ever but looking well, we longed for a 'Kodak' to perpetuate the group he and the Queen sitting side by side on spindle-legged chairs in the corridor, their heads together, audibly discussing the price of methylated spirits (this is for your private ear). The Queen has not mentioned your appointment to me;[1] either she has not read the Box or perhaps hopes to surprise me with the news. Bigge and Sir Fleetwood think you have done extremely well and congratulate you heartily. The former is very keen on Palace reform but as usual the Queen demurs and merely says, 'Then I must tell my maid my bed can*not* be mended for the present.' What an angel she is and how little she knows of the world we poor mortals inhabit.

WINDSOR. *November 19th 1897*
I was with the Queen more than an hour while she sat to a Danish artist, Jucksen, for her portrait in a picture he is painting of Princess Maud of Wales' wedding; she sat most patiently and

[1] As a Commissioner of Inland Revenue.

was so gracious to the artist. Then I flew to the Library where I found Burnand[1] being entertained by Mr. Holmes and very happy. Lady Downe came also to see the illustrations for 'The Pilgrim's Progress' and we were all enchanted with their beauty. We showed Mr. Burnand the drawings and this afternoon Mr. Holmes took him all over the Castle, corridor included, and he departed enraptured with his visit.

WINDSOR. *November 23rd 1897*

I am feeling better today which is lucky as I have a deal of running about, owing to the dense fog the Queen did not stir out this afternoon so I was often wanted. This evening at 6 p.m. we had an entertainment in honour of Prince Drino's eleventh birthday [*Prince Drino was the eldest son of Prince and Princess Henry of Battenberg and afterwards was created Marquess of Carisbrooke*], the cinematograph and some performing dogs both hailing from the Emperor, the living photos were on rather too small a scale and after an hour of that we were left somewhat exhausted, the process is marvellous but by no means perfect. Tonight we have a 'hen-dinner' and the children can join in in honour of the birthday. . . .

I gather you are becoming very indiscreet about me, your mother writes very sweetly but I *had* meant to tell her myself, and you should have denied it to 'Nunks'. I feel sure that before another week is out the whole Castle will be ringing with the interesting intelligence.[2]

Soon after this Bernard visited Windsor and wrote in his diary:

WINDSOR. *Sunday November 28th 1897*

At Windsor at Lady Biddulph's to see Marie. Dined with the Queen quite unexpectedly. About 10 at dinner—fortunately I had my tights and Jubilee medal on the chance. The usual procedure—

[1] F. C. Burnand of *Punch*.
[2] About the 'coming of Arthur'!

the Queen walking in across the corridor, bowing, we all following, ladies first, in order of rank. Very little conversation at dinner,
except in a low voice. It lasted little over half an hour. The Queen
as she rose said of the wind, which was howling outside, 'What a
melancholy sound!' I thought she seemed more infirm about
rising from her chair. When my turn came to be summoned to
stand before her in the corridor for conversation she immediately
put me quite at my ease by her great amiability of manner and
evident interest in what was said. She laughed more than ever.
She began by saying how sorry I must be at leaving Mr Balfour
and I assented, expressing regret. Then she remarked on his lying
so late in bed, thought it could not be healthy. I described how he
dictated his work from bed, and how the regime seemed to suit
his health. Then she asked me about my new office, and I told her
I should become one of the most unpopular people in the king-
dom, having to do with income tax and death duties. She said the
latter were dreadful things, to which I rejoined that they brought
in a great deal of money. Then she talked of Victor—such a
pretty boy, and of his approaching visit to Windsor. Then talk
turned on Ledbury and Lady Elizabeth's platform speaking. She
said 'I cannot imagine Marie making speeches on a platform' and
I said I was glad she had not inherited this taste for public speaking. She laughed and said, '*Nor her sister?*' So I think it ended.
This is the third time I have dined—twice at Windsor and once at
Florence, and the third conversation I have been honoured with—
and I had a stronger impression than ever of her charm, which
consists of extreme womanliness, and great commonsense, together with sincere and evident interest in what she is saying. No
mere making of conversation, but real sympathy and interest.

Marie to Lady Elizabeth Biddulph

WINDSOR. *November 29th 1897*
    You will have heard from Bernard of the Queen's wonderful
kindness. I can hardly believe that Victor arrives this afternoon as
Her Majesty's guest yet such is really the case and the Carriage is

ordered to meet him at 3.12 and a charming room is prepared for
him on the Ground Floor close to mine. He is invited to dine
every day in the Royal Nursery and will not be allowed to dawdle
over his food as Prince Maurice eats fast and will provide a good
example. I am so delighted at the prospect of seeing him again and
he will have such fun here and so much to see. I am sure he will
remember such an event for the rest of his life. The Queen has
invited him to remain until Friday. . . .

I had a very happy day yesterday with Bernard crowned by
our both being invited to dine with the Queen. Her Majesty was
most gracious and had quite a long talk with Bernard after dinner
about Mr. Balfour and his new office, etc. and I felt very proud
for his manner is so perfect, so easy and yet so respectful and he
looked so 'distingué' in his new knee breeches and silk stockings.
I only wish you could have been there, that would have been
complete bliss.

To B.M.

WINDSOR. *November 29th 1897*

Victor arrived safe and sound and, but for his cough, looking
very well, he was too sweet for words and very pleased to see me
and I felt very proud as I took him down the Corridor to tea with
the Royal children. He behaved like a perfect courtier and kissed
Princess Beatrice's hand without being told to do so. He talked a
great deal at tea and amused Mr. Tufnell the tutor very much by
announcing that V.R. meant Victoria Regina. . . .

It was delightful to see him playing so charmingly with the
other children and neither shy nor bumptious.

WINDSOR. *November 30th 1897*

Victor is basking in the sunshine of Royalty to such an extent
that I hardly see him. He positively refused to have tea with me
saying he *must* go to Prince Maurice and then have a good romp.
This morning I took him to see the chickens and kangaroos near
Frogmore and on the way home the Queen was behind us but a

good way off, however she sent a man flying after us to say we were to wait till she came up as she wanted to see Victor, so we stood by the side of the road and as the pony chair drew near, he tore his red cap off his head and bowed till his golden hair looked like an aureole in the sunshine flowing out in the wind. Then he kissed the Queen's hand and the Princesses' and conversed affably for some minutes introducing his Chinese doll, Ching-Foo with much pride. Frances was weeping with emotion and will I am afraid spend the rest of her life relating her adventures here and sight of the Queen. It really is very wonderful and I can hardly believe it! Victor lunched with Prince Maurice and went into the Queen's room afterwards and out with the children in a donkey carriage this afternoon and now I have succeeded with some difficulty in packing him off to bed. . . .

The Chinese Ambassador lunched here today and I sat next to him and discussed philosophy and education, the two things that interest him most in the world. He prefers our philosophy to that of the Germans and thinks it kinder and more human but he informed me he considers the English language very ambiguous.

WINDSOR. *December 2nd 1897*

Victor is more than happy and the two little Princes are perfectly devoted to him and he to them. They tell each other extraordinary stories and pay visits to all the birds and beasts on the Estate, all three of them packed into a charming little carriage drawn by a stout pony. This afternoon they played at soldiers and presented arms, and Victor was fascinated by the sentries when they suddenly saluted him rather to Frances's dismay. The Queen has given him a splendid box of soldiers which are to be kept in the Drawing Room at Ledbury and Cecilia Downe presented him with a delightful picture book so as usual he departs laden with gifts. Last night we had another grand tea-party and a game of 'Happy Families'. Mr. Tufnell, the tutor, asked Victor for Mr. Potts, the painter, 'Yes, he is at home, but he is not going out of his house today for I am collecting the Potts family myself.'

Considering he has never played the game before we all considered this rather sharp.

Bernard's diary

WINDSOR. *December 6th 1897*

Went on Sat. to L. Cust's at Windsor to see Marie and enjoyed my Sunday with her as usual. Victor's visit an immense success. He won everyone's heart from the Queen's down to the housemaids by his charming manner, naturalness, and good temper. The Battenberg boys devoted to him and he to them. They drove out together, saw all the animals, played games and told each other long stories, V. doing the lion's share by means of his Chinese doll Ching Fu, who told a story too, always. (The Queen said it was a great pity Marie did not shew him the Chinese Minister who came down one day to luncheon!) One day he ran away from his nurse and rest and saluted the sentries as he had seen the Princes do, so as to get them to present arms to him— which they did! Then he insisted on seeing St. George's Chapel, so Marie got the Dean to go with them. On entering he said to his nurse 'take off my hat' (tho' he had only once or twice been inside a church), then marched down the aisle and exclaimed 'What a beautiful East Window!' It was the West Window, as the Dean explained to him. He was fascinated by the banners and insisted on Marie taking him into every stall and reading the names of the Knights. Then they came to the altar and he said to the Dean 'Have you anything more interesting to show me?' He went every day to the Queen after luncheon with the Battenberg boys, without his nurse or mother, and seems to have behaved perfectly. Marie describes his first meeting the Queen, when they were walking on the slopes. He said he knew quite well what to do, and when she came near he tore off his cap, bowed very low, his hair flying in the air, and seized her hand and kissed it. Then he turned to Frances for his Chinese doll which he showed to the Queen. He seems to have behaved in the same courtly manner to the Empress Eugenie and altogether seems never at a loss as to his manners, and so natural and such a child, too. He is full of promise. The Queen was quite glad to hear from Marie that he was sometimes naughty, otherwise he would be *too* good.

The Duke of Cambridge seems to have been most amusing at dinner one night, talking politics and all sorts of tabooed subjects in his loud voice, addressing the Queen as 'Madam', abusing bicycles, school boards, etc. etc., allusion to 'Affie's' state of health! The Queen rather shocked at his not feeling Princess May's death[1] more remarked on this to his equerry, Gen. Bateson, who said, 'At that age people do not feel such things'. The Queen said to Marie she thought this a most extraordinary remark, as the Duke was only 3 months older than herself, and *she* felt things very much! It certainly was most tactless! H.M. much interested in the *army* question, and rather dissatisfied with the lukewarmness of Ministers, especially the Duke of Devonshire, who she thought very inert and lazy. The Spanish Ambassador, Casa Valencia, astonished them by *sitting down* after dinner in the Queen's presence. (V. curious in a Spaniard!)

I think and hope the question of counteracting Sugar Duties is 'off colour' just now. The Queen said the only two people who had ever out of mistaken politeness tried to end a conversation with her saying 'Do not let me detain Y.M. any longer' were John Bright and the Archbishop (Longley) of York (and Canterbury). She does not like Sir A. West. She is wonderfully well and the people about her say they do not see why she should not live another 10 years.

To show her curious naivete about money and ignorance of the world in which other people live, Marie told me she had said she really must forbid her maids to have her bed mended which they wanted, having been alarmed by what Lord S. and Mr. B. had been trying to impress on her as to the extravagance in the expenditure of Windsor and Buckingham Palace, which I have calculated costs nearly £40,000 per ann—furniture and repairs

---

[1] The Duchess of Teck, mother of the future Queen Mary, had died after a sudden operation on October 27, 1897.

inside and out, staffs of inspectors for these purposes *only*. On Mr. Balfour saying to her that she ought to have no anxiety on such matters and have enough, never deny herself what she wanted, she said that it was very good for her to have to deny herself things. Once she thought to economize by having fewer different kinds of bread at breakfast!

WINDSOR. *December 6th 1897*

A drive with H.M. and Lady Erroll this afternoon. They both slept and I had a hard task to rouse them from time to time. Grieg came this evening at six and played his divine music, he is a real genius. He told the Queen his great-grandfather hailed from Aberdeen and was called Greig. His wife sang, very funny to look at and her voice 'passée', but interesting all the same.

WINDSOR CASTLE. *December 7th 1897*

The Queen was very amusing yesterday about games at Public Schools, football she thinks very barbarous, cricket would not be so bad if the ball were softer. I was appealed to as to whether it could not be made of some kind of composition. I stood up for athletics but granted Rugby football was a desperate game. At dinner we had much talk (a 'hen' party) about music and musicians, the Queen as usual inveighed against Oratorios and said she could not forget the boredom of 'The Messiah' heard in York Minster when she was about 16. I could not agree about this and praised Handel and the whole tribe of oratorio writers, so you see I was in opposition all day long!

WINDSOR. *December 9th 1897*

We have a huge Investiture today and sat down forty or fifty to lunch, only six ladies to grace the manly board. Sir F. Carrington fell to my lot, very agreeable, on the subject of South Africa boundless admiration of Rhodes and firm belief in the future of Rhodesia, which he says is far the most pleasant climate of all those Colonies.

WINDSOR CASTLE. *December 10th 1897*

We had some lovely music this evening in St. George's Hall. Sir Arthur Sullivan came to conduct an Anthem he has written at the Queen's request for December 14th, and the choir from St. George's conducted by him sang it most beautifully, as well as several other things, 'Peace, Come Away', by Stanford and a piece by Loebgesang. The Queen enjoyed it all to the full, I have never seen anyone more worthy of music and moved by it than she is. It is only a pity we do not have it oftener. I am reading 'Tennyson's Life' in every spare minute, it quite absorbs me and I must at once begin re-reading his poems. These will all possess new meaning; he always left his wife once a year and travelled with a male friend, devoted as he was to her, and this consoles me not a little for our separations. I know I love you even better (if that were possible) when we are apart and realize the blank in my life in a way I never should if we never left each other from year's end to year's end.

WINDSOR CASTLE. *December 14th 1897*

I was invited to the Service at the Mausoleum this morning and it was most touching, the service was very simple, music heavenly, sunshine pouring through the narrow windows and the birds twittering in the garden outside, it struck me immensely. I dine with the Queen tonight and hope Princess May will not be too shy to speak to me. She looks pale and thin and as if she longed for sympathy but was too shy to seek it. Prince George looks ill. I am sure he is not strong. [*These were later King George V and Queen Mary.*]

WINDSOR CASTLE. *December 15th 1897*

I dined with the Queen last night, a party of six because of the Yorks. Princess May talked to me most confidentially for half an hour after dinner and was very affectionate and not a bit shy or reserved when once the first few words were over. Her poor father is in a terrible state but they have persuaded him to have

K

a resident Doctor and he is quieter in consequence. She was brave and pathetic, very touching and seemed glad to talk openly to an old friend. She enjoyed seeing Maud, I wish she would see more of her.

OSBORNE. *December 19th 1897*

We had a Ladies' Dinner last night, the Queen was rather sad and silent, brooding over General Gardiner's funeral, I think, about which I have carried some score of messages to the Gentlemen. It certainly is strange she should take such deep interest in the merest details of these functions. A cheerful ceremony is always treated with the utmost indifference. I suppose as some say it is the dim shade of inherited melancholy from George III. Minnie Cochrane is here for two nights and very cheerful, she departs tomorrow and won't be here till after Christmas again. Bring golf sticks, there is a course on the premises and Sirs F. and A. play most afternoons and look forward to games with you. If the weather turns dry I should almost advise the bike too. I believe Prince Henry[1] arrives tonight or tomorrow morning, we shall long to chaff but shall not dare! However, I hope the Friday 'Globe' may fall under his eye, most amusing and perfectly true. I read the speeches to the Queen but dared not venture on 'The Times' article, she thought them most bombastic but I am sure she will be too tactful to make any allusions to the young man himself.

OSBORNE. *December 20th 1897*

The Bigges expect you on Thursday as on Friday they all come up to the Tree here and I hope you will come too, it will amuse you. Then golf may be played daily and the roads are all gravel and excellent for biking if the weather keeps fine so you can do as you like about that, however I have no doubt you could borrow a bike with the greatest ease for they swarm here. Prince Henry arrived last night very late for dinner, he looked very ill and was

[1] Of Prussia.

most depressed and nervous in his manner, hardly speaking to the Queen above a whisper and tearing his pocket handkerchief to pieces as he talked; he had not seen a single paper so will have had a rude shock today; he went to London this morning and will I hope learn a few home truths on the way. The Queen ordered the papers *not* to be brought into breakfast this morning and copies of 'The Daily Graphic' were hurriedly concealed after she had thoroughly enjoyed the caricature. Do not breathe this! I am busy arranging with the clergy to take the various services here and correspond with Bishops, Deans and smaller fry in a most familiar strain.

OSBORNE. *December 21st 1897*
I drove alone with the Queen this afternoon and much enjoyed my tête-à-tête. I cannot say how much I love and admire her. We talked of people being sympathetic and the reverse and the Queen said, 'It makes the whole difference to me if I know people may be good and trust-worthy but if they lack sympathy I can never feel the same towards them.' I hope she feels this of me, I *think* she does and she mentioned Aline Majendie[1] as being after her own heart. . . . Mind you bring your tights, stockings, pumps and Jubilee Medal. I am sure you will be asked to dine.

OSBORNE. *December 23rd 1897*
I have just had the sweetest note from the Queen inviting you to stay from Friday to Monday and since that, a message that you are on no account to leave before Tuesday, as the Queen will not hear of you travelling on Boxing Day. It really is more than kind and thoughtful and I am full of joy and gratitude, it will be every-thing having you on the spot, and all the men are so nice and friendly that you will have great fun. . . .

[1] Miss Aline Majendie, daughter of L. A. Majendie, M.P., of Castle Hedingham, Essex, became a Maid of Honour in 1894. She married in 1903, as his second wife, Field-Marshal Lord Grenfell.

Bring your nicest clothes but top hat is not necessary as we have Church in the House and there would be no other chance of wearing it. Do not forget golf sticks, etc.

Letter in the Queen's hand

Dear Marie,

I find by some mistake that the message I thought had been conveyed to you about your Husband coming here for Xmas had never been given. I therefore write at once to say I hope he can come here on Friday staying till Monday. [*illegible*] hopes telegraph at once to tell him.

Dec. 22/97.   Ever

                                                                    V.R.I.

To Lady Elizabeth Biddulph

OSBORNE. *December 28th 1897*

I have employed my spare energy in walking with Bernard. We have had the happiest time together and he has been the greatest possible success, dining with the Queen three nights out of four passed here, and sitting twice next to the Duchess of Albany and last night between Princess Louise and Princess Beatrice, only one from the Queen, a most alarming position; however he acquitted himself admirably, kept the conversation going and even amused the Queen with an account of our Belgian adventures; she roared with laughter at my sketching difficulties in Bruges and said, 'I shall write to the King and tell him the population should not spit over the drawings of my Ladies when they travel in Belgium.' Altogether the visit will always be a bright spot in our lives and something for our children to talk of. I feel sure you must be nearly as pleased as I am. Bernard has just left with Princess Louise who has invited him to travel up to London with her and Lord Lorne, so he has done all most comfortably.

I have some charming presents, large gold spoons from the

Queen, a stand for miniatures from Princess Beatrice, a lovely old silver spoon from Princess Louise, and a lovely little silver tray from the Duchess of Albany.

Bernard's diary

December 23rd 1897

Marie remaining on this year in waiting it had been decided that I should spend Xmas at Albert Cottage with the Bigges and I arranged accordingly to go to them on Dec. 23rd, Thursday. The day before, however, I had a wire from Marie saying the Queen had invited me to stay at Osborne from Friday. She first asked me till Monday, then remembering that day was bank holiday said she could not hear of my travelling that day and asked me till Tuesday! On Dec. 23 therefore I travelled in a dense fog to Southampton, 3 hours late and stayed the night at the Bigge's, removing next day to Osborne House. Xmas Eve at $\frac{1}{4}$ to 6 I was present at the Household Xmas Tree at which the Queen gave her presents to the household. The Princesses were there, and the most handsome presents were given all round, Marie getting a case of large silver gilt spoons, the usual pocket book and some odds and ends, including a man of gingerbread, a German custom. When the Princesses left they fell on the tree and divided the spoil, filling waste paper baskets!

In the evening we dined with the Queen I sitting between Lady Churchill and Duchess of Albany, beyond the Duchess being Lord Lorne, then the Queen. I had much pleasant talk with the Duchess, books, education, philanthropy, Red Cross Society, etc. She is a most sociable and excellent and kindhearted woman with a very good head and good manners and has brought up her children *quite* admirably. In the drawing room I was summoned to talk to the Queen, and she spoke of my journey in the fog, of Mr. Balfour's and Lord Salisbury's kindness to, and popularity with, their families, Lady Salisbury's health, Victor. She said 'Your mother spoils him the most'. Nothing specially noteworthy.

I forgot that she gave me a Jubilee pin at the tree which Princess

Beatrice presented. I hope my son will always keep it! I wrote, as the custom is, to thank her Majesty.

Xmas Day

A most lovely warm sunny day, with frost at night. Chapel in the house—a long low ugly room, the building and ugly decoration of which cost between 5 and 6 thousand. The Rector of Whippingham preached a good simple sermon. Short service, with carol and hymn. Afterwards Lord Lorne and I had a second game of golf in the lovely grounds towards the sea and he won today! Called with Marie on Bigges and Edwards in afternoon, and after tea was summoned with the household to the Durbar Room to see the Royal presents set out on long tables round the room. The Queen in her chair was wheeled round to see her presents and examined everything with the most evident and lively interest and pleasure—a pretty and touching sight.

N.B. This happened on *Xmas Eve* after our own presents had been given.

The whole household, including myself, dined with the Queen, but not unluckily in the Indian room, which was full of presents. Baron of beef, woodcock pie from the Lord Lieut. of Ireland, boar's head displayed on sideboard. I was placed as on the evening before. A very pleasant evening. At night played as before with Lord Lorne at billiards and had a great deal of pleasant talk.

December 26th

Sunday. Church in morning, then walked with Marie to the sea. Lovely again. Dined with the household, all of them kind and some of them great fun, especially Sir J. McNeill, and Sir Jas. Reid. A great day for Xmas cards all round, the Queen sending one to Marie and one to Victor with their names written by herself on the back. Reid's joke sending vulgar cards to the gentlemen, especially to Mather. Walked with Lord G. Clinton and Colonel Davidson to Barton.

December 27th

Monday. Lovely day passed in golf, walks and talks with my dear wife. We dined again with the Queen (the third time out of four nights), I being placed between Princesses Louise and Beatrice, the Queen next beyond the former—a highly honourable but somewhat alarming position. Much talk with Princess Louise about Watts' statue, architecture and statues in London, Somerset House, very lively and amusing, but with H.M. listening and Lorne sometimes talking across! Towards the end H.M. joined in a good deal, announced Arthur Ponsonby's marriage to Dolly Parry. Princess L. said she was very tall and he short and the Queen said it was like the poor Crown P. of Italy and his tall wife. Then American Ambassador: the Queen said Bayard had talked so much and was so deaf she could not make him hear. Then came Marie's sketching adventures at Bruges and the Queen overheard Marie say how the Belgian boy had spat at her sketch and thrown stones at her. She was immensely amused and roared with laughter, her whole face changing and lighting up in a wonderful way. She said to Princess Louise 'I must tell Leopold'. Then repeated across the table 'I must certainly tell the King!' She asked how far Marie's sketch had gone—I said, 'There was not much left when I saw it!' at which she laughed heartily again. After dinner I talked to the Duchess of Albany and Pss. Louise while the Queen talked to the Clement Smiths and others. Finally she sent for me and I was able to say what an event in my life my visit to Osborne had been and thanking her for the pleasure she had given to us both. Much amusement caused by Marie upsetting a glass of lemonade over herself. Pss. B. and Pss. L. rushed forward to wipe it up, the Queen laughed and hoped it had not gone over the books! Billiards again.

December 28th

Tuesday. Golf with Lorne—badly beaten this time. Marie read the Queen this morning a letter from Lady Elizabeth thanking her for Jubilee portrait and for her kindness to 'my precious

Marie'. The Queen said 'It is not kindness—I do *love* you, dear' and then said, speaking of someone else's husband, 'Not like your husband, who is *most* charming', repeating the words! So I hope I was a success! She spoke pathetically and for the first time of her old age, blindness and lameness, of her losses this year—the Duchess of Atholl, Gen. Gardiner, etc., which had saddened this great Jubilee year, for which, nevertheless, she was thankful. Who can help doing all they can to make happy her last years! I feel it is a great privilege to be able to give up something for her, and I do give up a great deal in my dearest Marie. Very few people would have the courage to go through the work, late hours, etc., with such unvarying cheerfulness as Marie does, suffering as she must just now.

I returned in great comfort and splendour with Pss. Louise and Ld. Lorne, crossing in the *Alberta* to Portsmouth and so on to Victoria. A good deal of talk with the Princess. So ended my visit, auspiciously as it all went throughout, and next week I get Marie back.

Marie told me of a talk with the Q. about modern manners of children to parents. All the P. of Wales' children so nice in this way especially the Duke of York. But she had heard dreadful stories of modern children, of parents like Lady Lytton allowing her girls to visit without her, horrified to hear that no-one now learnt quadrilles, to hear of 'kitchen lancers' and Washington Posts! But modern manners not so modern perhaps. Her story of the young Crimean Officer whose letter to his mother was sent to H.M. to read: he began 'I have told all the fellows what a jolly old female you are'; Female! The Queen had no desire to read more!

CHAPTER XI

VISITING STATESMEN

Sixth and Seventh Waitings

*My brother, Arthur, was born on May 5th, 1898, which occasioned
the following telegrams from the Queen to my father:*

WINDSOR CASTLE. *May 5th 1898*
I am delighted at the good news and congratulate you and dear
Marie warmly on the birth of a second son.

V.R.I.

May 7th 1898
Rejoice to hear dear Marie and baby are going on so well, trust
no more lung trouble. Is Lady Elizabeth Biddulph quite recovered?

V.R.I.

*This is Bernard's account of the christening of the baby, Henry
Arthur Adeane Mallet.*

Tuesday, July 12th 1898
[Newspaper cutting: The baptism of the infant son of Mr. and
the Hon. Mrs. Bernard Mallet (Extra Bedchamber Woman to the
Queen) took place yesterday afternoon in the Chapel Royal, St.
James' Palace. Princess Henry of Battenberg, attended by Miss
Bulteel, was present on the occasion and stood sponsor in person.
The other sponsors were Mr. A. Balfour, M.P., and Mr. Adeane.
The service, which was fully choral, was performed by the Rev.
Edgar Sheppard, Sub-Dean of the Chapels Royal.]
Mr. B. of course, could not come, so I represented him. A very
pretty little ceremony, the picturesque choirboys in their red and
gold gowns sang very well, Victor having chosen one of the

hymns which he knew: 'Loving Shepherd of Thy Sheep', in which he joined lustily. My mother came up for it and we had most of the family in London and Lady Normanton, Lady Sligo, Mrs. R. Moreton and Miss Balfour and others. Register signed by Princess Beatrice, Charlie, me, Lady Elizabeth, my mother and Alick Yorke. Then tea most of the afternoon at Alex. Sq. where the Princess came on her way back to the Station. Altogether a successful little function giving the little man a good 'send-off'.

Sixth Waiting

OSBORNE. *July 20th 1898*

I got down to Windsor very comfortably. I dined with the Queen (a Ladies' party) and had a long talk with H.M. afterwards. She was as kind as ever and asked much about my illness and for news of Victor and the baby, adding, 'I hear he is beautiful'. Princess Christian was there and very affectionate. She is off to Nauheim in a week, does her three weeks cure and then goes to Clouds [home of the Hon. Percy Wyndham] for the manouevres on Salisbury Plain. Princess Thora has come here with us and is very cheery. I believe this house will be very full before long, all the Royalties like the country life and sea bathing. . . . The Queen insisted on sitting out last night on the Terrace but mercifully the Princesses refused to run the risk of rheumatism and kept with me them. I shall have to wear a shawl in the evening for the draughts are worse than ever and the country seems quite chilly after the stuffy heat of London. I am feeling very low and cannot get over leaving all my dear ones. It was a hard wrench parting yesterday and I shall be days getting over it and shaking down to this very different existence. I always dislike it at first so intensely that I wonder how I ever become reconciled. The first week is the worst; that past, I make myself a little happier and start a few feeble occupations. . . . This place is looking lovely though there are not as many yachts about as usual. . . .

I like to know we feel alike about Cyrano[1] and that you appre-

----

[1] Rostand's play, *Cyrano de Bergerac*.

ciate it so thoroughly, real poetry is so refreshing in this sordid world.'

OSBORNE. *July 22nd 1898*

We have just returned from visiting the *Blonde*. The Queen wished us all to see where Prince Henry died and the Captain seemed to take a melancholy pride in the whole sad story and gave us many details. Altogether it was mournful and depressing, even the sight of Lady Erroll in jetted cape and plumed bonnet squeezing herself into the conning tower failed to raise our spirits. . . .

I think of nothing but electric light [my parents were thinking of installing it in the house in London] and Lord Edward gives me advice at every meal. I hope you will enjoy Hatfield.

OSBORNE. *July 24th 1898*

. . . In the morning I went on board the *Alberta* with the Queen and Princesses and we steamed as near as possible to the *Blonde* and anchored close to her in Osborne Bay in order that the Officers and Petty Officers who were on board at the time of Prince Henry's death might come on board and be presented. The Captain also brought his dog, a spaniel, thanks to a strict diet of ship's biscuits and salad oil this animal not only survived three years of West Africa, it flourished. Poor beast, it appears it took an immense fancy to Prince Henry and never left his side for a moment. The Queen was much disappointed at not being able to go on board the *Blonde*, but it really was rough and we do not want any more broken bones in the Royal Family just now. Poor Princess Beatrice, it was her wedding day and therefore doubly trying, but although her eyes were red and swollen she took photographs of the vessel and talked as cheerfully as though life was beginning instead of ending for her. She must have *no* imagination, that is the only explanation I can offer. The Queen is very well, her eyes no worse and her power of enjoyment as keen as ever. She sends for me often as much for the sake of a little chat as for business I think, and is quite as well up in the details of my illnesses as you or my numerous medical advisers.

I have had a tiresome time trying to arrange some music for the Queen on Tuesday night. Tosti is impresario and gives me *no* help. He pitched upon Nordica, and actually engaged her, much to the Queen's disgust as she neither admires her voice nor her person and has emphatically declared, 'I will *not* hear Nordica', as on a former occasion she declined to meet Abraham! Ladies are therefore out of the programme and we must fall back on the male sex. Mr. Byard is coming and I have been doing my best for Plunket Greene. He was a failure last time but that was due to a plethora of Korbay's compositions, 'Strike him dead' nearly blew the Queen out of her chair, he had also been informed his Royal Mistress was deaf and you may therefore imagine how he bellowed. I hope he may curb himself this time and sing German.

I miss that darling baby more than I can say, I wish I had it here in a cage.

OSBORNE. *July 25th 1898*

Lord Ormonde and Sir Allen Young came to tea with us yesterday and the Dufferins dine tonight. He looks 1,000 and is very deaf. She seems to grow younger instead of older. The Crown Princess of Austria and her daughter arrive tomorrow with a vast suite so the musical evening is postponed till Thursday. I enclose a letter just received from your mother. I shall now certainly speak to Lord Cromer. [*This was about the possibility of my Uncle, Louis Mallet, being transferred from the Foreign Office to Cairo.*] Poor man, he is terribly anxious about his wife, she can never be better and cannot live more than a year but a hot climate is her best chance (they say) if she will return with him to Cairo.

OSBORNE. *July 26th 1898*

Summer has come at last and makes me long for an outdoor life, tea under trees and other country delights; our Sitting room at tea-time reminds me of 'The Black Hole of Calcutta', the butter melts, Lady Erroll pours out the tea as strong as brandy and we all perspire and wish we were in our own humble homes. The Archduchess Stéphanie has just arrived and I have to look after the two Ladies in Waiting and show them the sights; one, Countess Kothek is the daughter of the old Count who first loved Mama years ago and then fell a victim to Maud's charms at Dresden. She is a lively little creature, not pretty but with a flow of conversation very gratifying to the poor entertainers. This is really one of the most tiresome of our duties, but at any rate we ladies can muster sufficient French and German; the gentlemen are in despair with a Greek Colonel who speaks unintelligible French and an Austrian Count who is voluble but only in Viennese German. The Greek lady is the finest talker I have ever met, she never ceases for one moment and we are now obliged to take her in turn as the fatigue is too great for any ordinary individual. I am reading 'Hilda Stafford'[1] to the Queen in the small hours of the morning, a story by the author of 'Ships that pass in the Night' and equally gloomy and consumptive. We have abandoned the newspapers for the present and therefore H.M. complains that the Foreign Office do not send her sufficient news about Spain and the War, this to the despair of Fritz who foresees acres of cypher before him. I had a nice letter from Mr. Law this morning and a splendid illustrated copy of his new book on Hampton Court. He wants me to explore the pictures at Barton and Fritz proposes taking me there tomorrow morning. It seems I must penetrate next into Lord Strafford's bedroom as the best Van Dyck hangs over his wash-hand stand.

My parents were about to move from 9 Alexander Square to 38 Rutland Gate, a larger house necessitated by the appearance of Arthur, and were excitedly installing electric light.

OSBORNE. *July 27th 1898*

I have just had a visit from Lord Cromer. He was charming and

---

[1] By Beatrice Harraden.

spoke so affectionately of your father,[1] he seemed to think *you* had the first claim on him but I told him you were provided for and had been fortunate so far. He promises to do all he can for Louis and asked me his age, and when I told him he is old enough for any post, 'I like young men and he must have financial talent, it is hereditary. I will try and see him before I leave London.' Make Louis leave a card at once. I really think he will not forget, but he distinctly said it would be no opening for Louis to go to Cairo as a diplomat.

OSBORNE. *July 28th 1898*

I have been very busy about the music we are going to have this evening and other things and the Queen sends for me often. I must confess to fussing somewhat, I do not feel up to much responsibility and it is so difficult to please everybody. I do not know what I should do without Sir Arthur, he is such a help and so kind. Emily Ampthill has arrived with the remains of a chill. She is affectionate but inquisitive and we have to be a little bit on our guard.

OSBORNE. *July 29th 1898*

The music last night was a great success and I need not have been so anxious, but Tosti was in a bad temper and frightened me by saying Marie Brema's voice would blow the Queen out of her chair and that Norman Salmond had no fixed address and was mixed up in a divorce case. Imagine my feelings! I was in an agony and on the verge of hysterics, however Sir Arthur came to my aid, calmed Tosti, gave me courage and now the Queen raves about Marie Brema and I am covered with glory. I fully expect we shall have a Wagnerian Cycle at Windsor ere long. May I be there to see it. Tosti remained in a vile temper all the evening and played the accompaniments abominably. I felt deeply for the artistes.

[1] Sir Louis Mallet when at the India Office had been largely responsible for launching Lord Cromer on his great career in Egypt.

OSBORNE. *July 30th 1898*

Prince Christian Victor was here last night, in order to say 'Goodbye' before leaving for the Sudan. He did not appear in very good spirits and the War Office refused to pay his expenses and only gave him leave to go; in short they make themselves odious as usual. He hopes to hear more on his arrival at Cairo, Kitchener has asked for him, so he must intend giving him work. What do you say to the extraordinary doings of the Foreign Office?[1] I have laughed to tears over Sir Claude McDonald's dispatch and the interpolated criticisms thereon. Is Sanderson the guilty one, or could it be one of the younger men goaded by the everlasting tedium of their lives into calling an eminent diplomatist names? I must write to Lulu and hear what he says to it all. The Foreign Office must be shaken to its foundations and Sanderson tearing out his remaining hairs. The *Garland* comes to Cowes on Monday.

OSBORNE. *July 31st 1898*

The Queen is to visit the Prince of Wales on board the *Osborne* this afternoon. Sir James gives a most cheerful report of the invalid[2] and says he has never seen him look better, his cheerfulness is remarkable. He sleeps on deck where a comfortable tent has been constructed and is looking forward to plenty of society of a congenial character but the fact remains he must not be allowed to move for at least two months and that it may be six or eight before he walks easily. I hope to get to the *Garland* tomorrow but may not have a chance. I am curious to hear what the Queen will have to say about Bismarck's death, nothing good I expect. I think she has always placed him and Gladstone on the same shelf, how curious that one should survive the other so short a time. Was it not prophesied they should die in the same year?

OSBORNE. *August 1st 1898*

The Queen talked a little of Bismarck last night, she said he was

---

[1] See Appendix. [2] He had fractured his knee-cap.

'a very wicked man' and had the Crown Prince and his son at deadly enmity. Also that although he always took the credit for the war of 1870, it was really the work of the old Emperor and of Moltke and he had much less to do with it than was generally supposed. Her Majesty added Bismarck and Gladstone *hated* each other. It was very interesting and I could let my pen run on but feel it would not be safe. With the utmost difficulty H.M. has been persuaded to send a telegram to Count Herbert B. Sir Arthur tells me as a profound secret that the author of the marginal notes which have caused so much stir at the Foreign Office is George Curzon, and yet some people, i.e. Lord Cromer, talk of him as Viceroy of India! What do you say? I should not approve in spite of my faith in young men.

OSBORNE. *August 2nd 1898*

I am just off to drive with the Queen through Cowes rather agitated that my outward appearance may do credit both to my Sovereign and my family. . . . Princess Louise is here more amiable to me than ever and wants to know why you never play golf with Lorne at Wimbledon. She insists on the entire *Garland* party coming to tea with her this afternoon. It will be a shock when she sees how many they are!

To Lady Elizabeth Biddulph

OSBORNE. *August 3rd 1898*

I am delighted you are so thoroughly enjoying yourself. Ledbury is very pleasant at this time of the year one gets out and sees lovely country and delightful gardens. Here one feels the caged existence more than in the winter and a sort of fate pursues me if ever I venture a hundred yards from the house. I therefore spend the whole day in my room, latterly the orders have only come out at a quarter to seven so we sally forth with the bats. I have had very delightful visits from the *Garland* party and Princess Louise has invited all five to tea with her this afternoon. I am sure she will admire Jack [*Cator*] and pounce on him at once. (Do not say this.) Poor Aunt Annie has sciatica very badly and is quite lame and does not look well. . . .

Princess May is very stiff. I am sure she means to be kind but in her case it is often necessary to take the will for the deed. She has very good looks and her clothes lovely, hardly a trace of mourning.

OSBORNE. *August 4th 1898*

The more I think about Louis the more I feel he ought to accept Lord Cromer's offer. I have talked it over with Sir Arthur and he is of the same opinion. Lord Cromer told him the other day that *he* should not leave Egypt till it was our own! So that is a concrete safeguard and also shows his policy, and the Khedive's brother who came to see the Queen, in pouring out his grievances to Sir Arthur said the Khedive thought men of better social standing should be sent to Egypt. He strongly objects to individuals like Mr. Birch whom he said, with some truth, was not known in London society, so Lulu with his Foreign Office prestige and link with the Court would have a good chance, even of 'Khediveal' favour. . . .[1]

Chamberlain who was here last night talked the Queen over about the Vaccination Bill, I cannot conceive why but conclude he was instructed to do so. I do my best to counteract for honestly I believe the Conveyance Clause to be a real disaster to the country so does the Queen in her heart of hearts. Do not repeat this. Old Sarum arrives on Saturday and we think we shall have to pitch the tent for him on the lawn, the House is so bursting with guests. I have seen Henry Foley's letter re the Foreign Office scandal, he never mentions Norton, very loyal of him, but gives away Curzon freely. How different to Russian policy; there N. would be the scapegoat and sacked at once.

OSBORNE. *August 8th 1898*

Lord Salisbury seemed in excellent spirits last night and chaffed

[1] Louis Mallet spent two or three years in Egypt before returning to the Foreign Office as Private Secretary to Lord Lansdowne.

L

Ferdy Rothschild who however retorted on the Vaccinations Bill and boldly avowed he had voted against the Government. . . . The Queen speaks into a phonograph this afternoon in order to send a verbal message to King Menelik.[1] Wonders will never cease, and as Mr. Lang truly remarked, 'There will be no room for reserve'. The Queen has taken a great fancy to Mr. Lang. How soon will he be a Bishop?

OSBORNE. *August 9th 1898*

We have had a Council today, only Lord Cross and Lord James, I think the Queen would have liked a larger number and was a little piqued, but I suppose most P.C.'s were away. So that horrible Vaccination Bill is law. I am ashamed of the Government. They deserve a good beating. Many of their members voted against their consciences, Lord Denbigh for one, and I am *quite* sure Lord Salisbury disagrees with the Clause in his heart of hearts. His arguments were very feeble and he took refuge in cynicism. We may now prepare for an outbreak of smallpox and the effect of the Bill on me will be to have Victor re-vaccinated as soon as possible. I had a long talk last night with the Duchess of York. She is a thorough Puritan at heart, just like me, and cannot bear the prancings and millinery of the High Church party. She told me she had urged Maud not to be drawn into the net by the Cator family and confessed she could not bear to discuss religious topics with the mediaeval Mary Lygon. It really is very curious this tremendously prejudiced attitude. She is a clever woman with great ideas of her own, and if only she could break down that stiff manner she could become a powerful factor for good in society. As it is people say she gives herself airs! The Italian Ambassador is here and so delighted to see me that he at once suggested you and I should pay him a visit at Alexandria near Turin where he has a palazzo with forty spare rooms. He has been given a Command of a Corps d'Armée there.

[1] Menelik was Emperor of Ethiopia.

Seventh Waiting

BALMORAL. *October 14th 1898*

The Queen welcomed me as affectionately as ever and the Empress Frederick talked to me for some time on various family topics. Princess Victoria Schaumburg-Lippe was also very friendly and seemed glad to see me again. She has never grasped my new name and introduced me to her husband as Marie Adeane. They seem a devoted couple and she has changed much and for the better in her personal appearance, being now a graceful good-looking woman instead of a particularly plain girl. I went to the Queen just before midnight and after nearly twenty minutes delightful talk, mostly about my friends, H.M. sent me off to bed for which I was truly thankful.

BALMORAL. *October 15th 1898*

I cannot say I think the Queen as well as when I left here in August, the Empress of Austria[1] was a terrible shock and she said to me, 'I cannot help feeling not only for myself but for those I love' and the Queen of Denmark's demise although not unexpected has cast a gloom over everyone, the House too is rather overpoweringly full of visitors and I think the Queen feels obliged to talk more than she is inclined to and gets rather weary.

I am just back from the Memorial Service at Crathie Church for the Queen of Denmark, it lasted nearly an hour and the music was good as Sir W. Parratt played the organ and conducted the choir but the coldness of the Scotch ceremonial made it far less touching and impressive than our own church service and did not move me a bit; only I felt sad, for the Queen looked feeble and depressed, and one could not repress the thought that she whom we mourned was but a little older and up to a few months ago had been more active and younger in every way than our beloved Sovereign. On the other hand the Prince of Wales has taken a new lease of life, the complete rest and discipline of an invalid existence has made him look younger and better than he has done

[1] Assassinated at Geneva by a madman.

for years and he has borne the trial with the greatest patience and good temper; it seems to have drawn him closer to the Queen and to his children and altogether seems a blessing in disguise. He walks with ease and will not have a stiff knee; he wears a sort of splint with springs that supports the leg and you would hardly tell he had anything the matter with his leg. I read to the Queen Lord Rosebery's speech last night. She approved and thought it strong. I wonder what will happen. I cannot believe in a war, but we must stick to our guns this time unless we mean to be the laughing stock of Europe.

BALMORAL. *October 17th 1898*

After dinner last night the Empress [*Frederick*] asked me to stay with her while she made a drawing of Dr. Storey, Lord Rector of the University of Glasgow, a magnificent looking man of about sixty. The sitting lasted two hours and the conversation between the two was brilliant. We discussed theology, philosophy, Jewish intellect, and religious education of children, besides literature and a host of minor subjects; the Empress has a talent of putting everyone at their ease and drawing out clever people. Dr. Storey had expected to be both alarmed and bored, needless to say he was neither. I was so excited by the discussions that I found myself joining in with some vehemence and emitting Jewish facts learned from Aunt Annie and Connie which were new to my illustrious hearers. I fear I may have been too forward and rather tremble.

BALMORAL. *October 18th 1898*

In spite of a gale the Queen drove yesterday in a shut Landau with Edith and myself and was quite lively and talkative. She showed us a most interesting letter from the Sirdar. I find my confidential work increases with each Waiting and the interest therefore deepens, Sir Arthur always discusses politics with me and lets me have many a glimpse behind the scenes, and this makes existence here tolerable. I like working with him so much.

I have much talk with Count Seckendorf about art and pictures and Italy, he is also very interesting about the War of '70 in which he took part and was at Sedan. 'The Debacle' is he says a most dreadful picture of the whole campaign and may have been written by an eye witness. I am reading 'With Kitchener to Khartoum' to the Queen but the style is too journalistic to please her, although she appreciates its picturesqueness of style.

BALMORAL. *October 18th 1898*

Busch's 'Bismarck' is exciting not only the Household but the Royal Family; Princess Beatrice is having it read aloud and I do not envy the 'lectrice' when she reaches the outbursts against the Battenbergs. The beloved Empress is as tactless as usual and is furious with her son [*Wilhelm II*] for going to Constantinople.

BALMORAL. *October 21st 1898*

I do not fancy from what Lord George Hamilton says, that the Government are best pleased at having to place George Wynd-ham. It appears he is almost the best hated man in the House of Commons, they have never forgotten his part in the Scott-Gatty affair. I must finish in a hurry having been constantly interrupted and now I have to lunch with the Queen, a very rare honour and must change my dress.

BALMORAL. *October 22nd 1898*

I had not time the other day to tell you of Mr. Fitzroy's[1] début here. The Queen and Princesses were rivetted by the likeness to Charles II, which I had warned them of and thought it most re-markable. He was very much at his ease, rather too much, I thought, I do not believe I really like him. He is so cynical and makes fun even of his poor little wife, because she is fond of her children. He has secured a tremendous place and looks extremely

---

[1] Later Sir Almeric Fitzroy, K.C.B.; Clerk to the Privy Council for thirty years. Directly descended from Charles II and Barbara Villiers, Duchess of Cleveland.

self-satisfied. I spent most of yesterday afternoon arranging the programme with Mr. Borwick and Mr. Kennerly Rumford and in the evening we had lovely music, very refreshing to the soul, it was all too short and one longed for more. Next week we are promised Albani which I shall not like half as much. The Queen thought 'With Kitchener to Khartoum' was flippant and she would have no more of it, the portrait of the Sirdar which Steevens gave us quite annoyed her, he is supposed to be a hero in every sense, 'sans peur et sans reproche'. I do not think anyone here fears a war with France and as no doubt they are well informed we need not tremble in spite of all the newspapers say.

BALMORAL. *October 24th 1898*

I had a most delightful talk with the Empress on Saturday evening, we discussed education both in England and Germany, she goes in for the Froebel system heart and soul and implores me to send Victor to a Kindergarten. She also wants to know Mrs. Humphry Ward[1] and suggests that I should arrange a meeting at Windsor, but do not mention this; it would be very interesting.

BALMORAL. *October 25th 1898*

I have had to pen letters to Lord Rowton, the Bishop of Ripon, Sir W. Parratt, Dr. Story, Lady Churchill, Lady Bigge and the Dean of Windsor, by the Queen's command, besides arranging various matters with the Minister at Crathie and telegraphing to singers and pianists who are to perform here next week. Add to all this a long political discussion with Sir Arthur, a summons to the Queen and you will acknowledge I have not spent an idle morning. . . . Colonel Money who brought the despatches from Omdurman dined here last night and was most interesting. He gave us many horrible details of the battle, but said our men hated the massacre of the dervishes and were full of admiration for their

---

[1] Mrs Ward was a best-selling novelist of the period. Her husband was on the literary side of *The Times,* and Mrs Ward later became a protagonist of the 'Anti-Suffrage' movement against votes for women.

courage. Horrid things happened after the battle, the dervishes dug up the bodies of our 21st Lancers and cut off their heads to prevent their going to heaven and our Sudanese troops rushed about the battle field setting fire to the killed and wounded with the same object. It seems awful that such barbarism could not have been prevented on our side. Colonel Money dined with the Sirdar the eve of his advance to Fashoda. They knew the French were there and Colonel Money advised Kitchener to send up a Company of 'friendlies' and wipe them out, but he did not dare. It would have really been the best thing and saved these awful complications and the shadow of war which seems to be hanging over us.

BALMORAL. *October 26th 1898*

The news from France is bad for them and better for us. No-one here believes in war and of course they have accurate information, still the situation is far from pleasant and I expect there must be a revolution to clear the air.

I had a long walk nearly two hours with the Empress yesterday afternoon and a very interesting talk about art, literature and French politics. German affairs I steer clear of. She is rabid on the subject of the German Emperor's pilgrimage to Jerusalem.

BALMORAL. *October 28th 1898*

We all went to the Glassalt with the Queen yesterday and had a pleasant though chilly time. The Queen is in excellent spirits, even discussing Fashoda at length and most amusing about it all. At dinner in the evening the Queen and Empress discussed the state of the Italian Army with much heat, contradicting each other so vigorously that we all shook with internal laughter, it was most amusing to see two people who are never contradicted, playing the game with each other. Neither gave way and the altercation ended by the Queen turning to Princess Beatrice and the Empress to Sir F. Lascelles and continuing their pet arguments in an undertone. Tomorrow the Queen gives Colours to the new battalions of the Cameron Highlanders in front of the Castle, it will be a pretty sight.

BALMORAL. *October 29th 1898*

We have been out all the morning seeing the Queen give new Colours to the new battalion of the Cameron Highlanders. The Queen spoke so well and her voice was as clear as a bell, she never hesitated and what she said was short and to the point and yet with that touch of womanliness which she always imparts to all her utterances, public and private. No time for more, I must fly to lunch and cope with eleven officers in kilts and bonnets. The two hundred men are feeding in the ballroom.

BALMORAL. *October 31st 1898*

We expect the Sirdar and Mr. Balfour at three. I read a letter from Slatin yesterday, he does not seem to love Kitchener over-much and seems to have been hardly treated. The news from France is *not* so good, we are by no means out of the wood and I believe the Cabinet are rather nervous. We were very foolish not to stop their steamer from taking supplies to Fashoda, carelessness somewhere I suspect. I cannot however believe in war and from this quarter everything will be done to avert it.

BALMORAL. *November 2nd 1898*

A. J. B. is too charming to me, and treats me like a friend and an equal. I sat by him at dinner again last night and we discussed Dreyfus and the Leeds Festival. After dinner he talked to me for nearly an hour and was most interesting about John Morley and his great undertaking, i.e. 'Life of Mr. Gladstone'. He thinks it a thankless task and one which can but be a 'succès d'estime' and thinks John Morley will regret it when his turn of office comes again. Mr. Balfour talked confidently of going out in two years, but I doubt the others coming in. Kitchener has conquered us almost as effectually as the Sudan. We were more or less preju-diced against him, but he is certainly a gentleman and can talk

Alick and the Sirdar (by Marie)

most intelligently on all subjects, he also has a sense of humour although of rather a grim order and there is no doubt he is a marvellous soldier; what he lacks is the softness so many strong men have hidden away under the roughest exterior, and there is that in his eye which makes me truly thankful I am neither his wife nor his A.D.C.

BALMORAL. *November 3rd 1898*

I had a nice little chat at tea-time with Mr. Balfour about you. He was so kind and friendly but remarked that you *never* looked him up. I said you did not like to bother him, and he replied, 'Tell him it is a pleasure to see him.' So I do hope you won't continue to be modest. He said he feared your work was dull and I acquiesced but added that you were working hard on the business of the office and doing your best to make work for yourself. I cannot say he has enquired after his godson [*my brother, Arthur*]. I believe he has forgotten all about it! Alas! he departs tomorrow; I think he has rather enjoyed his visit if one can judge from the fits of hearty laughter at Uncle Alick's jokes and his raptures over Marchesi and Hollmann's music.

BALMORAL. *November 4th 1898*

A. J. B. was more beloved than ever last night and roared so loud at Nunk's imitations of Lord Cross that he could have been heard ten miles off, he simply doubled up with laughter. He is a most satisfactory person to amuse and I really think he has enjoyed his stay here very much and was quite sorry to leave at 6 a.m. this morning. His last words to me were, 'Give my very best love to Bernard', so I hope that will make you happy.

BALMORAL. *November 5th 1898*

We have been much interested by the speeches of last night. The Sirdar was composing his while he was here and Mr. Balfour tried to help him, but as you may imagine, their styles were very different and Kitchener complained that A. J. B.'s was far too mild and aesthetic. Poor man he said he would sooner fight a dozen battles than make a single speech. I am not sure I do not think it was rather tactless to talk of finance so much to City magnates, but no doubt it was the same feeling which prompted him to speak with contempt of the sex whenever he talked to us Ladies!

Nunks and I had a lovely time wrestling with the various artistes who have been performing here this week. Mme. Marchesi has a fierce Sicilian husband who took offence and was quite ready to stab 'Nunks' to the heart; the truth was he overheard Mr. Balfour saying to the Duke of Fife that Mme. Marchesi had enjoyed an 'accidenté' past. She certainly looks like it, but the darling Queen has decreed that she is very good, a perfect wife and mother so we have to agree! Then Janotha is a living lunatic, a genius no doubt, but quite impossible to cope with. She arrived with a huge black cat in a basket and countless images of the Virgin, one of which was gummed on to her pocket handkerchief in order that she might kiss it whenever she blew her nose! She would eat nothing because it was Friday; the Queen gave her her books but she would not look at them until she had shown them to the Madonna, murmuring, 'Look, look, read, read.' She threatens to visit me in London, I only hope she won't give you a fit.

BALMORAL. *November 7th 1898*

'Biggie' was rather cross with me yesterday because the Queen had made me read some War Office box to her and he thinks it absurd that military messages should go through the Ladies! But that is the natural result of having a Sovereign of 80! I am sure I wish she *would* see her Gentlemen oftener. I frequently am invited to put my nose into other people's affairs and dislike it particularly, but I am sure the tendency now will be for me and my colleagues to do more and more, and in the state of the Queen's sight and considering her age it is quite inevitable. I did my best to smooth down difficulties and was quite calm so he softened and we remain as good friends as ever. I only tell you this to show that I have not always a bed of roses to lie upon. Dear little Dr. McGregor preached yesterday in his usual animated style. He is a most extraordinary figure to look at but immensely clever and a real saint, none of the courtier about him! The Queen last night at dinner begged him to stay here another day, he promptly replied that he had promised to meet his wife at Elgin and could not disappoint her. He is liked all the better for this by everyone.

BALMORAL. *November 9th 1898*

I have been out trotting with the Queen this morning to the Kirkyard to lay wreaths on the tombs of various members of the Brown family and other old retainers. Her Majesty in excellent spirits and the weather quite glorious at last, were it not for the joyful prospect of seeing you on Saturday I should almost wish to spend the rest of my Waiting here. We are a very happy little party and 'Nunks' keeps us in roars of laughter.

BALMORAL. *November 10th 1898*

We had a most cheerful Ladies' Dinner last night, the Queen in excellent spirits, making jokes about her age and saying she *felt* quite young and that had it not been for an unfortunate accident she would have been *running* about still! These are her very words. After dinner Princess Beatrice and Bessie played on two pianos very well and we all plied our knitting needles. I have nearly finished reading Marion Crawford's 'Corleone' to the Queen and she has been much thrilled by the story as if she were a girl of eighteen! It is quite a treat to read to anyone so keen and I have enjoyed it immensely. Another lovely day, I have just returned from walking with 'Nunks'. We visited Mrs. Wally Brown who digressed upon her daughter's marriage and announced to our intense amusement that the 'funny-moon' had been very pleasant. I call this a first-rate expression and mean to adopt it in future.

WINDSOR. *November 15th 1898*

Mrs. Humphry Ward arrived at twelve and the Empress did not see her until one, so I had a pleasant talk with her. At one I took Dorothy over the State Apartments, and was chased back by a Page as the Queen needed me, but I showed her a good deal and think she was pleased. Mrs. Ward was fascinated by the Empress and they conversed on every sort of topic, Dreyfus included of course.

The Russians shook us very much by saying that no injustice towards the Jew is possible. They *all* ought to be exterminated. Princess Lobannoff at lunch remarked: 'Jews! What are they? Little heaps of dirt and rags, how can anyone speak to them?' What would she say if she met the Rothschilds at dinner?

Bernard's Diary

November 1898

Marie came out of waiting on Thursday, Nov. 17, after a more than usually interesting time at Balmoral. More confidential work and more interesting visitors, Empress Frederick, Mr. A. Balfour (for 5 days) and Kitchener. Political excitement over the Fashoda question less at Balmoral than in London, apparently not so much panic. Kitchener in high favour—asked to sit on the Queen's left hand at dinner, and at an audience in her room told he might sit down! It seems he talks well if tackled and drawn out as he was by Mr. Balfour and the Queen, but he is very brusque and dumb, as when in talking to Princess Beatrice about the Arab women of whom he came across a body of 2,000 in the bush he said they were jabbering 'like *all* you women do'. He is strong on the necessity of our having the whole watershed of the Nile, including the Bahr el Gazal province. The Nile tributaries flowing from West to East are the important ones for the Nile water, hence the importance of this province, which Lord Cromer on the other hand thinks a useless swamp.

Marie asked the Queen to satisfy a correspondent who wrote

to H.M. what her surname would be. She said she thought Guelf D'Este of the House of Brunswick (*not* Hanover).

The Welf (Guelph) family descended from a South German Count of that name, who died about 825. The male line became extinct in the seventh generation, with the death of Welf III in 1055. His sister Kunigunde (c. 1020–1055) married Azzo II, Marquis d'Este and had two sons. One, called Welf IV (born between 1030 and 1040) was created Duke of Bavaria, and his descendants continued to be known as the Welf family. The other, Folco, was the ancestor of the Dukes of Ferrara and Modena, who were known as the d'Este family. A descendant of Welf IV in the fifth generation, Otto das Kind (born 1204), was created the first Duke of Brunswick-Luneberg, from whom the Electors of Hanover were descended. The male descent of the Hanoverian dynasty therefore goes back to the d'Este family, and not to the Guelphs.

This confirms the Queen's view of her surname.

CHAPTER XII

SPRING AT CIMIEZ

Eighth Waiting

In the second week of March, 1899, the Queen took Marie with her to Cimiez, Nice, for about a month. The next batch of letters come from there.

WINDSOR. *March 9th 1898*

Admiral Fullerton telegraphed this morning, 'Sea very rough. Strongly advise Queen to postpone journey'. So here we are and quite likely to remain as nothing will induce the Queen to cross the Channel on a Friday, although it is the usual day for leaving Balmoral, and I have even known it to be Friday and the 13th of the month. If we do not start on Saturday we shall wait till Monday and all this uncertainty is very tiresome as our books are packed away in boxes, also our work so we have no employment and the men have no clean shirts and are growling like grizzly bears at the delay.

WINDSOR. *March 9th 1899*

This afternoon drove with the Queen who seemed as wonderful as usual and very well, blinder I think and perhaps a *little* deaf but well in health and full of interest in all that concerns me and mine. The Duchess of York is shy but very friendly and I hope I may see a good deal of her. I do not think I shall be able to bring her back as she talks of Easter Monday but she seems rather to regret it which is flattering. We discussed the Church question as we drove and the Queen was very wise but very emphatic especially about Confession. She remarked how foolish Lady Wimborne has been and I make her laugh by telling her of the sobriquet

'Deborah of Dorset'. We also discussed Lord Herschell and the Queen spoke of him with real affection and said his visits to Balmoral had always been a pleasure to her. She was interested to hear we had known him so well. The only topics here are Byngo's illness and Lady Stratheard's popularity, it appears that in spite of her twang and crude americanisms the Royalties like her very much and she evidently amused them. She remarked about her elderly spouse, 'When he is ill he is terribly fussy but when he is well he is lovely!' The Choates[1] seem to be extremely difficult people with no idea of how to behave in polite society. He sat down plump next to Princess Christian and under the Queen's very nose and talked very loudly about English politics and other subjects better left alone, and she is not at all 'distinguée'.

We are to make an attempt on Saturday at starting, but I quite expect we may not move before Monday.

WINDSOR. *March 10th 1899*

The appointment of this Mrs. Haughton as a Woman of the Bedchamber in the place of Lady Cust is rather mysterious and disgusting. I had thought that either Victoria Grant or I would have been promoted but the Queen has kept it all a profound secret from all the Ladies and told Sir Arthur that she wished to give it to the widow of some officer killed in action, so the choice devolves on the War Office. I do not expect we shall ever be promoted and I ought not to grumble but it does seem a little hard, especially as we are by no means millionaires.

HOTEL EXCELSIOR REGINA, CIMIEZ. *March 12th 1899*

We have just arrived after a most successful day, a case of 'a calm sea and prosperous voyage'. I cannot pretend that the Royal train shook less than that patronised by other mortals and certainly the Irish stew made at Windsor and kept tepid in red flannel cushions could not be compared with the excellent dinner provided in the train that goes round Paris, but Lady Southampton

[1] Mr Choate was the American Ambassador in London.

and I shared a 'salon à deux lits' and were very comfortable; she is such a dear, kind woman but hardly an exhilarating companion for a long journey. I fairly scandalized Dossé our elderly respectable courier by begging him at Tarascon to procure me a 'Libre Parole' and the 'Intransigeant', but greatly to my disgust neither of them mentioned the Queen or the English nation, in fact they ignored us completely in their report of the news of the world. Thousands of people lined the harbour at Boulogne and waited patiently for hours just for a sight of the Queen and there was a certain amount of cheering. Here, as far as I could judge there was very little cheering but the crowds were responsible and respectful; those who have been here before say that the reception was cold compared with other years. The Prince of Wales and Princess Louise were on the platform at Cannes looking very well; he has taken to golf determined not to be behind the times. . . . The weather is glorious, perfect summer, everyone in white dresses and flowery hats, I feel like a little black mole and a dowdy one too, for this place is smarter than Paris and the assemblage in the other portion of the hotel would, as regards clothes, put any Marlborough House Garden Party in the shade.

CIMIEZ. *March 14th 1899*
I have just got my first letter from home and feel better already for seeing your dear handwriting; either the post is very slow or I am fearfully impatient, anyhow I began to feel deserted and forgotten, especially as the Duchess of York, said that 'dear Georgie' wrote daily and she had already received numerous letters, which I am bound to say I do not quite believe! The heat is intense, I do not feel inclined to walk ten yards and my clothes are quite unfitted for the climate, but I have already made up my mind that I do not like Nice; it is garish and very dusty and most unattractive, nothing picturesque about it, even the villa gardens are tiny and covered in dust, and houses everywhere, no escape from them unless you drive for miles. Coming abroad only to see huge hotels and hordes of smart people depresses me more than

M

I can say, I long to be away in the hills amongst the flowers and orange orchards having my meals out of doors and sketching, instead of which our existence is just the same as if we were at Windsor or Balmoral with the exception of taking our meals in a Dining Room so hot that all appetite fades away! The sun does not appear more than it can help and we have not yet enjoyed a typical Riviera day. I feel like the slave that freedom is the only boon worth having in this world.

We did contrive to drive to 'La Bastide' this afternoon, starting at 4 p.m. and getting home about 6.30 p.m. That is certainly an ideal abode and I should be more than happy there for months; it is sufficiently removed from the madding crowd and had a glorious garden where tulips, anemones, irises and forget-me-nots grow wild and in great masses. Lady Salisbury is a wonderful woman, she is rather deaf but looks the picture of health and was most amusing. Lord Selborne is still an invalid and looks ill, the Edward Cecils were out on the mountains so we missed them. I drove with the Queen yesterday to Villefranche, beggars were the chief excitement. The Queen clasped a sky-blue purse full of francs which she opened hurriedly from time to time to appease the awful deformities posted at regular intervals along the road. The Queen was delighted to recognise old friends and they were equally charmed at the prospect of constant 'largesse'. The 'Dames de la Halle' appeared today with vast bouquets for the Queen and the Duchess of York, the latter had to submit to a smacking kiss on either cheek from the fattest and most 'garlicky' of the worthy fish-wives, and they also insisted on embracing Colonel Carington and Sir James Reid. Bessie and I escaped by the skin of our teeth!

CIMIEZ. *March 16th 1899*

The Queen has been much taken up with her family and I have not seen much of her; the Connaughts arrived yesterday morning after an awful crossing from Alexandria. Their boats were nearly washed away and one day the whole party were forced to remain in their berths as all the cabins were flooded and they were battened down. The *Surprise* is a good sea-boat so it must have been 'touch and go'. Captain McNeill who went with them up to Omdurman gave me a long and interesting account of their adventures. The Duchess insisted on riding over the battle field in spite of Kitchener and the Duke's protests and the sight was too ghastly for words, quite unfit for any man to witness, much less a woman. Thousands of vultures and the hottest sun have done but little to thin the ranks of these terrible corpses and Captain McNeill told me he felt sick for days after. He also explored with the Duke the battlefield at Atbara where the dry air has mummified everything; dead men, camels, tanks, the battle might have been fought yesterday. The corpses sit in the trenches or lie about just as they fell, like some hideous nightmare. A tribe have pitched their tents in the very midst and the children play with skulls and slaughtered mahdists as Victor would with his nine-pins. It seems that Kitchener was far from agreeable or even civil, or was in such a hurry to get rid of his royal visitors that although they had travelled for twenty-nine nights and days to reach Khartoum, Saturday to Monday was the limit of their stay there. The Duke of Coburg arrived last night. The Queen says he is terribly cut up about his son's death, but the gentlemen declare he is much as usual and he declines coming up here and prefers the 'dépendence' of the 'cercle de Mediterranée' which looks as though he intended a few 'larks' on the sly. We have been busy all the afternoon leaving cards, I should think fifty have been showered on me and I have had to get some printed in order to return them 'en règle'. . . .

I have a charming bedroom, very lofty with two windows, on the Queen's floor. With the aid of a couple of screens and quantities of flowers it makes quite a pretty sitting-room. The bed I have tucked away into a corner, and I receive Bishops, and Generals with equal equanimity.

CIMIEZ. *March 18th 1899*

I cannot imagine why the whole of our Royal family should have decided to descend 'en masse' upon their august relative today, about 2 p.m. the hotel was literally crawling with Royalties and one could not take a step without falling foul of one or other. The Princess of Wales and her daughters look very seedy and Princess Maud has dyed her hair canary colour which makes her look quite improper and more like a little milliner than ever. The Empress Frederick looks sunburned and robust, her lady, Mme. Faber du Fauré, whom I knew well ten years ago was delighted to see me but remarked that I had lost all my complexion. She supposed it was the result of matrimony. I longed to tell her I should never have recognized her. Time has been generous in the way of fat and she is quite a typical product of beer and wurst. Mme. de Papignon turned up too and required much attention. All this time I was pining to be alone with Violet[1] and enjoy a good gossip. At last I was free but only for five minutes, then back I rushed to the door to see off batches of Royalties, and finally as we were settling down again a Page rushed into my room, 'The Queen is dressing and Mrs. Mallet is to drive with her'. Then hurried 'adieus' and still more hurried toilet and I was off, leaving Violet to the tender mercies of Colonel Carington, who contrary to his usual manner, is most kind to me and mine, and has behaved all day like an angel. I think Violet enjoyed her luncheon with the Household and was most grateful. I have just been ordered off to practise hymns in the Chapel for the service tomorrow. More than aggravating. I think the Queen is rather overwhelmed by her family and the Coburg Succession problems, endless discussions, some of them rather stormy, I imagine. The Duke of Coburg's life is not one that would be accepted at any Insurance office, and yet he talks as if he were sure to outlive the Duke of Connaught who is as hard as nails. I dare not write all I hear, it would not be safe, but I hope for the Queen's sake some decision may soon be arrived at. The Queen paid Lady Salisbury a visit

[1] Miss Biddulph.

on Thursday and gave me a most amusing description of it. Lady Salisbury in a huge hat covered with lilies-of-the-valley, discoursed upon Lord Salisbury's tiresome resolution to attend Lord Herschell's funeral, which postponed his arrival at Beaulieu and said, 'I entirely agree with Sir William Jenner who said, "I never mean to attend any funeral but my own." '

CIMIEZ. *March 20th 1899*

The wind has been like a knife and several of our party have colds, while a Prefect died this morning of pneumonia. He is much regretted as he was an amiable man and very friendly to the Queen. I have not much to chronicle as the Queen has been so taken up with her family, that I have had an easy time though I am not a bit more free to come and go. The Bishop of Ripon preached a good sermon yesterday morning though it was more topical than practical and I led the hymns with vigour, the rest of the choir consisting of Fritz Ponsonby, Sir Arthur and Rankin, the fat Highlander. Princess Beatrice presided at the organ and played very well. We had an early service at 9 a.m. to which I was invited, very quiet and nice, only the Duke and Duchess of Connaught, Princess Beatrice, Princess Thora and Bessie Bulteel.

My 'culte' for the Duke of Connaught increases as time goes on, he is such a gentleman, so courteous and kind, and they are both very simple in their ways and rather enjoy hardships. They are worried to death about this Coburg succession and I believe they want to renounce it altogether, in which case the Duke of Albany would step into £300,000 a year and a very good position at his uncle's death. Of course he would be obliged to become German, enter the German army, and give up his happy healthy English life; it is rather nice of the Connaughts longing so to stay in England and wishing their son to do the same. All this is a dead secret so do not breathe a word of what I tell you. Dr. Bemkart from the *Surprise* who was with that unfortunate Prince Alfred when he died has been over here twice. He told the Duke and Duchess of Coburg the boy would not live a week and he died just two hours after the time prophesied. They truly refused to believe it, laughed him to scorn, packed the poor youth off to Meran and now lament and weep at his having died quite alone. It appears the end was paralysis of the larynx caused by the state of the brain, which in its turn was the result of the terrible fast life he had led in Berlin from the time he was 17; put into the 1st. Prussian Corps, the fastest of all the Regiments with a thoroughly bad man to look after him. He simply had no chance whatever and humanely speaking his life has just been drained away. How strange Royalties are, their children seem to lack the ordinary care bestowed on our own humblest middle class. Such a thing could never have happened to any of the boys I know and if it had the parents would be blamed by the whole of society.

I am reading the Queen 'Jaquissara' by Marion Crawford and she enjoys it immensely. I also do a certain amount of business about 1.30 each morning, such as reading despatches from Lord Curzon, Sir Julian Pauncefote, etc.

The 'Pelican' pen is smashed, the dry climate corroded the ink and when I tried with the aid of two footmen to unscrew the top in order to clean it and refill, the screw broke clean off, so I am sending it to Sir J. de la Rue to get it mended. I love it and hate writing with any other.

CIMIEZ. *March 21st 1899*

I went off at 9.30 to the Marché aux Fleurs with Lady Southampton, Bessie and Colonel Carington. Never did I set eyes on anything more beautiful. There were literally cartloads of daisies, anemones, cyclamen, violets, carnations, hyacinths and orange blossom, besides a dozen other flowers I have no time to mention and all to be had for a few pence! We got a girl with a huge basket to carry our purchases which she did on her head in a very graceful manner and Lady Southampton bought as much as she could carry to send to England by the Messenger. Victor shall have another boxful by the Saturday Messenger.

There has been a good deal of tiresome business today, scandals etc., with which I do not care to mix myself up and into which in my present confidential post I am probably being dragged. I am always rather outspoken and so invariably get the worst of it. The Duchess of York with whom I have just had a long talk is most sensible and reliable, my admiration for her increases and if only she could shake off her shyness she will make a model Queen. As for the Princess of Wales, her restlessness is alarming and her one idea is to be constantly travelling, she looks ill, so do her daughters, and I hear she dreads the possibility of reigning. I do not think she will have the chance yet awhile, the Queen was never better and when I tell you she wanted of all things to sally forth at a quarter to ten tomorrow morning in order to see the Préfet's funeral cortège you may imagine how youthful are her ideas; even I am not energetic enough for that! After much talk with Dossé and the detectives I decided to tell the Queen the thing was not feasible, in fact I put it rather more strongly and hinted at danger. It would have been the height of imprudence, for the crowd will be immense and deputations are expected from every town in the Department. Sir Arthur gives me full marks for this step and calls me a sensible woman. I should indeed be useless if I lacked all moral courage and the Queen would be the first to despise me.

CIMIEZ. *March 23rd 1899*

We spent part of yesterday afternoon in Nice flattening our noses against the shop windows and longing for hats and jewels. The principal wares displayed there is a wonderful collection of second-hand jewelry at a Russian pawn-broker's. He lends money to the miserable wretches on their way to Monte Carlo and they are generally unable to redeem their pledges, so he acquires splendid jewels for next to nothing and can afford to sell them cheap. I felt quite inclined to buy a magnificent pair of turquoise and diamond ear-rings, price 260 francs.

Today Lady Southampton and I have been to 'La Bastide'. Lord Salisbury had just arrived and Lady Gwendoline rather more grubby than usual gave us a dismal account of their journey, fog in London, a rough crossing and snow at Avignon. Arlington Street is full of influenza and she said they fled before the plague. Private: There is a tremendous struggle going on as to whether Mrs. Horace West can come to Court. The Prince of Wales is pushing it with might and main, the Queen says it has once been decided against her by the Lord Chamberlain and is not for revision, nor am I, but Sir Arthur calls me a prude and a hard woman. Like *all* men he is taken in by rouge and powder and canary-coloured hair and I have no patience with him. I am sure I have no personal feeling against the woman, only if she can be presented why not twenty others of doubtful character, we shall soon have Mrs. Dick Grosvenor, Mrs. Stracey, etc., etc. 'L'affaire West' is fast becoming a rival to 'L'affaire Dreyfus' and some day I shall make you laugh over many details which won't bear writing.

CIMIEZ. *March 25th 1899*

Sir Arthur gave me a most interesting letter from Colonel Grierson, Military Attaché at Berlin to read to the Queen. It contained a description of Rhodes's sayings and doings while dining with the Emperor. They discussed the Raid and the famous telegram and Rhodes delivered himself as follows: 'I was a naughty boy but I knew my own people would stick to me and did not intend anyone to punish me but them.' The Emperor was quite fascinated by him and said, 'With Rhodes as my Minister I could venture anything.' He got the Concession in three days, it would have taken the Foreign Office three years to settle the preliminaries. Rhodes proposed the Emperor should annex Mesopotamia to which he replied, 'I have had that in my mind for the last ten years.' This throws much light on the pilgrimage to Jerusalem.

The Queen paid a visit to a Zoo Garden near here belonging to a certain Comtesse de la Grange, 'ci-devant cocotte', and was presented with a new-laid ostrich egg; this was carefully blown by the chef and its contents manufactured into an omelette which Her

Majesty pronounced delicious. On the egg the doubtful Comtesse had scrawled her name, 'Just as if she had laid it herself,' remarked the Queen quite naively! Then added, 'Why cannot we have ostrich eggs at Windsor? We *have* an ostrich.' 'Yes, mama, a male one,' was Princess Beatrice's amused reply.

I went with Princess Thora and the Duchess of York to tea on board the *Venus* yesterday. We climbed ladders till our legs nearly fell off and came home in pouring rain, but we had a cheery drive and I am very fond of Princess May. She will be a blessing to England some day. This afternoon such a pleasant drive with the Queen. We went up the valley of the Paillon right into the country and I enjoyed the peace and absence of automobiles more than I can say, they make driving here a hideous nightmare and kill at least three people a week.

Enclosed in this letter is a Household Menu for Luncheon adorned with a painting of a gay young woman dancing a sort of can-can, with Marie's remark: 'What do you think of our Menus? I hope you don't imagine we have conversation to match!'

Household Luncheon
Rissoto à la Milanaise
Grilled mutton chops
Poulets aux nouilles
Asperges à la sauce
Tapioca pudding
Meringues aux fraises

CIMIEZ. *March 29th 1899*

I am just home after a drive to Beaulieu with the Queen and 'Chrissey'[1]. We went to the new Hotel there, a perfect palace, to enquire after the Grand Duchess of Oldenburg. She appeared, a little woman limp and sallow in a pink hat covered with scarlet poppies. She and the Queen embraced in public to the intense delight of those inhabitants of the hotel who were not at Monte

[1] Helena, wife of Prince Christian of Schleswig-Holstein.

Carlo. The Queen was very cheerful and full of small talk and 'Chrissey' entertained her with an account of her doings in Paris, omitting to mention however, the slightly improper play to which Reggie Lister conducted her, 'Les Femmes de Chez Maxim' Louisa says 'too appalling for words!' Dear old Mr. Brabazon[1] turned up this afternoon looking rather as if he had been up the chimney, hands and shirt equally grimy. He was however very delightful and will come again on the chance of my being free to go out sketching with him. Leoncavallo, the composer, is coming this evening to play some of his new Opera to the Queen, which will be a relief to our otherwise sombre evenings. The Queen could not lead a quieter life and I suspect it is good for her, for she looks particularly well.

CIMIEZ. *Easter Sunday*

I have had charming little Easter gifts from the Princesses and a dear little egg of lapis lazuli from the Queen tied on to a bunch of pink roses. Princess May gave me a green enamel egg. Thora one painted on olive wood, 'Chrissey' three paste buttons and Princess Beatrice a very artistic little medal. Very kind and friendly of them all, and nice souvenirs to possess. The day is so beautiful, glorious sunshine and the air scented with roses and orange blossom and just as everything is looking its best people are flying home. I should like to spend April and May in the depths of the country here, that would be heavenly indeed with you and the children and lots of books and drawing materials. . . . I was much distressed at Victor's hair being shorn off before my return and I fear the hair has not been kept as I intended. I wanted to put it into a frame and keep it always, and I had a good cry when I got Mama's letter yesterday. She need not have been so interfering, it seems as if I am to have nothing to do with my own child. You ought to have prevented its being done before my return.

[1] Hercules B. Brabazon, a Sussex squire and friend of the family, who was a very fine impressionist water-colour artist and now fetches a fair price on the market.

CIMIEZ. *April 3rd 1899*

The Queen is quite furious about Victor's hair being cut off and especially during my absence. She wanted to see him once more with it because she always admired it so much and told everyone what a lovely colour it was. Last night she said with immense emphasis, 'My dear, you *must* let it grow again. I wish it.' I murmured vaguely that I feared it might take years. 'Never mind, dear, I cannot think of that lovely hair all gone.' I have written to Mama so that I hope at all events she has preserved the shorn locks but I quite expect to hear that they were left to Carlé, who will make them into a fine wig which he will sell for £5. The Queen is very vehement on the Church question and full of wrath against Lord Halifax,[1] 'your cousin' as she says turning to Louisa Antrim, and intimating that she ought to keep her relations in better order! Mr. Goschen dined last night, also Sir J. Hopkins, Admiral commanding Mediterranean Squadron. The Queen chaffed Mr. Goschen at dinner about the *Surprise* which is a wretched little ship and much too lively for the insides of the Royalties who fear to use her. 'I think it would be a good thing if you were to try her yourself, we should then soon have a better boat at our disposal.' It was most amusing and tickled the Admiral very much. Old Goschen said very little and looked down his nose, they all saw the likeness in George Goschen to you and I really felt as if you were in the room. I can see the resemblance so strongly. I hope you will have good weather and good golf at Littlestone.

Mr Goschen, afterwards Lord Goschen, was First Lord of the Admiralty and reputed to have been the prototype of Sir Joseph Porter in H.M.S. Pinafore. At the time there was a rhyme about him which ran: 'If Goschen had a notion of the motion of the ocean. . . .' I remember his son as having a resemblance to my father.

[1] The 2nd Lord Halifax, who lived for 95 years, was a celebrated High Churchman, who worked for closer relations with Rome. His son became Viceroy of India and Foreign Secretary.

CHAPTER XIII

PAINTING AND MUSIC
Ninth Waiting

Bernard describes Arthur's first visit to the Queen.

May 16th 1899

Marie took Victor and the baby (1 year 1 month old) to see the Queen at Buckingham Palace at 11 by appointment. She had heard of V's being at Windsor on Sunday and said she must see them. V took some time to answer her questions. He said afterwards he had to *think* so much before answering. She gave him a box of soldiers and deplored the cutting of his hair. The baby unluckily was frightened by the spectacles she put on to examine him with and rather cried and would not look at her. However, she had a good look at him and said she would kiss him so that he might say he had been kissed by the Queen. He would not turn his head so H.M. had to kiss him on the back of his head! Victor's first interview with her was much more amusing, but he was nearly 2.

Bernard and Marie then set off for a holiday in Mrs Yorke's yacht. Here is his account of what happened:

May 18th 1899

State Ball. Packed up house and left on Friday night for the *Garland* for Whitsuntide. Went in *Garland* (with Mildred Buxton[1]) on Sunday morning from Southampton to Yarmouth, where church, and in afternoon drove to Freshwater to A.

---

[1] A first cousin of Marie's, Mildred Hugh Smith had married Sydney Buxton, who later became a Cabinet Minister under Mr Asquith and later Governor-General of South Africa and Earl Buxton.

Elliott's. Yarmouth a fascinating little place. Left 4 a.m. Monday for Exmouth—a rough passage, I ill once and Mildred quite succumbed. Walk in evening and on return found wire telling Marie she was to go with the Queen to Balmoral. This quite spoilt the rest of the trip for me. *All* plans upset, the yachting and our pleasant week in London. Miss Chaine's illness the cause, but we thought it very inconsiderate. (The Queen herself knew nothing of our movements, of course.) On Tuesday we all went to Exeter and met Mrs. Yorke. Saw Cathedral and drove in afternoon to visit the old Miss Merivales and Barton Place which I had never seen. Quite a Jane Austen little country house in lovely country, which is now at its greatest beauty.

There was a muddle about the beginning of this Waiting and Marie is full of grievance at having been summoned before she need have been, and writes rather miserably in consequence.

WINDSOR. *May 26th 1899*

The provoking thing is I need never have come until today and could have said 'Goodbye' to Mama but they got into such a state of excitement and muddle here they wired all over the place, to Swindon, Ennismore Gardens, and goodness knows where! and Mama was quite alarmed. I quite hope it may be arranged for Mrs. G. to relieve me in about ten days but cannot be sure.

BALMORAL. *Undated, May*

I was too tired with bad neuralgia to write last night the long journey and an evening drive with the Queen. Oh, how I wish I had one quarter of her strength! We had a glum journey, even Aline depressed, it seemed so cruel rushing further and further from all our loved ones and now here we are plunged into winter with a vengeance, 10° of frost every night and there was snow on the ground two days ago. The trees and grass look more wintry than when we left them in November, not even a birch leaf out and not a single wild flower showing its head. The house is colder than I have ever felt it. We are all very gloomy.

BALMORAL. *May 29th 1899*

I have my hands full writing to thank for the Queen's presents and congratulatory letters. There were 3,000 and 4,000 letters received on the 24th [*the Queen's birthday*], many more than the Jubilee brought forth, the Queen is much pleased by these spontaneous outbursts of loyalty and affection and it is quite certain she has never been in better health or higher spirits during her whole long life.

(Later) Just home from a long trot, one and a half hours, beside the pony carriage, first to the Graveyard to lay wreaths on the tombs of Mrs. McDonald and John Brown, and then a meandering about the garden paths, it has suddenly become extremely hot and we all swelter. The fat Rankin and still fatter pony could hardly get along. The Queen was very sweet and affectionate and told me interesting family secrets which I may tell you some day and finally gave me a dear little brooch with '80' on it in memory of her birthday. I always feel fascinated when I am with her and forget all the inconveniences and worries connected with her service.

BALMORAL. *May 30th 1899*

I hope my plans are settled at last and I must say the Queen has been far more kind and considerate than ever any one of her family or surroundings. She really is thoughtful and anxious to help whenever difficulties are pointed out to her which is *not* always done. For instance it was only on Sunday she realised that we were yachting together. She evidently imagined I was gallivanting alone and was really distressed when she found your holiday had been spoilt and has been most sympathetic ever since through Sir James, although never discussing the subject with me. . . . Sir James is most kind and very helpful. He declares the Queen really likes to have me and that I am useful in the writing etc., in short that she feels confidence in my head as well as my heart, so that is gratifying and tides me through the very depressing days, so long they are too! You can read 'The Times' till nearly 10 p.m. by the light of the sun. A gale is tearing down the Valley and the cold is intense today, in contrast to yesterday which felt like spring. The Queen is in excellent spirits and most amusing, commenting on the wretched health of the Prince of Wales and his children with evident pride in her own strength.

BALMORAL. *May 31st 1899*
I am really astonished at the Grand Duchess of Hesse's talent for decorative art; it is wonderful and she could earn her living at any moment and a very good living by making designs for wallpapers, chintzes, etc. She draws unerringly, never rubbing out or correcting a single line, and her taste is excellent. It really is genius thrown away but it makes her very happy and she works as hard as if her livelihood depended upon it.

BALMORAL. *June 1st 1899*
I have been busy all day, a great relief, painting this morning with Princess Thora and the Grand Duchess of Hesse, and driving for two and three quarter hours with the Queen this afternoon. We worked at a table, painting, burning and staining it and nearly finished the whole thing. The Royal Family are providing a Stall for a Bazaar at Bagshot on July 17th and every article sold at it is to be of Royal manufacture. It is an excellent outlet for the artistic energy with which the Family is gifted and really the things are very pretty and very artistic. The Grand Duchess is most amusing when describing her life at Darmstadt and her loathing of Germans is most extraordinary. Though anything but British by birth she adores England with passion and declares a cottage here is preferable to all the Schlosses in the Fatherland. . . .

BALMORAL. *June 2nd 1899*
There was great commotion last night and a Special Messenger

sent by special train to London with some documents that Mr. Balfour said he must have by the Meeting of the House today. It required the Queen's signature and no-one knew it was of such vital importance until Mr. Balfour wired at 7.30 p.m., saying he must have it by 12 today. We all thought the Government must be on the verge of collapse but although, unlike Sir Arthur, Sir Fleetwood would reveal nothing, I gather it was not of such importance as that. No doubt tomorrow's paper will reveal the secret. You will see in the papers that the unfortunate Duchess Marie of Mecklenburg-Strelitz is engaged to a French Count. The Queen told me the whole horrible story two days ago. She believes the servant drugged the poor girl and outraged her from revenge, as it appears the Grand Duke had ruined his wife, then they managed so badly that everyone knew about the baby, and finally the stingy mean parents and grand-parents gave the man £5 to hold his tongue. He keeps a hotel at Lübeck. It is an incident worthy of Russia in the 17th century and most disgraceful but evidently the Mecklenburg-Strelitz family are the meanest and most immoral in Germany though, according to the Queen, the richest.

BALMORAL. *June 5th 1899*

Much painting and music today with Princess Thora and the Grand Duchess. It makes such a difference to our lives having them here and we feel less like nuns in a convent. A propos here is a neat little limerick contributed by Gerry [*Liddell*]:

> There was an old monk of Almeria,
> Whose life grew drearier and drearier,
> Till he crept like a mouse,
> To the top of the house
> And slept with the Lady Superior.

The Queen was very chatty last night and poured many interesting secrets into my discreet ears. I long to write them down but dare not. She talked about her four score years and said what a wonderful blessing it was that they were not 'trouble and sorrow' but 'joy and peace'. It is the greatest comfort to know that this is the case and I always think that the Queen enjoys life with the best of us and in the best and highest way. She said too she *loved* her Jubilee hymn, it was all so simple and true and I said I could never sing it without tears in my eyes and she added, 'I always cry, too.' This is the most touching thing in the world, these little Sunday evening talks with the greatest of Queens, who before God, is the humblest of women, and it is the greatest privilege to serve her be it ever so feebly.

BALMORAL. *June 6th 1899*

I am now in such constant attendance on the Grand Duchess and Princess Thora that I have to work hard to get through with my business and I was an hour with the Queen this morning reading and talking, then lawn tennis, and finally no time to write to you by early post. We have been enjoying a fourth-rate Circus this afternoon much less than the Queen; a performing pony leapt the barriers and careered amongst the audience till rebuffed by my parasol it took to its heels and tore round the field and was captured by heated men after a splendid chase. Gerry [*Liddell*] is the greatest fun and makes our life quite gay, one of the few real sunbeams I know in life. Edith Lytton gets rather on my nerves, she always contradicts and has not the remotest sense of humour yet I cannot help admiring her immensely and her blind devotion to her children is very touching.

Bernard's Diary.

July 17th 1899

Marie returned from Balmoral and we went to Hurst[1] to be with the children and my mother. I got a few days of golf at Rye, whither we both went on Friday to Monday (to the Mermaid) to meet the Albert Grays. Fine weather. Then Marie went to Maud Cator's, and July 10 to Windsor again for 3 weeks. I went

---

[1] Hurst was Lady Mallet's house at Sedlescombe in Sussex.

down on Sat. last (15th) to see the presentation of New Colours to the Scots Guards—an extremely pretty sight.

Marie says the Queen is wonderfully well and keen. Perhaps memory not *quite* what it was. She is in excellent spirits and full of jokes. Horrified at 'Messaline' and made Marie read all the criticisms. It ought never to have been licensed, she says. She was very funny at the evening concert about it, as she told Marie, 'I spoke to Signor Tosti about it—I put my fan quite over my face' as, indeed, Marie had observed her doing. It is delightfully young, modest and naive! She is distressed about Lord Salisbury, not seeing him because of Lady S's illness, which is very serious— tappings, pneumonia and then stroke. There can be no real hope and he is broken-hearted. But it is a bad moment for his with-drawal from politics! The Transvaal crisis seems to me the most serious of all the present Government have enjoyed. . . .

July 19th

Went down to Windsor as Marie had 3 hours free and rowed her on the river after tea.

July 20th

Received telegram inviting me to dine and sleep at Windsor.

Sat between Mr. Elliot and Lady Erroll at dinner. The Queen talked to Lord Lorne about Mr. Choate's behaviour when he came to Windsor. It seems he talked *across* her at dinner and sat down besides her afterwards; also never called her 'Your Majesty'. Very odd that Harry White had not coached him at all. After-wards the Queen went down and sat in the Quadrangle. We all followed and were taken up one by one to talk—rather alarming, as she had Princesses Louise and Beatrice on each side! She told me of Victor having sent her flowers tied with red, white and blue ribbon, and seemed pleased that he had thought of her! (She carried the flowers in her hand that morning, Marie said, and was very sweet about it all). She was also much amused, as she told me, at the baby being able to hum the tune of God save the Queen, taught by Victor!

Victor has been at Windsor since last Saturday and stays till next Monday, 10 days! The Queen heard he was seedy and thought a change would do him good! I hear he has been behaving well and is a success with grown-ups and with the children. I think he must be a more than ordinarily attractive child, and he specially shines in society, tho' I don't think he is cheeky! The first evening he followed one of the Battenberg boys till he found himself running into the Queen's room. Someone told him to kiss her hand, which he did, and he says she then kissed him and he ran out of the room as fast as he could! A very informal presentation which I am afraid he will forget. I think, however, at his age he ought to remember *something*, especially as he is mad over the war, and the weeks have been historical in this respect.

Victor had two more interviews with the Queen. As no-one was with him it is difficult to say what passed, but H.M. told Marie that he had described one of his imaginary battles to her and rather astonished her with his military knowledge, talk about his guns being 'put out of action', 'bringing up his reinforcements', etc.

H.M. continued to overwhelm the family with kindness for next day (Tuesday, 6th) I received an invitation to dine.

To Lady Elizabeth Biddulph

WINDSOR. *July 13th 1899*

The Queen heard of the death of the poor Duchess of Rutland on Tuesday evening and was much depressed. She was known to have heart disease but never thought of her own health. The old Duchess of Abercorn, 87, dined here last Monday and I showed her and Lady Lansdowne various sights on Tuesday morning. She was as young as a kitten and really only looks about 60, walks three miles a day and thoroughly enjoys life. Sir J. Reid says if people live to 80 they may then go on for years and will only die of old age. The Queen is the picture of health and in excellent spirits, we had lovely music last night, Marie Brema and Plançon. On Saturday we have Suzanne Adams and Ben Davies and on Monday the Queen's Band with soloists, so we are quite gay. Of course we are all black once more for the Cesarewitch so I cannot wear the elegant grey dress which I purchased at a vast expense for this very occasion and have to fall back upon what I have worn here the last four months. We go to Osborne on the 21st.

WINDSOR. *July 17th 1899*

I was with the Queen most of the morning and again for an hour in the afternoon when she sat to Orchardson. Then came the Circus and being pleasant to guests, etc. and the day has flown.

OSBORNE. *July 22nd 1899*

Our journey yesterday was piping hot but the sea breezes cooled us, at the end of it we spent a very pleasant hour having tea on the deck of the *Alberta*, chatting to new officers of which there are several. We were greeted with the gloomy tidings of that awful accident on board the *Bullfinch* and passed close to the *Australia* where the dead and dying were lying. The Queen was much distressed and Admiral Fullerton had his hands full signalling to enquire the condition of the wounded. . . .

The Queen was much better last night and less drowsy, I gave her your message of thanks and she was most kind and gracious.

OSBORNE. *July 23rd 1899*

The weather is very thundery but we have just had a tremendous storm and tropical rain and hope for another as the air is still as heavy as lead. The Queen feels it a good deal and particularly dislikes thunder but she works quite as hard only permitting herself a little extra gossip with me and I fear a good deal with 'Munshi'. He is ubiquitous here and I am for ever meeting him in passages or the garden or face to face on the stairs and each time I shudder more. . . . What did you say to Lady Erroll about modern authors? She tells the Queen and everybody else that your opinion is quite wonderful on this subject, and the Queen said last night, 'Lady Erroll tells me your husband says there are no good English writers now and he is so clever, he *must* know, but *I* think Edna Lyall writes very well.' I am going to read her a little paragraph in the 'Spectator' about Mary Ansell, which will make her mind easier, as it is so sensible as usual. Sir Arthur swears by it. I wish we could make St. Loe known to him. I do not believe the 'Spectator' has a more constant reader or admirer. We had a long talk about the Transvaal today but do not agree. Sir Arthur has been reading the Reports (Confidential) of the Boer's military strength, they have the quick-fire guns, which we have not yet got, and better arms in every department. He thinks we ought to smash them while we can and then disarm them and withdraw the thousand men we are now forced to keep at the Cape. This is all Chamberlain and I find Joe talked to him in this strain.

OSBORNE. *July 24th 1899*

The Queen was much pleased with my extract from the 'Spectator' and remarked, 'It is a very sensible paper, and I believe no longer as Radical as it used to be', I hastened to reassure her and pointed out its many merits. The Transvaal news has become somewhat graver. Sir Arthur lectured me long this morning with many maps, I can see his point of view but cannot agree that the Dutch are disloyal. I dined with the Queen last night, just a Household dinner without any guests and we had rather a long dreary evening, 'faisant pieds de gru' in the Drawing Room. Princess Christian and 'my Puss' as she calls Princess Thora have just arrived rather upset at not having found luncheon on board the *Alberta*. Interrupted by a long interview with the Queen and now I must fly to tea under the cedar tree, a pleasant innovation.

OSBORNE. *July 25th 1899*

How amusing your meeting Rosalind Carlisle.[1] If only she knew what the Queen thinks of her it would make her 'sit up', as the boys say. I hope she won't ask me to lecture on my particular branch of women's work. Last night a Reuter telegram announced Kruger's resignation and there was a sensation at the Ladies' Dinner in which the Queen was indulging. This morning the statement was contradicted, it is now confirmed, what are we to believe? I do not think the outlook is more peaceful. 'Chrissey' is very friendly, almost too much so for I have to sit in her room by the hour and exercise the greatest tact not to say anything that may be repeated with interest.

OSBORNE. *July 26th 1899*

The music last night was a pleasant variation to our dull evenings. They seem longer and more trying in this canary-coloured Drawing Room than anywhere else and somehow we are not a very lively party. Bertha Lambert can only talk of herself and bores me to tears and dear old Lady Erroll is always wanting to hold prayer meetings in our Sitting Room and asks me twenty times a day to join the Mother's Union. Susan [*Baring*] is my only solace, Fritz Ponsonby is love-sick and pines for his Ria and Sir Arthur very irritable on the Transvaal. Mrs Lecky has this morning sent him Olive Schreiner's shriek to present to the Queen and he cannot make up his mind what to do. People are such a bore with their prejudices and partisanships I hope you may be having a satisfactory conversation with Lord Cromer at this very minute. I am quite ready to supplement it on Saturday. . . .

Madame Nevada who sang last night is a sort of trick songstress and shakes and 'roulades' high staccato notes like a motor car in Bond Street. She does not give me much pleasure, and as for her

[1] Rosalind, Countess of Carlisle, was a Stanley of Alderley and a cousin of Marie's. She was a very strong-minded radical and teetotaller, but also an autocratic ruler of the tenants at Castle Howard, where her husband had to play second fiddle, being a gentle, artistic man.

accompanist, Signor Ducci he made us simply burst with laughter. He wanted to play a March of his own, 'The Victorian Era', and we all snubbed him in turn, but when presented to the Queen he boldly asked if he might play it and she could not very well refuse, so down he sat and thrummed for ten minutes; the Queen never thanked him and was much annoyed at his presumption. But he was delighted at the success of his ruse and appeared in the seventh heaven.

OSBORNE. *July 27th 1899*

There are still wrangles about Coburg and I trust our dear Duchess is not going to be put upon. The Queen is rather shocked at finding General Négrier, who has just been sacked by Gallifet, possesses a high class in the Victorian Order, given him at the last Manœuvres by the Duke of Connaught. Gallifet seems to be doing well and purging the Augean stables. I am alone this afternoon, everyone is out, Bertha with Princess Christian at a function at Ryde, Susan sailing in the *Sheila*, only Lady Erroll survives and I dread an open air Prayer meeting tête-à-tête under the cedar. I drive with the Queen about 7 p.m., she ought to take Lady Erroll but dreads the Mother's Union quite as much as I do.

CHAPTER XIV

THE BOER WAR

Tenth Waiting

OSBORNE. *February 1st 1900*

I am not very happy about the beloved Queen, she has changed since I was here last and looks so much older and feebler that my heart rather sinks. She has had a very bad cough and has not quite got rid of it and last night she slept soundly while I read to her and seemed so feeble; she keeps a brave face and optimistic but not so much as I had been led to expect and I am sure she realises the vital mistakes that have been made quite as much as we do; this is very satisfactory and perhaps she may say more to her Ministers than we have any idea of; she wanted to know if you had been in the House and heard A. J. B. She seemed to crave for an outside opinion and she was not angry when I hinted that public opinion censured the Government, only sighed. Against the Press she is very irate. The 'Morning Post' is banished from the Palace and we are forbidden to touch it, it is now ranked with 'Modern Society' and I do not fancy Lord Glenesk will bask any longer in Royal favour. H.M. was very funny about Spenser Wilkinson, 'They tell me,' said she, 'he has never been a soldier and is a crammer. I think he had better go to the Front at once', but all the men here believe in him and in the recesses of the Equerries' Room a surreptitious copy of 'The Morning Post' is eagerly devoured every morning.

[*I remember Professor Spenser Wilkinson as a bearded old Fellow of All Souls in 1914. He had been I believe, Military Correspondent of 'The Morning Post' during the Boer War and was then Professor of Military History at Oxford University. He was a keen member of the Oxford Cyclists Battalion of Territorials and had invented a famous*

tactic for dealing with cavalry. The cyclists were to bicycle along the
road and when the Cavalry charged, to dismount and twiddle the wheels
of their bicycles very fast, which was believed to panic the horses. I have
not heard of these tactics being applied in actual warfare!]

I had a very cordial reception from everyone, and 'Chrissey'
and Thora were most cordial and the Queen very affectionate,
full of enquiries about Mama and you and the children, insisting
on all my little anecdotes of Victor and his soldiers, altogether I
feel quite happy. Sir Arthur is *not* cheerful but I have not had any
talk with him yet. Lord Edward *looks* ill and Sir James is rather
grumbly. Edith Lytton is very sweet and affectionate.

OSBORNE. *February 2nd 1900*

I find from Sir Arthur that your information about Buller is
not correct, he is *going* to move but has not done so yet. The
Queen is absolutely confident Ladysmith will be relieved and
dislikes even a hint that it may be an impossible task, but last night
Sir John McNeill had the courage to tell her the truth and what
he thinks, which is that the situation of Ladysmith is almost
hopeless, he is not a pessimist and his opinion is based upon
knowledge of the country. What has not yet come out but what
the Queen told him is the fact that they are now eating their
horses, but even so I believe they may hold out for six weeks, if
they have sufficient ammunition. We are all forced to take the
ultra-optimistic line in public, but in the privacy of our own
rooms we indulge in more reasonable talk and I do not find
myself the least more grave and pessimistic than my colleagues.
Bigge is really furious with the War Office but blames the system
and hopes this war will cause drastic reforms. I cannot help feeling in the air that there is some truth in the story that neither the
Queen nor Lord Wolseley knew of Roberts' appointment until
after it was settled, but I have nothing definite to go upon. As for
Lord Salisbury he is effete and extinct and Edith Lytton who
knows him and his entourage intimately says he will now draw
more and more into his shell until he becomes quite inaccessible,

the truth is he is not quite 'human'. The Cecils are a species apart they cannot be classed with ordinary mortals. If only I had more confidence in Lord Rosebery's immortality I should plump for *him*. Sir Arthur says A. J. B.'s Manchester speeches have done incalculable mischief, why, oh why did he make them? The weather is vile, heavy snow and damp air. The Queen did not go out this morning, the rarest of all occurrences but she drove this afternoon in spite of the sleet.

OSBORNE. *February 4th 1900*

Pray send me any news you can, we might be in the Sahara for all we hear in this place. Everyone is afraid of his or her neighbour and a deadly level of caution and dullness drives me nearly mad. I feel sorely tempted to say something outrageous in order to enjoy the consternation that would promptly ensue. Lord Wolseley arrived on Friday at 8 p.m. and left on Saturday at 8 a.m. so we did not enjoy much of his company. I dined that night with the Queen and kept ears and eyes open but beyond the most blatant optimism I learned absolutely nothing. He seemed bursting with health and spirits treating everything as a huge joke. Cracking up Lord Dundonald to whom he *refused* a Command and who had to pay his own passage to the Cape. And labouring hard to convince us the war would be over in a month, at any rate the worst of it; this sentiment I have heard every day for the last three months so I am not likely to be taken in! You may be right about Buller, Sir Arthur is quite capable of trying to deceive me. My work consists in writing to widows and orphans and communicating with Miss Norman at Netley. . . .

My evening task is now no light one, the Queen sleeps soundly and yet adjures me to keep her awake, even shake her if necessary, this I cannot bring myself to do, so I read and rustle the paper and wriggle on my chair and drop my fan and do all in my power to rouse my Sovereign, but she would be so much better off in bed and so should I! And yet I fear habit is stronger than nature in this case. Do not fear my being over-worked. I feel intensely lazy and am awfully bored, sitting for hours alone in my room. I am sorry Edith Lytton has gone, I do not know the Duchess of Roxburghe at all, so she will be no resource. Mr. Lang is here and preached very well this morning. Of course the war was the text and he steered very cleverly between pessimism and optimism and everyone was pleased, he is in high favour with all the Royalties and will soon be a Bishop.

OSBORNE. *February 5th 1900*

It is bitterly cold today but I have been out twice this morning. A gloomy little funereal service in honour of poor Prince Henry's burial day. These reiterated memorial services are very trying but I really think the Queen enjoys them, at any rate they are the only lodestones that draw her within the precincts of a church! This afternoon I have had a cheery drive with Princess Thora whom I continue to like more and more, and who is full of good sense and very open-minded. She talked just as we do about the Government and is quite disgusted with Lord Salisbury and Mr. Balfour, sad too, for she considers they have missed such a splendid chance of making themselves immortal! But she says she only dares to talk openly to me and a few others as Princess Christian is furious with her and everyone else unless they 'lard' the Government with fulsome praise. As to news I believe it is true that Buller can do nothing because of the weather, there as here it is 'pouring cats and dogs'.

OSBORNE. *February 6th 1900*

I am very fond of Evelyn Moore [*a Maid of Honour*], who nearly always shares my views as to politics and like all people who peep behind the scenes is disgusted with the way the business of the country is carried on; she thinks Mr. Goschen is feeble and effete, as we consider Lord Salisbury. He is doing his best to wreck the Admiralty but mercifully he has young and fresh blood in the shape of the Sea Lords to keep him from utter ruin. She says her brother, Admiral Moore, who is a Junior Sea Lord, thinks well of Austen Chamberlain and likes him. Admiral Fullerton and Prince Louis of Battenberg came here last night to discuss the Royal Yacht. It is a most unfortunate business, but will have to do now although she *must* be but a make-shift. It is really disgraceful that the Sovereign of the first Maritime Power in the world could have no better vessel in which to put to sea, but £500,000 has been spent and the vessel cannot be used for another purpose and Goschen won't ask Parliament for another grant, so the Queen must lump it. Fifty feet off her mainmast, ten feet off her funnel and the destruction of the fo'c'sle will not tend to improve her appearance. No-one but Sir William White is to blame, but you would not choose an R.E. who constructs barracks by the mile to build your country house. The Queen seemed brighter yesterday and better, less sleep too at night. I am keeping and arranging all the war telegrams she gets, they are awfully dull and mostly about transports, their arrival and departure.

OSBORNE. *February 7th 1900*

At one I have to play duets with Princess Thora and 'Chrissy' is sure to pounce this evening and carry me off for a couple of hours gossip in her room, talk which would be pleasant enough if I did not always have to keep my tongue intently bridled but sharply bitted; however I am extremely fond of her and her violent opinions and very often absurd tirades against any Government people make me chuckle inwardly and smile outwardly too! Thora is very sensible and level-headed and ought to have a chance. It would have been for instance a godsend to Russia if the Csar had married her instead of the angelic but somewhat cow-like Princess whom he adores, but who cares for little beyond her husband and her children and cannot rouse herself to reform either society or politics.

They profess to have no news here and even the Queen is rather disgusted with Lord Salisbury and A. J. B. and the tone is quite changed. I bet on Rosebery, with odes and elegies and judicious flattery he has been smoothing his path here for many a long day. I cannot admire his character but I do recognise his genius, and I feel certain he is the coming man. I read extracts from Chamberlain's speech to Her Majesty last night and she highly approved and remarked, 'He is a strong man', but of course George Wyndham is the hero of the hour. I only hope he will be able to sustain the reputation he has made for himself. Last night too, we talked of the chocolate,[1] the Queen as usual truthful as the light, said 'I did not think of it myself, I said I wished to give something to each of my soldiers but I could not decide what form the present should take; then three alternatives were suggested and I chose the boxes of chocolates.' The gift has been appreciated beyond the wildest expectations and the invalids at Netley talk more of the chocolate than of their wounds. They have not yet received it but they will do so in time. I feel more than ever what a splendid sense of proportion the Queen has, but it can only be realized by those who come in direct contact with her, even those just outside the inner circle get such distorted views of her opinions and prejudices.

OSBORNE. *February 8th 1900*

The Queen discovered it was my birthday and has sent me a splendid signed photograph, the best I have ever seen, I think. You must present me with a frame for it, an adequate one will cost a small fortune. It is very sweet of her for she is awfully anxious in spite of all she says to the contrary and I do *not* think her well. Never broach this to a soul! I cannot help feeling uneasy I wish warmer days would come and better news. The last straw is the very serious illness of Sir W. Lockhart who was doing so well in India, and who can ill be spared just now; he has dysentery badly. Roberts and Kitchener have gone to the Modder River; also a profound secret; from Buller there is no more news beyond the list of casualties. The Captain Talbot[2] wounded must be the Bishop of Rochester's son.

[1] A small metal box with the Queen's portrait, containing a slab of chocolate, was given to all soldiers and sailors as the Queen's Christmas present.

[2] This was undoubtedly Neville Talbot, who was Junior Dean of Balliol in

The Duchess and I drove with the Queen this afternoon Her Majesty sitting with her back to the horses, so funny, to be out of the wind. We made feverish efforts to keep the conversation alive but the Queen slept peacefully on my shoulder and was hard to rouse.

OSBORNE. *February 9th 1900*

Not much news today, there really have been no telegrams at all and Buller must be fighting but the long delay makes one anxious. The news about MacDonald is not reassuring, but the soldiers here say the Highlanders should not have been used again so soon. The Queen is anxious some notice should be taken of the Irish Regiments but as they seem to run away on every occasion it is not easy. There has been a good deal of rushing about today, messages and arrangements for a Knighting into the bargain. I had to entertain the M.P. for Sunderland at lunch, very amiable but distinctly middle-class. We got on very well and I discussed coal and shipping as if I hailed from the Tyne.

OSBORNE. *February 10th 1900*

The news is as bad as possible. Fritz told me the truth last night but no-one of the other Ladies knows and don't let it out or I shall be suspect. Buller has retired again! Another 'Spion Kop' disaster and I feel certain from what I have heard and seen that he can never reach Ladysmith. It is too awful to contemplate, I fear the garrison will never consent to surrender and that means certain death to at least half the forces. No-one can explain or excuse Buller's conduct in changing his plan of campaign when he got to the Cape, I firmly believe all would have been well had he stuck to it. Hely-Hutchinson and Milner ought never to have been allowed to interfere. One thing you may be certain of, when the War Office profess to have no news they have only disaster

---

my time at Oxford. As a chaplain in the First World War he helped to found Talbot House at Poperinghe in memory of his brother Gilbert. He was afterwards Bishop of Pretoria. A splendid 6ft. 7in. giant.

to reveal. I very much doubt if the policy of deceit is wise but it may be better to let the public down gently and the truth gradually leaks out. The poor darling little Queen was as brave as a lion last night, never letting me know by sign or word of the bad news but made me read a cheerful telegram from Roberts about MacDonald and the accounts of the sick and wounded and then I just tried to make her laugh and told her funny things out of that article in the 'National' on children's ideals. Still she looked so anxious and care-worn and the worry will tell upon her health, she does feel so intensely for everyone and the optimism is a good deal put on in order to make herself believe all is well, when she knows it is not, quite the Sophie Palmer frame of mind. How amusing her letter is. I am very fond of her and she is clever and her family. I will do what I can about the photo but I expect the Queen would give one outright. I tremble for Gerald Balfour, his life is in great danger. Where is he living? As for Lord Salisbury I hear his one idea is to get off abroad. I only wish he would do so at once and resign. Evelyn Moore has the worst opinion of Goschen and she knows the truth from her brother, they are both old and effete. We are suffering from the effects of Anno Domini.

OSBORNE. *February 11th 1900*
We had our little service of Intercession this morning like everyone else, with special hymns and a tactful little sermon from Mr. Clement Smith. We had the prayers for our poor brave soldiers, for the sick, the dying and the mourners, but I can't enter into the Old Testament spirit shown in the prayers for victory and boasting of our cause as righteous, it may be, but that of the Boers from their point of view is equally so. It is like praying for rain or any other special object which I never feel inclined to do, to me it seems one should pray for spiritual and not temporal blessings and war is so eminently unchristian, so full of evil that I cannot bring myself to pray that we may slaughter our enemies. I ought to have been a Quakeress and joined the Peace Society! I am quite out of place in these war-like circles where the

only cry is 'Let us slay the Amalekites!'. The Queen is secretly distressed at the bad news but outwardly as cheerful as ever. We had a Ladies' Dinner last night and she talked very openly, said Chamberlain has assured her over and over again that the Boers could never put more than 50,000 into the field and that Buller had said there would be *no* hard fighting. This quite disposes of the boasts of the Intelligence Department. The Government have treated us all round to a tissue of lies! Now they cannot pack off useless Militia Regiments fast enough. Evelyn Moore's brother who manages all the transports, writes that he has just received orders to send out 12,000 men and several more naval guns. Do not mention this. The rising in Egypt and Mauritius is far from agreeable. I tremble for the future. We are all, from the Queen downwards, making things for the troops, caps, cholera belts, socks and waistcoats, the Queen turns out khaki comforters as if her bread depended on it, and says so sweetly, 'I like to think I am doing something for my soldiers, although it is so little'. She told me she made many things during the Crimea, 'but they *would* give them to the officers, not at all what I intended.'

OSBORNE. *February 12th 1900*

My midnight séance was very nice, the Queen was chatty, she made me read her the special war hymns and then said, 'I fear wars will never cease as long as the world exists.' We discussed the question most openly and I dared to say what is always in my heart, i.e. the lack of Christianity and civilisation shown in killing each other as the only way of settling a quarrel; the Queen did not quite agree and put the other side very fairly, how much good it did a nation to have to think of others and suppress luxury even for a short time, how good it will be for all those smart idle young men to miss a Season and rough it with the troops; 'it is rather like the stopping of duels which were of course a great evil when carried to excess but men were more chivalrous when it was in fashion'. Perhaps outwardly so, say I, but it must have been the bane of society and I can never see that it stopped intrigue or put and end to scandal. I see my poor friend Tait is dead, wounded for the second time, poor boy, I shall never forget his golfing conversation with the Queen at Balmoral. Sir J. McNeill, our chief military authority here, predicts the end of Ladysmith. He thinks nothing can save it and the garrison cannot fight their way out on account of the miles of barbed wire with which the Boers have hemmed them in, they would be massacred to a man. He had the courage to tell the Queen his opinion last night and she took it well, although I am certain she did not believe him. We shall have an awful battle on the Modder soon but thank God Methuen won't have anything to do with it. Now we see why he was not superseded.

OSBORNE. *February 13th 1900*

Oh, such a dismal day! I never have seen such a snow storm for years and the North East wind batters the windows and freezes me as I sit in my chair. Pray do not let Victor attempt skating unless you are with him, there are such crowds of 'roughs' on the London ponds and he might be seriously hurt.

Now the Government have revealed their scheme I am more in the Slough of Despond than ever, the soldiers here sniff and sneer and Sir Arthur is frantic. Even Princess Beatrice is roused to wrath and inveighs loudly against the Government and Thora is furious. It appears the Queen's wishes which were most sensible have been quite disregarded and the amateur rabble that is to protect our coasts is not even likely to be lured into voluntary regiments. How can they get away for a month's drill when it is often impossible to secure them for four days at Easter? But, oh, this Party Government, what a miserable thing it is, votes! votes! votes! In spite of their grand majority, their late victories, the discomfiture of Sir E. Clarke, they tremble when they think of the next Election. It makes me sick.

Lord Cross made an ass of himself as usual last night, very squiffy after dinner, he began to pay his usual fulsome compliments. I am supposed to have turned from him too haughtily but

o

his ignorance and intemperance disgust me. He evidently knew nothing and asked who Colonel Kekewitch was, and announced that all the Militia would be called out in three weeks; also, with intense pomp, that Lord Roberts would be in Bloemfontein in a week! He does not have the same success as he used to in Royal circles, thank goodness. The Buchanans arrive this evening for two nights and Fritz Ponsonby has gone to town to see his wife make her debut in Mrs. A. Paget's tableau as 1) the Pacific Islands, 2) the Virgin Mary. 'Most extraordinary,' was the Queen's only remark.

OSBORNE. *February 15th 1900*

The successful advance by French has cheered us all, he is a good man and I perceive the youngest General we have in South Africa. I firmly believe in youth versus age, not extreme youth, but if a man cannot command or rule or administer by the time he is forty, then he is not fit for anything, and Generals verging on seventy *must* be past their prime. (Very private): The Queen is as disgusted with her Government as you are, but declares Lord Salisbury is not to blame, that his hands are tied. 'I have often told him to put his foot down and I have said over and over again they are too timid,' she said this afternoon while driving alone with me in a shut carriage. 'They do not take my advice or the advice of experts about the Army and civilians *cannot* understand military matters; General Peel was by far the best and strongest Minister for War we ever had and the present Lord Derby the worst.' I feel I hardly ought to put these words on paper but you will lock them up or burn them as you think best and at any rate keep them to yourself. A telegram from Prince Christian Victor has just arrived and he is very well and back at Chievely, so Thora is very happy again.

OSBORNE. *February 16th 1900*

We were roused this morning with the welcome news of the relief of Kimberley and have been in great spirits all day. The

Queen already looks better and I only hope the tide has turned and we may have no more serious reverses. Lord Rosebery's speech is splendid, Lord Kimberley's not bad, and Lord Salisbury's feeble as usual, and I hear Rosebery was furious at not being answered or even alluded to; he is the soul of vanity and cannot stand being ignored. If only he would act when in office as he does when in Opposition I should believe in him but that is just what he does not. I went to Ryde with the Queen and Princesses this afternoon to the Children's Ward of the County Hospital which the Queen opened when I was here last summer. It was delightful to see her talking to the children and giving them toys, they were rather too young to appreciate the honour, for the oldest was five and all the rest averaged two years old. I like the Duchess of Roxburghe so very much.

OSBORNE. *February 19th 1900*

We took Holy Communion yesterday with the Queen which I have never done before. It was a touching little ceremony, the Queen stood at the Altar rails leaning on her stick and supported by Princess Thora, she cannot kneel on account of her lame leg and the service is shortened by the sentence being said generally and not separately to each person. Old Waite the page and three of the maids and three of the Gentlemen formed the whole congregation. The news today is extremely good. Lucas Meyer has left Ladysmith and the Boers are melting away there as they did at Kimberley, but this is a secret. The Queen is in the best of spirits and the effect on her health is wonderful. The prolonged strain was beginning to tell on her and I did not feel happy about her, she is very much alive to our danger from foreign powers and quite on the alert, distrusts the Russians as much as you do but always declaring the devotion of the Czar to her and England is genuine only he lives in a fool's paradise and really knows nothing of what his Ministers do in his name. Alas—I fear he is a weakling and his Empress a rabid pathetic 'hausfrau'.

WINDSOR. *February 20th 1900*

The news is quite splendid, triumphant telegrams have been pouring in from Buller all the afternoon. I expect the Boers will be dished at Ladysmith as they were at Kimberley.

WINDSOR. *February 21st 1900*

The Queen has just sent me the kindest possible message by Princess Thora to say she intends to invite Victor to stay here very soon for a few days change. It is really very sweet of her and so wonderful in the midst of all her anxieties and affairs of State to think of Victor's health and my pleasure. These are the traits which endear her more than ever to my heart and ready to fall down to lick the dust from her feet! She even apologised for not inviting the baby but I said Minnie[1] could look after Victor if he might have a crib in her room next to mine and Victor is to lunch with the Ladies and have tea in the Schoolroom and go out with Prince Maurice and the tutor so I am sure he will have a very happy time. . . .

We are waiting anxiously for news but none is forthcoming that may be revealed to us. Therefore Ladysmith cannot have been relieved nor Kronje beaten for both events are hopefully expected.

The Queen said lots of characteristic things at a Ladies' Dinner last night. Princess Thora remarked that her dog, Pat, did not like Buckingham Palace. 'I can *quite* understand that,' said the Queen. Lord Salisbury is having an Audience at this moment. I hear the most lamentable accounts of his condition, mental and physical. He is quite played out, I wish to goodness he would retire or resign one or other of his great offices.

WINDSOR. *February 23rd 1900*

The Queen has just sent me a message by Princess Thora to say she invites Victor to come tomorrow and stay for a whole week. I am more than overjoyed, it will be so perfect for him and for me and such a time for him to look back upon one day. I wired to Frances and wrote at length about clothes and toys but there is

---

[1] Minnie was Marie's lady's maid.

no time for suits to be made and I leave it to you and so do your best to rig him out. The new white jersey and pair of ready-made knickers from Gooch look quite nice. He is to lunch with us and have tea in the school-room and go out once a day with Prince Maurice and the tutor, and Sylvia Edwardes is wild with joy at the prospect of reading to him and playing with him the livelong day.

[*Sylvia Edwardes, who was a Maid of Honour and whom I remember as being extremely nice to me during this visit, afterwards married Count Gleichen to whom I was A.D.C. when he commanded the 37th Division in 1915. When foreign titles were dropped he became Lord Edward Gleichen. He was a good soldier and a first-rate Intelligence Officer and was abominably treated, particularly by General Sir Henry Wilson, whom he looked upon as a friend. He suffered, as did Prince Louis of Battenberg, from having had a German name and title, but he was one of the most patriotic Englishmen I ever knew.*]

WINDSOR. *February 27th, 1900*

The Queen has not taken me to Netley after all, as she thought I should prefer spending the day with Victor. I must confess to a slight feeling of disappointment as I should have liked to see the wounded at Netley and to have heard their stories besides the historical interest of going with the Queen; but in some ways I am rather unlucky for I never come in for the functions. . . .

We got the glorious news of Cronje's surrender about 10 this morning. Lord Roberts laid special stress on its having taken place on the anniversary of Majuba! I do not think the Boers can affect to despise us any longer and I trust this crushing blow may completely demoralise them. We are pining for further details but shall not hear them yet as the telegrams will go straight to the Queen. Emily Ampthill has just arrived and is furious with the Government and with some of the Generals, she thinks Lord Salisbury a perfect disgrace and thinks he ought to resign as soon as the war is over. She also has the latest news of Lord Lansdowne and most of the other Ministers. I thought the Queen tired last night but always thinking of others as usual. She sent a splendid doll by me to Mrs. Haughton for her baby. She is a most unresponsive female, reserved to a fault. The Queen is really very angry with the Duc d'Orléans, he is a horrid mean little beast and ought to be kicked out of the British Isles at once and delivered to his own countrymen who would very soon pick his bones.

WINDSOR. *February 28th 1900*

Victor looks better each day and is intensely happy but his restlessness and unceasing activity is rather trying and he refuses to do the smallest thing alone and won't look at a book. He is perfectly mad on the subject of soldiers and now wishes *you* were a General or at least a Colonel. The inspection of the Berkshire Volunteer Territorials in Khaki took place this morning in St. George's Hall as a drizzle prevented the Queen from going out. It was somewhat dull and unimpressive for they could only march past the Queen who was seated in a chair with her feet on a little Indian carpet, and then face about and listen to the Queen's little speech, so simple and worthy. There was no cheering and no music but afterwards they had a sort of stand-up luncheon in the Waterloo Chamber. Princess Christian proposed the Queen's health and they then cheered to the echo. Victor was rather disappointed because the men wore their top coats and the full khaki uniform was thus shrouded. The Queen was less tired than I could have believed after her six and a half hour expedition to Netley, two of which were spent seeing and speaking to the sick and wounded but she told me her interest was so keen that she felt no fatigue whatever and she had mastered the details of the serious cases and was full of plans for helping the maimed men. She told them they might work her a cushion. I have just seen the very latest cipher telegram from Buller and all goes well and he is about four miles from Ladysmith but the progress is slow and as White has only just enough horses for the guns and his men are rather sick he cannot break out till the right moment comes. The 8th Division is ordered out but it ought to have gone three weeks ago and if the Queen had had her way it would have been at the Front.

This has been, as you say, an historical day and one to be remembered all one's life; the bells are pealing and from my window I can hear distant cheering, the good news is confirmed and Buller wired that he has been into Ladysmith and that the Boers have melted away like snow in springtime. The unfortunate besieged are however in rather a bad way, they have been eating horses and mules for some time past and Buller himself says, 'The troops will need nursing before they are fit for anything in the way of campaigning.' I saw the beloved Queen before luncheon, beaming with joy and surrounded by loyal telegrams from all sorts of people. She was so delighted and her face had lost that look of tension it has worn through the last anxious fortnight. She spoke of the joy and then sighed for the sick and wounded, telling me to arrange with the Dean for a Prayer of Thanksgiving on Sunday and for a cheerful hymn and then so characteristically asked how Victor was enjoying his visit and gave me for him the most gorgeous box of soldiers I have ever set eyes on. I really do not know how to be grateful enough, and Victor has had another ideally happy day playing with the children and driving with Prince Leopold in his tiny cart with the pair of Shetland ponies no larger than fair-sized dogs. I drove with the Duchess of York this morning and am to dine alone with her in her room this evening as her mourning is too deep for her to be present at a rather large Queen's dinner. She is very nice to me and I am devoted to her and we talk quite openly about everything, politics included.

Victor made his farewell bow all alone to his Sovereign and I hear from Miss Stewart and Thompson the Page, that he acquitted himself like a born courtier, bowed low, kissed her hand and thanked fervently for his happy visit. The Queen told me he behaved quite perfectly and said, 'I shall have a lot to tell my baby when I get home'. This pleased her immensely, she thought he looked rather pale today but really he is alright again. . . .

The Queen told me all about her giving up the visit abroad and was rather pathetic. I will write details tomorrow.

WINDSOR. *March 7th 1900*

The Queen has just told me that both Houses of Parliament have asked permission to come and give her a hearty cheer when she arrives tomorrow morning and they are to be drawn up in the Quadrangle at Buckingham Palace. It will be an interesting sight and if you care to come to my room with Victor about twelve, I could find you a good place to see it from. . . . The Queen will take a long drive tomorrow afternoon, Thursday, probable route Embankment, Farringdon Street, Holborn, Oxford Street, the Park and home. I expect the Princesses will go with her and we shall not be wanted. The great news will be in all the papers to-morrow morning and the excitement will be madder than ever. I do feel very pleased and proud to think I shall see and hear everything. The Queen is in the best of spirits and enjoying her well-earned popularity. She said, 'I know people will say I was *advised* to go to Ireland but it is *entirely* my own idea, and I must honestly confess it is *not* entirely to please the Irish, but partly because I expect to enjoy myself.' This, at eighty-one, beats the record. With such intense vitality and power of enjoyment there can be no serious decay of mind or body. I feel bursting with admiration and loyalty and proud to have seen such a day.

Her Majesty tells me another battle is imminent: this the 'Revers de la Medaille'. Sir Arthur has just looked in to tell me the battle is raging and the Boers fleeing in all directions.

[*In the end Marie did go on the drive through the streets with the Queen. There is a little note to Bernard telling him where to look out for her saying, 'You will see me and I hope cheer me.'*]

WINDSOR. *March 11th 1900*

There seems to be something of a crisis here today, Sir Arthur was sent fleeing to London at two, to see Lord Salisbury about the insolent proposals of peace prepared by Kruger and Steyn. They insist on complete independence. Lord Salisbury for once agrees with the Queen and a 'stinker' has been sent in reply but Lord Salisbury won't let anything be publicly known before Tuesday. The Queen told me all about it three days ago, she was so bursting with indignation that she could not keep it to herself and she wants it to be in the papers tomorrow, but Lord Salisbury clings to the old diplomacy, hence the delay. There has been another battle close to Bloemfontein, we are victorious and have 50 prisoners. Lord Rowton has unexpectedly appeared on the scene, swelling with importance, he is the greatest bore and the worst adviser but the powers-that-be all swear by him and are as ignorant as a new-born baby as to his true character and reputation.

CHAPTER XV

DARKENING SHADOWS

Eleventh Waiting

WINDSOR. *July 18th 1900*

I arrived last night and by some mistake the Housekeeper declared I was not expected so no room was forthcoming for a while and there was some crossness and a general blaming of everybody all round, however I remained calm and did not fuss and am now in the rather stuffy little Chintz Room, so called I suppose because it does not contain one inch of that fabric! Harriet remains on until tomorrow, rather a bore for me as I am quite superfluous and would much rather have remained on at Hurst or with you, however it is useless fretting and as the Queen grows older one must allow more and more for these little caprices and try not to resent them. Harriet is very amiable but I can see she has had friction with some members of the Household and she is not as popular as she used to be. How curious it is that when people have power they seem to lose the talent for wielding it. I have had a pleasant morning with 'Nunks' and Gerry and picking up the threads, always amusing after some months absence, and now I am going to Eton to try and see Mr. Benson, and if not to leave a note asking for an interview tomorrow.

Captain Towse has just been to have the Victoria Cross from the Queen. He has lost both his eyes, a bullet went in at one eye and came out at the other, scooping them both out, I forget at which battle. He is so handsome, only thirty, and luckily has a dear little wife who came with him, a most pathetic sight.

They went to Osborne and immediately Marie was laid low with a very bad attack of lumbago which kept her in bed for several days in very hot weather in a rather stuffy room. There is an amusing cutting from the Daily Mail *describing the Queen's journey to Osborne as follows:*

The Queen left Windsor for Osborne yesterday and despite the scorching sun Her Majesty looked the coolest among those travelling to the Royal ship.

Her Majesty was wearing a white shawl and white hat trimmed with black and white feathers and carried a white parasol . . . passing through a florally decorated Waiting Room, assisted by her Indian attendant, entered the Royal Saloon which is kept beautifully cool by blocks of ice.

There was much more ice than usual, several pailfuls being placed at each end of the room and blocks of ice surrounded by flowers were laid in various parts of the carriage. Four lovely bouquets were in the Saloon, the Queen's being composed of carnations.

The little Princes of Battenberg took with them to Osborne their cages of pet birds.

The Hon. Mrs. Mallet, one of the Ladies-in-Waiting, was so affected by the extreme heat that she had to be led to her Saloon by Sir James Reid, the Queen's physician.

OSBORNE. *July 24th 1900*

The Queen is certainly less vigorous and her digestion is becoming defective after so many years of hard labour! If she would follow a diet and live on Benger's Food and chicken all would be well but she clings to roast beef and ices! And what can you then expect? Sir James has at last persuaded her to try Benger's and she likes it and now to his horror, instead of substituting it for other foods she adds it to her already copious meals just as poor Princess Mary thought it banting to eat biscuits as well as bread. She is very sleepy in the evenings and goes to bed earlier although not early enough. There is an awful row about the Royal yacht, it is rotting from stem to stern and the Queen vows she won't take it at any price. Goschen declares if she persists he will resign altogether, the fat is in the fire and the Admiralty having behaved

Reid to the rescue (by Marie)

abominably are terrified. Of course 'Old Sarum' knew nothing about it till Sir Arthur broke it to him last week and then he was furious and said, 'Sir W. White should have been dismissed', etc., etc., but he ought to have known. It may be disagreeable for the Government if they have wasted half a million.

OSBORNE. *July 25th 1900*

The Queen has just sent us an immense War Office telegram to read from Roberts, not good news nor encouraging. The Army seems to be suffering from creeping paralysis and I expect the Campaign may not be over for another six months, even a year. I am reading all I can about the Chinese, the question is most interesting and on the whole my sympathies are not with the Europeans. Of course this massacre has put them in the wrong for the time being but 'spheres of influence' have much to answer for in the matter.

OSBORNE. *July 26th 1900*

I am decidedly better today and feel life is less of a burden. The drive yesterday went off without too much pain and the Queen was very cheerful and affectionate and marked her approval of my efforts by again inviting me to dinner. But this hot weather does try her and there is no denying it, and of course when she devours a huge chocolate ice followed by a couple of apricots washed down with iced water as she did last night she ought to expect a dig from the indigestion fiend. Sir Fleetwood and Sir Arthur have gone to Portsmouth to inspect and carp at the ill-fated new yacht, I do not believe for one moment the Queen will take her, and that will be one more reason for a Dissolution. I have laughed till I have cried over the 'ineptitudes' of the Westminster Gazette of the 24th. It is the wittiest sketch ever penned and I long to put it in A. J. B.'s room to greet him when he arrives on Saturday. How true, how sadly true is every word of it. I quite howl over his failure, but I dare say many people who have gauged him as you have, knew in their heart of hearts it must come to this.

OSBORNE. *July 27th 1900*

We have just had a perfect thunderstorm, indeed a meeting of four thunderstorms just over our heads, nothing the Queen dislikes more but the air is clearer now and that will be a relief. The Queen looked sad and tired last night but she slept well in spite of eating two ices at dinner. I am still improving and have peregrinated to Sir Arthur's room for the first time today. He is benign but Sir Fleetwood becomes less sociable year by year but more fussy, he is really the pearl of the two though not in some ways so easy to work with. . . . No news from anywhere, the Chinese lies continue but they won't deceive us. We have a Dinner party tonight and the glorious Marine Band from Portsmouth should come. Aline tells me Mr. Lang played a curious and not absolutely straight part in her brother's election at Portsmouth. The truth is he was horrified and disgusted by Lord Salisbury's speech about the Drink Commission and preached a sermon telling his parishioners to vote Radical, and he turned the Election.

OSBORNE. *July 28th 1900*

We heard some interesting experiences of the War last night from Colonel Norcutt, who commanded a Brigade during Colenso, Spion Kop, Vaal Kremtz, Ladysmith, etc., he says the men are true heroes and so good-tempered and uncomplaining. It only shows what Englishmen would be if they did not drink. Vaal Kremtz was the worst, forty-eight hours lying down without food or drink and being shot at all the time without the possibility of returning fire.

OSBORNE. *July 29th 1900*

I think I have discovered what excites Mr. Balfour's interest most and that is medical details, he quite revels in the Hospital

Reports and is very strong over the inefficiency of Army Doctors and hearing someone ask after my lumbago he enquired how I had been cured and what drugs I had taken! It amused me so much. He had a long talk with the Queen after dinner and confidently spoke his mind, for he murmured to me afterwards that he had been 'most indiscreet' and felt rather uneasy, I consoled him and vouched for the Queen's discretion and felt rather proud to have been, as it were, taken into confidence by him.

A very amusing incident occurred later in the evening about 11.30, just as dear old Lady Erroll had taken off her hair and picked out her teeth someone knocked at her door. She said, 'Come in!' in reply! Then she opened it and there stood A. J. B. in the passage, he could not find his room and was at his wit's end. He had tried Aline's and was trembling with bashfulness. She directed him as well as she could and he eventually found his bed! These sort of jokes are constantly occurring, all the passages are alike and no-one ever plays the host. The poor 'ineptitude' is rather unhappy about the remarks on his temper. He took some pains to explain to me at lunch that he did not funk the Hospital Commission but loathed Burdett-Coutts; he acknowledged things have been very bad indeed and that radical reform is necessary, so I hope and trust something may be done. I cannot help suspecting from internal intelligence that they mean to dissolve in October, but it depends on whether the war is over. A. J. B. tells me Roberts promises that in a month, but we have had these promises before. I gather the entire Cabinet is down on Buller, a little unfair in my humble opinion.

OSBORNE. *July 30th 1900*

A. J. B. was very lively last night and very fascinating, and I do not think he is as cynical as he appears to be although it may grow and could turn him into a second 'Sarum'! Lady Erroll attacked him with enormous courage on the temperance question and he professed child-like ignorance and told her to send him her statistics. Dear old soul, she is very happy today in spite of my prophecy that this Parliament will never meet again—nor will it and the changes even if this Government returns will be great. Black Michael[1] refuses utterly to return to the Treasury and hints at retiring altogether. Goschen is so sick about the Royal yacht that he may go too, and no doubt Joe will boss the show. We had a lovely war discussion after dinner led by Princess Thora. A. J. B. was very frank and discussed publication of despatches etc., they will all be made public at the end of the war. He thinks Roberts has erred on the side of leniency, the Germans would have packed home many more officers with 'fleas in their ears'. . . .

How awful is this murder of the King of Italy. The Queen is terribly upset and it makes her nervous, though we all assure her she is safe in England. She vows she won't go abroad again and is terrified at the Princess of Wales going to Hamburg. This tragedy is the direct result of letting Sipido[2] go scot-free, no crowned head will be safe for the anarchists wax bolder every day. We might be living in the Middle Ages instead of the twentieth century. Horrors and wars are quite as frequent, let us hope individuals are more enlightened but sometimes I doubt even that! The Queen says she always prophesied the massacre of King Humbert. He scoffed at all precautions and believed in the devotion of his people. He was a brave man but I believe most immoral.

I am sending for my mourning trappings, we never escape jet for long.

OSBORNE. *July 31st 1900*

We seem to have shock after shock and everything is so sad I hardly know what to do or what to say. The telegram containing the news of the Duke of Coburg's death came at eight this morning. I heard Sir Fleetwood's voice in my passage at that unwarranted hour asking for Princess Christian and I guessed at the

---

[1] Sir M. Hicks-Beach, Chancellor of the Exchequer.

[2] A young Belgian anarchist who shot at and missed the Prince of Wales in a Brussels railway station. It naturally created a great deal of talk at the time and I believe the Queen was much upset over it.

disaster and simply trembled for the beloved Queen. However they wisely decided to let her dress and have some food before they told her and she bore the blow both heroically and angelically, bowing to the will of God, as she always does and only murmuring, 'My people will feel for me.' She telegraphed to Lord Roberts herself this morning, 'I know the Army will sympathise with my great grief.' Mercifully says Sir James her health has been better these last few days and it is everything to know she has strength to bear the shock. Had it occurred last week I should have been very anxious. She was prepared in a measure, for the last week we have known he was hopelessly ill but the Doctors thought he might live for six months or that the end might be as sudden as it was. He was sitting in the garden at 6.30 p.m. and then going to bed at 9 p.m. he was sleeping as peacefully as a child and at 9.30 he was dead. He was saved intense suffering, there is much to be thankful for, but it is awful to reflect that his own acts have largely contributed to his premature death. Sir Robert Collins who is here and knew him well declares he was the most gifted of all the Queen's sons and capable of great things but, alas, intemperance was his ruin as it is of so many. Poor 'Chrissy' is quite miserable, in bygone days he was her favourite brother and she has other domestic troubles that drive her wild with grief, I do pity her from the bottom of my heart and love her too, and am thankful she is here to comfort the Queen.

I have been interrupted by a summons to the Queen. She gave me her hand to kiss and I knelt down to take it in mine and so we remained for a full five minutes, trying to be calm enough to speak. The Queen cried so gently and seemed so patient and resigned in her great sorrow and finally a calm came over me and I was able to control my voice for I wished to spare her tears if possible, of course they came but she did not sob and then talked over the sad details and recalled his early days here, his birthdays had always been spent here (he would have been 56 next Monday), of his childish likes and dislikes, to her he was once more the happy boy and I could see that. And then she said the sympathy

of her people and individuals help her, she knew they were thinking of her, and well they may; how often has the Queen sym-
pathised with broken mothers' hearts all this year! She said the
trials and sorrows of the last few months were almost more than
she could bear and, alas, I cannot help feeling there may be more
in store.

August 1st 1900

I have been writing hard all day, thirty telegrams to answer at
a time and any amount dropping in all day, besides letters innumerable, so please forgive the shocking scrawl. . . . I have been
with the Queen twice today for quite a long time, she is more
angelic than ever and never murmurs, but the children and sons-
in-law she has lost were not old, most of them in fact in the prime
of life, and this adds to the sadness and she dwells on it but never
murmurs. It is really a mercy she had not seen much of the Duke
lately, the blank is not so acutely felt, if it had been anyone here,
even a member of her Household, it would have been more of a
shock; and the wretched man has been spared the most horrible
tortures, it now turns out that for the last two months he has been
fed from a tube but the Doctors thought fit to keep it a secret even
from his wife, a most unjustifiable thing, and poor 'Chrissey'
dwells so much on the fact that had she only known she might
have seen him again. From what I hear the disease and suffering
existed for two years at least, but this is a State secret. The Queen
slept well last night and her health continues excellent, Sir James
is quite satisfied and so are the Princesses, and her grief is so
natural tears one moment and almost a smile the next at any
quaint telegrams: 'Sincere condolences. Poem follows.' I think I
am a little bit of use to her and comfort, and that rejoices me more
than anything in the world. You will enter into my feelings on
this, the privilege is truly great and worth any sacrifice. It is a
humble way of serving Queen and Country and brings a rich
reward. 'Chrissy' and Thora also like having me here to pour
out their sorrows in my ears and to them I act as a sort of safety

valve, so altogether I could not wish to be away just now. Aline is a great dear and an immense help, for Judy[1] is the greatest fool in Europe and Annie Roxburghe is rather 'duchessy' but *not* to me. I think it is only the Churchill manner, she is kind and good at heart only bored to tears by the life here.

OSBORNE. *August 2nd 1900*

Received another shock, attempted assassination of the Shah. Blow upon blow and the darling Queen is seriously alarmed for the safety of her sons and grand-sons now journeying to Coburg. I am not surprised at her anxiety for these crimes are as catching as the measles and there seems to be a deep-seated anarchical plot which is to involve all the Sovereigns of Europe. We have extra detectives here, I am happy to say for our extra policemen look very beefy and beery and are proverbially stupid. I spend hours thinking how I could preserve the Queen if she were attacked when I was driving with her and have come to the conclusion I could do *nothing*, owing to wanting room for her legs the place opposite to her is always left vacant.

We had a very trying dinner and evening yesterday, the Duchess and I the only visitors at the Royal meal, conversation was wellnigh impossible, but we discussed the merits of different kinds of tea, and the Queen quite brightened up and declared she was the only person in England who could not get good tea! After dinner I read the leading articles and obituaries on the poor Duke from six different newspapers, while the Princesses answered telegrams and the poor little Queen looked so crushed and sad, and the effort not to let my voice falter was so intense that I was completely exhausted and hardly slept all night. Princess Beatrice is so dreadfully self-absorbed and unsympathetic I could shake her, 'Chrissy' on the other hand is not very discreet but the greatest comfort. I have scribbled thirty letters and twenty telegrams already today and am quite tired out.

[1] The Hon. Judith Harbord, daughter of Lord Suffield. Maid of Honour. Afterwards married a clergyman named Sullivan.

OSBORNE. *August 3rd 1900*

The Queen is well today and had a good night but she looks so sad, poor darling, my heart aches for her. The evening yesterday was a shade less gloomy and the attempt on the Shah offered a topic of conversation although by no means an exhilarating one, the worst is that Aline and I who both possess a sense of humour not shared by our female colleagues occasionally had much ado to keep a solemn face and when Princess Beatrice remarked, 'The papers say William [*Emperor William II of Germany*] will be the next, dear Mama', we nearly burst. His sermon is most extraordinary, the Queen says, 'blasphemous'. I think he must be a little mad in spite of his undoubted genius, but then Lombroso contends that genius and lunacy are one. . . .

We have a funeral service here tomorrow and are draping our clothes with crêpe. Sir W. Parratt and some choir boys from Windsor will do the music and that is my only consolation. It will be awfully trying. Bigge and Edwards are both unhinged and very cross. I keep out of their way as much as possible.

OSBORNE. *August 4th 1900*

We have just had a touching little Memorial Service in the Chapel here with beautiful prayers and heavenly music and the Altar draped in purple velvet and covered with white flowers, nothing gloomy or morbid about it, and all so very simple, only the booming of the Minute guns from the *Australia* in the Bay and the presence of the Queen and her children to distinguish it from a similar service for the lowliest of her subjects. I suppose our Court is the simplest in Europe, but its very simplicity is dignified and touching. The Queen bore up bravely, poor 'Chrissy' tried not to sob but looked too awfully old and sad, it was trying for us all and I do not think there was a dry eye in the congregation, not so much out of love for the departed, but out of the deepest sympathy for the darling little Queen who seems called upon every day to bear some fresh sorrow. Now there is a piteous story of Princess Louie.[1] Her Prince Aribert has made up his mind to divorce her on the pretext that she is too fond of the English and has no children, he has no real cause and does not even attempt to trump up one. He has squandered all her money, i.e. her allowance from England, her jewels, etc., and has now seized her despatch boxes and broken open her locked drawers. Princess Thora says all he will find are letters from her calling the Germans pigs and brutes, but I fear that will strengthen his case. It appears every rotten little German Principality can make its own 'Haus' laws and can issue edicts for divorce and re-marriage with the greatest possible ease. I call it horrible and thank my stars I am not 'Made in Germany'.

OSBORNE. *August 6th 1900*

The weather is truly appalling. I never remember such gales at this time of year. I have just been driving with the Queen and we were nearly blown out of the carriage, conversation was not very easy and I think the Queen looks tired but she is really well so there is nothing to be anxious about. The 'Anhalt' business is a great worry and no-one seems to know the best course for Princess Louise to pursue or how it will end. Your account of Canford interests me much and I wish I had heard all the talk about South Africa. The Duchess of Roxburghe thinks Winston Churchill much improved by his last experience, but one must not expect too much of the son of such parents. Lord Salisbury and Lady Gwendoline are going to the 'Schluct' so we shall have distinguished company, but the mere look of the fat old cynic enrages me.

OSBORNE. *August 7th 1900*

The Queen has just held a Council to prorogue Parliament. Only the Duke of Devonshire and Mr. Akers-Douglas and

[1] This refers to Princess Marie Louise, who in 1956 published her own autobiography, *My Memories of Six Reigns* (Evans Brothers). She was the second daughter of Princess Christian and sister of Princess Thora.

'Charles II'[1] turned up. The Duke seemed in good spirits but his manners are atrocious and it makes me quite sick to see him pick his nose vigorously at luncheon and explode into almost senseless fits of laughter. I had Akers-Douglas for a neighbour and much enjoyed a talk with him; he asked most affectionately after you and wanted to know how you liked the Inland Revenue, I replied with much caution that you wished you had more to do there and he said you ought soon to get a move up. I do not see how, do you? He confessed that A. J. B. was completely unhinged last night but made excuses for him, pleading insufficient notice of Burdett-Coutts's attack, etc., and of course he is too essentially a Party man ever to acknowledge his Chief in the wrong; all this is very well for the inner circle but it won't do for the general public and each time A. J. B. loses his temper he loses his prestige in the country; they won't understand the technical ins-and-outs and only judge from what they read and hear. I am perfectly certain he has lost a great deal of influence this year, although with the exception of Fritz Ponsonby the men here won't acknowledge it. We had another Ladies' Dinner last night and a gloomy evening but the Queen is really extraordinarily well and I am quite happy about her and think the enforced rest entailed by this deep mourning will be very good for her.

OSBORNE. *August 8th 1900*

The Queen was much more cheerful last night and discussed A. J. B. with me, saying, 'I am sure Mr. Mallet will be vexed at Mr. Balfour's curious loss of temper, it really is most extraordinary.' She made me read the whole debate from 'The Times' and as usual her judgment was faultless, utterly free from Party prejudice. It is a privilege untold to be able to talk to her freely and hear her real opinion about men and politics. I can see she is very much disappointed with A. J. B., and I do not think quite pleased with 'Old Sarum's' frank desertion of his post in a time of such pressing need. Sir Arthur is perfectly furious with him.'

[1] Sir Almeric Fitzroy, Clerk to the Council.

CHAPTER XVI

THE END OF AN EPOCH
Twelfth Waiting

This letter describes the rigours of the journey to Scotland, for which evidently the Court paid none of the expenses!

BALMORAL. *October 24th 1900*

I really had a very good journey on the whole and nothing to complain of. The officials at King's Cross were very civil and passed my luggage free although I had twice the weight allowed, and a whole compartment in the corridor of a Third Class Carriage was reserved for me where I made myself very cosy with pillows and rugs for the night, and should have slept well but for the flaring gas-light over my head which had no cover and could not be extinguished, so I rested but could not actually sleep. I wired for a tea-basket at Edinburgh and had a capital breakfast in the train there at 7.40 a.m. and another at Aberdeen about 11.40. There I met Edith Lytton and we did the rest of the journey very comfortably together. . . .

The Queen is growing very old and feeble, and each time I see the change, even since August. She has grown so thin and there is a distressing look of pain and weariness on her face; it makes me very sad. We are quite a family party, 'Nunks' and Edith Lytton and Gerry close by at Birkhall, the former looks well and enjoys being Master of the Household. I fear he only stays on another week. Lord Salisbury seems very flourishing, quite awake and alive and in excellent spirits. He was most amusing last night at dinner criticising Buller and saying how much better it would be not to make speeches and adding, 'I know at least one Cabinet Minister who never opens his mouth without making a mess of

LONDON AND NORTI

ARRANGEMENT

co

HER MAJES

From BALLAT

ON TUESDAY, THE **6**TH, AND WEI

	GUARD.	FOR MEN SERVANTS.	DRESSERS AND LADIES' MAIDS.	COUNTESS OF LYTTON. HON. MRS. MALLET. HON. EVELYN MOORE. MISS BULTEEL.	QUEEN'S DRESSERS.	Her Majesty AND PRINCESS HENRY OF BATTENBERG.	PERSONAL SERVANTS.	PRINCE VICTORI. BATTENE FRAUL MARGE — HON HARR PHIPF
ENGINE.	VAN. No. 210.	CARRIAGE No. 870.	SALOON. No. 73.	SALOON. No. 153.		Royal Saloon.		SALO No. 5

<-------------192 feet 8 inches-------------> < ----------

Seating plan for or

ESTERN RAILWAY.

CARRIAGES

Y'S TRAIN

to WINDSOR,

Y, THE 7TH NOVEMBER, 1900.

RINCES EOPOLD AND AURICE OF TENBERG AND ENDANTS. THEOBALD.	SIR ARTHUR BIGGE. SIR THOMAS DENNEHY. CAPT. PONSONBY. SURGEON BANKART.	MAJOR COLBORNE. HERR VON PFYFFER. INDIAN ATTENDANTS.	FOR PAGES AND UPPER SERVANTS.	DIRECTORS.	DIRECTORS.	FOURGON.	GUARD.
LOON.	SALOON.	SALOON.	SALOON.	SALOON.	CARRIAGE	TRUCK.	VAN.
o. 50.	No. 131.	No. 71.	No. 72.	No. 180.	No. 306.	No. 100.	No. 272.

·········· 403 feet 5 inches ·········· >

M'CORQUODALE & CO., LIMITED, Cardington Street, London, N.W.

e Queen's journeys

it.' I murmured to Sir Arthur that the same could be said of an eminent person at that very table! I longed to cut Lord Salisbury open and extract news to send you but not one scrap have I heard.

BALMORAL. *October 25th 1900*

I must say Lord Salisbury has been very amiable during his brief stay and quite communicative on certain matters. He talked to me last night about China[1] for nearly an hour and said nothing very new but cut poor Sir C. MacDonald, his beloved friend, to pieces, stating soldiers made shocking diplomatists, etc. I nearly burst with suppressed giggles, he said MacDonald should have packed his carpet-bag at once and taken to his heels, not stuck to his post, the first duty of a diplomatist is to *run*, and he added that before the disasters Sir Claude was to leave Peking on account of his health but the enforced business of the Siege had completely cured him and he wished to remain in China. 'People eat too much meat,' murmured Lord Salisbury, after having just devoured a huge beefy dinner, washed down with beakers of port! He attributes all the troubles in China to the Empress, 'old brute' he called her, 'Catherine and Semiramis combined'! He thinks she is far too astute to return to Peking; he also had a fierce dig at the Missionaries and hoped their ardour would be well damped for at least a generation. In fact he was excellent company and I felt myself highly honoured although it was but propinquity that procured me the favour. Not a hint has been dropped about the Ministry and we are all as ignorant as new-born babies, Lord Salisbury meets Arthur Balfour in Edinburgh today and has five hours confabulation, then journeys south. Princess Thora is awfully anxious about her brother. Lord Roberts wires he is seriously ill but there are no complications and he has the best of nurses and doctors. It seems as if the poor darling Queen is never again to be free from anxiety.

[1] The Boxer Rising had left the foreign legations besieged in Peking.

BALMORAL. *October 27th 1900*

We live in a constant state of anxiety about Prince Christle and I really think the sudden telegrams add to the trial for as each one arrives Dr. Bankhart is called in and all the shades and symptoms are discussed, today the account is certainly serious, pneumonia and other complications but I have a strong feeling that he will pull through and come safely home. Still there must be awful suspense for another ten days at the very least and it is so bad for the Queen in addition to the worse anxiety about the Empress Frederick. The acute attack in her case is over but I am convinced she will not last long. Do not breathe a word of this. The dear little Queen makes heroic efforts to be cheerful but her face in repose is terribly sad; I do not want to live to be very old; the penalties are too great.

News had arrived of the death in South Africa of Prince Christian Victor, the Queen's grand-son.

BALMORAL. *October 30th 1900*

Words fail me to describe the pall of sorrow that hangs over this house, the Queen is quite exhausted by her grief and that dear unselfish Princess Thora just heart-broken, she cared more for this brother than anything on earth and was justly proud of his exploits and valour. Another three weeks would have seen him home again and all his letters were full of the joy of seeing friends and relations and dogs and all he most loved. God's ways are so inscrutable, we cannot bear these trials without true faith and *that* the members of our Royal House have a large measure of, for their trials are nobly borne and they shine in adversity.

Princess Thora is admirable, although she and her mother will miss him every hour of every day, and she insisted on breaking the sad news to the Queen herself, knowing that in this way it would be less of a shock, she thinks of everyone but herself. . . .

The Queen is dreadfully shaken and upset and as she was not at her best before this shock you may imagine how anxious we feel about her health.

*The next letter contains details of a short funeral Service for the Prince
and describes the Queen's grief.*

BALMORAL. *November 1st 1900*

When she breaks down and draws me close to her and lets me
stroke her dear hand I quite forget she is far above me and only
realise she is a sorrowing woman who clings to human sympathy
and hungers for all that can be given on such occasions. I feel
thankful for my unreserved nature and power of showing what
I feel, for I believe it is a comfort to her, just a little. . . .

I believe it is quite true Lord Lansdowne is going to the
Foreign Office, at least Lord George won't deny it and the Queen
talked to me about it yesterday in the Carriage, saying that he had
begged to be relieved of the War Office, but do not quote me.
Lord George gave me a most interesting but flippant report from
Sir C. MacDonald to read today. Such strange language, quite a
school-boy style, saying the Siege was 'great fun on the whole'.

The final paragraph was most interesting. 'The Russians are
behaving like wild beasts, ravishing women and plundering and
murdering on each side and the Sikhs were heard to say, "These
brutes shall never cross our frontier nor have a chance of invading
India." ' So as Sir Claude MacDonald concludes, 'Good may
come out of evil.'[1]

BALMORAL. *November 2nd 1900*

I feel you will be depressed by the Government assignments as
I am, I see the all pervading influence of Chamberlain and it is
quite evident that Lord Salisbury has 'thrown up the sponge'. It
is comic to think of him in Lord Cross's place [*Lord Privy Seal*],
while that poor old dodderer is plucking his beard and reviling
the Government. Uncle Alick says his motto has always been, 'No
Cross, no Crown' and that he considers the Queen will totter in
the Throne once his support is withdrawn. I do not mind Lord

[1] This refers to the Boxer Rising and Siege of the Legations in Peking. Sir
C. MacDonald was British Minister in Peking. The behaviour of the various
national contingents of the Relief Force was evidently not at all uniform.

Selborne at the Admiralty and I do not care a 'blue penny' (as
V. would say) where Ritchie goes as long as I do not have to talk
to him, but I tremble to think they could not find anyone better
than Brodrick for the War Office, and I suppose we may promptly
chant a Requiem for the promised reforms. They have not had
the pluck to promote Lord Cromer and I expect Chamberlain
opposed him and dreaded the influence of a really strong man in
the Cabinet. Well, it is not more disappointing than I expected
but I cannot say I feel happy, Chamberlain will evidently be our
next Prime Minister and A. J. B. has sunk into complete insigni-
ficance. If you had been Joe's Secretary instead of A. J. B.'s you
would have been Governor of Jamaica ere this. He certainly
knows how to reward his friends.

We remain in the same melancholy state here, Ladies' Dinner
every night, gloomy evenings, silence only broken by the receipt
of consoling telegrams in divers tongues and by the replies sent to
them. The Queen is quite angelic and does her best to keep up,
but the effort is very great and cannot be good for her. The curious
thing is that she said to me, 'After the Prince Consort's death I
wished to die, but *now* I wish to live and do what I can for my
country and those I love.' Do not repeat this but it is a very remarkable utterance for a woman of eighty-two, and this is not
the first time she has made the same remark. I wonder if she
dreads the influence of the Prince of Wales?

BALMORAL. *November 3rd 1900*

Existence is very monotonous and I feel dull and depressed.
However, determined to improve the hour I had a spinning lesson
this morning and got on so well that I could hope ere long to spin
you a fine suit for next year's golfing. Uncle Alick has bought
himself a lovely wheel which he has lent me.

Lord George [*Hamilton*] is always very nice to me and most
communicative, so I pumped him about A. J. B., etc. He thinks
him still too much addicted to 'Souls' and fears the influence of
Harry Cust, not that he would get power over Mr. Balfour but

that he will hang on to him like a leech and the intimacy cannot fail to damage him in the eyes of the House. I am sure he does not think very much of Sandars as a Secretary but he is devoted to Harriet S. and forgives much for her sake. He loves Mr. Richmond Ritchie his own Private Secretary and says he could not do anything without him. I should like to work for a Chief who trusts and values one in such a way. Lord George fears Winston Churchill, Arnold Forster, etc., and not Arthur Elliot and his type. I think he dreads the Cabinets in November, expects a deal of wrangling. I dare say you will see in the papers as soon as you get this that George Wyndham is to go to Ireland and Gerald Balfour to the Board of Trade, while Lord Dudley is to be Lord Lieutenant. I do not expect Gerald will relish this snub nor the decrease in salary but perhaps he will be 'sopped' by a seat in the Cabinet.

I drove with the Queen this afternoon and she said Lord Lansdowne would not act in any way without Lord Salisbury, in fact he is to be a sort of 'dummy' to do the entertaining and tiresome interviews with Ambassadors and not to have any power. Lord Salisbury told the Queen that many more Ambassadorial afternoons would certainly shorten his life.

BALMORAL. *November 5th 1900*

The Queen is still far from well but I hope the change to Windsor will do her good. She has so little appetite and yesterday we had a thick fog worthy of London, which made her perfectly miserable.

BALMORAL. *November 6th 1900*

I actually made the Queen laugh at dinner last night by conjuring up a vision of 'Nunks' as a Bishop in full canonicals, I really thought I ought to have a medal. She was a little brighter yesterday but still ate so little. I could kill the cooks who take no pains whatever to prepare tempting little dishes and would be a disgrace to any kitchen. How I should like to work a sweeping reform, we are abominably served just now. The footmen smell of whisky and are never prompt to answer the bell and although they do not speak rudely, they stare in such a supercilious way. As for the Queen's dinner it is more like a badly arranged picnic.

Mrs. Dick Chamberlain has astonished the world, I hear she always alludes to Lord Roberts as that 'psalm-singing old fossil'. She ought to be caged but no doubt she will settle down and marry a peer.

WINDSOR. *November 7th 1900*

I had a very comfortable not to say luxurious journey. . . . I was introduced to Mr. Harrison, one of the L.N. & W.R. Directors who is a member of the South African Hospitals Commission and was most thrilling. His countenance grew quite black when he mentioned Mrs. R. Chamberlain and he says she did untold harm at the Cape and used the language of a petroleuse. He thinks the one cause of all the trouble was under-rating everything at the very first, thus there are no nurses, no stores, no comforts, and the hospitals were make-shifts, everyone declared the war would be over in six weeks.

WINDSOR. *November 8th 1900*

The Queen seemed a little better last night, it was the relief of getting the agonising interview with Princess Christian over and the latter was quite heroic and very calm and resigned; seeing her like this helps the Queen more than anything, but poor things, they cannot realise the full tragedy as yet, they will feel the bitterness when one by one other people's sons come home. Their sympathy for others in like sorrow is wonderful. How true it is that grief makes the whole world kin.

The servants here are too irritating, the Queen only ordered one small dish—nouilles—for her dinner last night and it was entirely forgotten, so she had nothing. The cooks should be drawn and quartered and the Clerks of the Kitchen strung from the Curfew Tower; their indifference makes me boil with rage.

I have just been over to Ascot to see Lady Ponsonby. She was pleasant and clever as usual and told me Louis had a standing invitation to stay, but I begged her to send him a special one and she promised to do so. The Park is most beautiful, the trees laden with golden leaves and the bracken a pinkish brown and I longed to sketch but it is too cold by 3.30, before which we can rarely get out. We have Ladies' Dinners every night so we lead a nun-like existence, however the males of the party include Lord Lawrence and Captain Drummond, so far from attractive that we do not regret it; the 'Munshi' has also returned after a year's absence in India, why the plague did not carry him off I cannot think, it might have done one good deed!

WINDSOR. *November 9th 1900*

Princess Louise [*Duchess of Argyll*] came into my room for half an hour after luncheon and was quite affectionate and kind about everyone, she is at her best when people are in real trouble and this is a redeeming feature in her most complex character. She told me she had seen Mama and you. I do trust she will make up her quarrels now and be a help to the Queen. Another State secret has come to me, Lord Kitchener is ultimately to be Commander in Chief, India, but I expect this must be buried for weeks if not months. Princess Louise was scornful about the Government and down on Lord Salisbury, thinks Cranborne's appointment absurd and unnecessary and wishes George Wyndham had stayed at the War Office. I must say I do not agree; he is Irish and a little 'blarney' will go down well and they will like his good-looks and good-manners. It is rather sad to realise how self-satisfied Betty and Gerald [*Balfour*] were, so cocksure of being the only people in the world for Ireland and never perceiving they were hated by all parties.

WINDSOR. *November 12th 1900*

The Queen is a little better and has got through the Council and had half an hour's drive and is none the worse, but she did not have a good night and Sir James is still anxious but not as much as he was yesterday. She dines alone tonight with Princess Beatrice, extraordinary event but the Ladies are to join her in the Drawing Room after dinner. I do not feel happy but still there is much to be thankful for. Our luncheon today was quite amusing and I had Lord Lansdowne and Lord Selborne as my share and enjoyed them both. I spoke to Lord Lansdowne about Louis and he was kind and sympathetic, said he hoped to come across him and was interested to hear he had been in Egypt. I hope something will come of it. He also asked me to lunch at Lansdowne House after Christmas. As for Lord Selborne he is the most charming friendly creature, so simple and not 'puffed up', we discussed old times and our dancing days and then plunged into Education. . . .

It was comic to see Lord Cross and Lord Salisbury both glaring at the Privy Seal of gigantic size and weight, Lord Salisbury chaffing Lord Cross and the poor old boy did not like it and looked most lachrymose. Sir M. White Ridley came to the Council but shirked the luncheon, still in the sulks I fear and Ritchie looked such a bounder that I longed to pour the soup down his back. His face shone with triumph and he ousted Lord Salisbury from his place of honour and seated himself between Lady Erroll and Aline, who both wished him at the bottom of the sea.

WINDSOR. *November 13th 1900*

The Queen is decidedly better today, slept seven hours and has had naps during the day. She enjoyed her coffee and egg for breakfast but she still has bouts of pain and Sir James is not easy. There is no reason why she should not be herself again if she could be made to take more nourishment and I *do* feel more cheerful. Sir James is devoting all his energies to getting her better and I have the utmost confidence in him. He is very nice to me and tells me everything which is a comfort.

The Mafeking nuns were a great success, such nice humorous women, very Irish with brogues and sparkling eyes and no

Q

nonsense. There were nine of them at Mafeking but these two were so exhausted after the Siege that they were sent home for the sake of health, they return to Mafeking next week. Their account of the Siege was most interesting and their devotion marvellous. They only changed their clothes and had a wash on Sundays while there was a truce, and slept in a bomb-proof shelter in the grounds. They had all the night-nursing for seven months and much of the day nursing too, and ten bombs burst on their Convent. Mother Theresa told me the Boers frequently took deliberate aim at her and the other nuns as their dresses made them scapegoats. The Boers also fired on little children, they are uncivilized brutes. They adored Baden-Powell and they spoke most highly of the whole Garrison, they would *never* have surrendered. In short, Mafeking seems to be a model in every way and Englishmen the best of fellows when there is no drink about. The Queen was so sweet to them and their attitude to her dignified and charming, perfect manners. I showed them over the Castle, they said it was heavenly and they went back to London very happily.

Aggy Jekyll sent me a note begging me to go to have tea with her and Timmy in College [*at Eton*] so off I went and found myself in the distinguished company of the Captain of the School, Hely-Hutchinson.

WINDSOR. *November 14th 1900*

The Queen was decidedly better this morning after a good night but a large luncheon party and shouting to the Princess of Wales exhausted her and she was in pain and very feeble after it. Of course we must be anxious for the next few days but there is no reason why she should not pick up again and regain her appetite, but she resents being treated as an invalid and as soon as she feels a tiny bit better she overtires herself and collapses. She is less meek now and that is a good sign, a reaction after so much anxiety is only natural after all, but Sir James has never been so anxious before in all these years.

Bernard's diary

November 11th 1900

Spent this Sunday at Windsor with Marie where I heard sundry pieces of political gossip, among others that Sir M. Ridley was furious at being turned out for Ritchie—not unnaturally. The world however imagines that he wanted to go. Cross also very angry and Chaplin. I gather that Lord Londonderry stays at the G.P.O. in the Cabinet, and Kitchener goes ultimately to India. Lord Salisbury's speech at the Mansion House about the War Office on Friday did not give satisfaction in the highest quarters—'not what he really thinks'. I had not realised that Prince Christian Victor's death had been such a shock to the Queen. That and all the strain of the last year has told terribly on her, and all about her are really anxious for the first time. Marie says the change in her state since August is alarming; loss of weight, size, appetite &c. One fears it must be the beginning of the end. But she is strong and has no disease and may probably be nursed back into comparative strength again. One prays indeed that it may be so. Not a hint of all this appears to have reached the outside world.

November 18th

Another Sunday at Windsor. The Queen much better but often depressed and nervous. She seems to have given up many of her old habits, sitting up late &c., for the time. The Bullers there last night. Marie had some talk with them and asked him how soon the war would be over. He said it would be all right when Roberts had left! 'Lord how these soldiers love one another.' The Queen sent a message that she did not want to have a discussion with him on the other generals, he might talk to her as much as he liked about her grandson as she wished to hear all. At luncheon with the household next day he sat by Lady Erroll, who immediately fell upon him with her temperance. Alcohol poison to the brain &c. He took it all very well, but at last told her that he had had his pint of champagne every day during the campaign, and very good champagne too. He also said they had lived on the best all the time, the only privation being an occasional lack of butter. His men were never without their full ration, and he never moved without his commissariat, which accounts for his very slow progress and also for his extreme popularity with the rank and file.

Interesting occasions were the kissing hands of the new Ministers on Monday, the reception of the Colonial troops and the two Mafeking nurses. The Queen sent for Marie in the afternoon and told her to ask Sir Fleetwood Edwards for the insignia of the G.C.B. which she intended to present to Prince Albert, Princess Christian's remaining son at tea time as a surprise! Naturally it was not in the house so the ceremony is postponed. Rather like a fairy tale.

WINDSOR. *November 16th 1900*

The Queen is still better and although seeing the Colonial troops was an exertion she got through it well and made them a most touching little speech in a strong voice. Poor men, they all looked wrecks more or less, for they were invalids one and all, but they are fine men and have good honest faces, the Australians far the finest and most refined. Their chaplain introduced them and explained who they were, etc. Poor man, he had his foot bitten off by a mad horse on the veldt and has lost his leg, I cannot imagine a more horrible accident.

Poor Princess Christian came and had a long talk today. I cannot say how much I admire her christian fortitude and resignation, she is so brave but truly heart-broken, but for the Queen's sake she is determined to keep up and it comforts her to have some definite object in life so she will continue her good works very soon and announces her intention of coming to lunch often at Rutland Gate. I trust the cook will turn out well.

WINDSOR. *November 19th 1900*

I drove with the Queen again this afternoon and tried to cheer her a little. I was rather successful and I suppose that is why she takes me so often, but I wish she would not, for poor Judy is getting quite hurt and 'huffy' and I should not mind staying at home one bit. I only hope and trust I shall be free tomorrow.

This drive on November 19 was the last time Marie saw the Queen.

WINDSOR. *November 20th 1900*

I have not seen the Queen all day but Sir James assures me she is much better and more herself in every way.

As the new century came in it seemed all too clear that the Queen could not last much longer. It is, however, strange to read the following letter from her doctor from Osborne dated January 4th 1901:

Dear Mrs. Mallet,

Just a line to tell you that the Queen is now much better. She has continued to improve ever since she consented to be treated as an invalid; and she now causes me no present anxiety. How far she may still improve it is impossible to say at her age: but I hope she may continue her invalid habits for some time longer, and so give herself every chance.

I am still of opinion that the foreign trip would be a somewhat risky undertaking, but we shall see a few weeks hence.

I have had rather an anxious time and have been very closely tied: so H.M. is to give me a little chance of air and exercise, and Sir F. Laking is coming here for a week or so. But I am told I am still to stay here and not in May Cottage which seems to me very unnecessary! However it may yet be altered.

Susan is in bed with a feverish chill and rheumatism but otherwise she is all right. I have been very little with her since she came, so I am longing for Sir F. Laking's arrival! You may have heard that Susan is to have a small house at Windsor Castle—a great boon for us.

With kindest regards and wishing you and yours every happiness for the New Year,

Yours very sincerely,
James Reid.

But the Queen did not rally for long. She died at Osborne on January 22nd 1901.

Marie was not then in waiting. She was in fact ill at home in London. My own memory is of Gerry Liddell coming to see Marie the very evening the Queen was dying. She was always great fun, so I managed to get her aside to sing to me a Scottish song which ran 'Pussy's got the measles and she's dead Puir Thing'. On singing this to Nannie the next morning I got a fearful rocket for such frivolity when the poor Queen lay dead. I remember also the black clothes everywhere, and I saw the funeral procession from Lord Rothschild's house in Piccadilly.

I find the Earl Marshal's Command to invite Marie to 'assist at the Interment of Her late Most Sacred Majesty of blessed memory' at St George's Chapel on February 2, with the instruction: 'Gentlemen: Full Dress with trowsers. Ladies Morning Dress.' The words 'with trowsers' written in specially in longhand seem somewhat inappropriate in an invitation to a lady. Bernard was not invited, but he describes Marie as returning more dead than alive from emotion.

It was the end of a long chapter in her life.

POSTSCRIPT

Marie's description of the new court of Edward VII is an interesting comment on changes at Windsor.

April 4th 1901

I left Kensington Palace at 4.45 p.m. with H.R.H. Princess Louise, Duchess of Argyll, to accompany her to Windsor as lady in waiting—by the King's command; this is rather an awkward position for the Princess has her own lady who would naturally expect to be taken, but I can only surmise that there being no ladies in residence it is considered better to import someone who knows the ways of the place. We only reached Paddington just as the train was starting and owing to faulty arrangements there was no reserved compartment and we were packed in with a vulgar looking woman of the 'nouveau riche' type. The Princess was received at Windsor by Capt Fortescue and we drove to the Castle where the rest of the household were waiting to welcome her, the King being out driving.

I am given the chintz rooms in the Lancaster Tower and the Princess is just above me. It is the greatest relief not to be in my old rooms where I have passed so many busy happy hours with my beloved Mistress close at hand. It is quite impossible to believe she is not still there and I feel a summons must come at any moment, the emotion is almost too much for me and I am terribly nervous. I am invited to dine with the King, the hour 8.30 instead of 9.15.

11.30 p.m.

Leading in was the order for dinner and my partner Prince Edward of Saxe-Weimar who placed me on the King's left hand. Before dinner H.M. spoke very kindly to me and gave me his hand to kiss and during the meal he talked a good deal and tried to put me at my ease, in fact no one could have been kinder, nevertheless I was so paralysed with terror that I could not eat and felt in an idiotic state. We talked of Mama and of Hardwicke's career, the King praising him much; then of pictures, finally the distribution of the Maundy in Westminster Abbey, which curious ceremony I attended this morning and was able to give an account of. The King said he had only once seen it when he was quite a boy.

Princess Louise then talked of my children and H.M. at once suggested they should come here on Sunday to play with the Duchess of York's children. Dinner ended we were led out by the gentlemen into the Red Drawing Room and quickly passed on to the Green where smoking became general, Princess Louise lighting her cigarette with the rest. I was the only individual who did not indulge! The party consists of Prince Edward of Saxe-Weimar, Sir Arthur Ellis, Mr Bertie Mitford, Sir D. Probyn, Sir F. Knollys, Capt Fortescue, Fritz Ponsonby, equerries, Sir E. Commerell, groom, Lord Suffield & Lord Edward Clinton who still remains Master of the Household until a successor is appointed, Herr Pyffer, German Secretary or 'the Swiss Waiter' as I call him remains on. The White Drawing Room where for the last two years of her life the Queen sat after dinner, is now used as a card room, one table being for whist the other for bridge, the King delights in the last-named game and plays every evening, Sundays included till between 1 and 2 in the morning.

Alick Yorke completes the picture in a letter to Marie from Windsor dated May 27th 1901.

I write to tell you my feelings and experiences on returning here for the first time since the great change. I feel continually in a dream, and cannot yet realise that the beloved presence which hallowed this spot is gone for ever. But in justice to all in Power I must say that kindness is the prevailing note and both the King and Queen and the Princess are as cordial and genial in their manner as possible, and all the household very considerate and kind. The moving of inanimate objects such as furniture and pictures does not jar and I must say the 3 drawing-rooms are more comfortably and artistically arranged than in the old days, but still it all seems as if someone was taking a liberty and I should wake up to find things and people restored to their old places. It seems so strange to see dear old Mr Wayte toddling after the King and the Indians waiting behind the lovely young Queen's chair—for beautiful and young she looks beyond comprehension considering the years which have so lightly passed her by.

I have had neuralgia in all my teeth which is most trying. I said I could not play bridge, but have had to sit up till the King retires, which he has done hitherto at 12.30 or thereabouts. I do not see any change in his manner which is as cheery and kind as before, but a certain seriousness of demeanour is added to it which reminds me often of his beloved mother, and Fritz tells me in doing his work he is so like Her in the questions He asks and criticism He makes. The chapel is much improved by the varnish being taken off the wood, and I hear the King is going to put in a new East Window to the dear Queen's memory. St George's Hall is being scraped and rearranged and the pictures are all being overhauled. Holbeins and Sir Joshuas and Gainsboroughs are being found in lofts over the Armoury and I do not doubt when all is completed the best works of art will be brought to the front and the collection enhanced thereby.

I have heard nothing about future arrangements, but fancy the pensions will not be large for the Ladies and Gentlemen, as the vast amount of servants dismissed will absorb a lot of money and men like Mr Lloyd will get the Lion's share.

The first night at dinner I sat one off the King and felt my spoon rattle against my teeth while I was eating my soup. Lady Gosford is very nice and at her ease and the Maids look so pretty in their widow-like mourning, and 'old Charlotte'[1] seems very proud and happy in her present exalted position.

[1] Miss Charlotte Knollys was Woman of the Bedchamber to the Princess of Wales for many years and continued to serve her when she became Queen Alexandra.

Marie continued all her life to keep in touch with the Royal Family. She several times was called upon to act as temporary Lady-in-Waiting to Princess Christian and Princess Beatrice, and went abroad with them on visits to their German kinsfolk. When Princess Ena married King Alfonso of Spain she was invited to the wedding in Madrid. Marie and Bernard were often invited to Court functions, weddings, Coronations and other great occasions. Queen Mary was always a particularly kind friend, and always came to the annual Amateur Art Exhibition organised by Marie and her freinds.

Marie took up local government work with great zest, and worked for years as a Poor-Law Guardian for Chelsea, and also for various charities. She survived my father by little more than two years, and died on March 5, 1934. She always enjoyed talking of her life at Court; but I think she had no regrets at returning to the quieter life which enabled her at last to give her full time to her family.

APPENDIX

The Foreign Office scandal here referred to is thus described in a cutting from the Daily News.

THE AUTHORSHIP: PREMIER OR PRINTER?

With an 'intelligent anticipation' of the situation which is *not* one of its characteristics, the Foreign Office has, on the eve of Bank Holiday, made capital provision for the thorough enjoyment of the British public, which above all things appreciates humour, whether gay or grim.

A Parliamentary Paper in relation to the China question issued by the Foreign Office last night is an epitome of the most amazing and amusing blunders ever issued from the press.

Embedded in a despatch and reading directly as part of it there appears an annotation (obviously from the pen of the Foreign Secretary or one of his immediate lieutenants) in the way of criticism of Sir Claude MacDonald's grammar, and, as will be seen below, a most comical and ludicrous effect has consequently been produced.

When we have read into the despatch the annotation—as it is printed, in fact, in the Paper as issued from the Foreign Office—we experience no wonder that the British Minister at Peking should be discovered writing of himself as Sir C. Ma*d*Donald!

At a late hour last night the chiefs of the Foreign Office discovered, or, more probably, had their attention directed to their identification with the latest edition of 'Jokes', and Mr. Curzon sent out a hurried note to 'able editors' appealing to them to observe that 'pars 2 and 3' were 'marginal notes' embodied in the text by mistake!

Happily for the gaiety of nations, this note in several instances arrived too late.

The Paper contains statements as to Sir C. MacDonald's communications with the Ministers of the Tsung-li-Yamen with regard to the non-alienation of the Yang-tsze region.

We append the first enclosure. We have placed the annotation at the side, but in the Paper itself it is actually printed after the first paragraph.

Enclosure 1

Yamen.

Sir C. MacDonald to the Tsung-li

MM. les Ministres,

Peking, February 9. 1898

Your Highnesses and your Excellencies have more than once intimated to me that the Chinese Government were aware of the great importance that has always been attached by Great Britain to the retention in Chinese possession of the Yang-tsze region, now entirely hers, as providing security for the free course and development of trade.

Strictly speaking, this is not grammar. China has not been mentioned, only 'Chinese Possession' and the 'Chinese Government', neither of which are of the feminine gender. 'Hers' can only refer, according to the ordinary rules of grammar, to Great Britain.

However, I suppose we must not be pedantic, but must leave Sir C. MacDonald and the Yamen to use bad grammar if they prefer.

I shall be glad to be in a position to communicate to her Majesty's Government a definite assurance that China will never alienate any territory in the provinces adjoining the Yang-tsze to any other Power, whether under lease, mortgage, or any other designation. Such an assurance is in full harmony with the observations made to me by your Highnesses and your Excellencies.

I avail, &c.,

(Signed)

CLAUDE M. MACDONALD.

The Daily News *has a little gibe at the 'marginal note' itself: 'It may be worth pointing out that the biter is himself bit, "Neither of which are of the feminine gender". "Strictly speaking", is that grammar? But we must not be pedantic. Let us rather be grateful. The Foreign Office has justified itself after all. Who will dare to say any more that the Foreign Office gives us nothing for our money?'*

Bernard's comment on this 'scandal' says that Curzon thus annotated a revise to go to the department and presumably to Lord Salisbury. The department, in the person of Norton, sent it down to the printer without crossing out the annotation! Hence the row. Curzon rushed to F. O. and rang up the resident clerk at 1.30 a.m. saying they would be the laughing stock of Europe. Sanderson (Permanent Under-Secretary) said he felt inclined to commit suicide! Lord Salisbury complained to Lord Cromer that everyone would take for granted that he was the author.

The Hon. G. N. Curzon was at that time the ambitious young Parliamentary Under-Secretary. Evidently he was already an expert at sarcastic marginal comment, for which he became only too well-known as Foreign Secretary after the First World War.

COURT OFFICIALS MENTIONED
IN THIS BOOK

Compiled from Marie's notebook. It may be noted that several ladies, including Marie herself, are referred to as 'the Honourable'. This title was granted by the Queen, the ladies to rank with the daughters of barons.

AMPTHILL, Emily Theresa. Lady in Waiting 1885–1901. d. of George Villiers, 4th Earl of Clarendon K.G. Secretary of State for Foreign Affairs. m. 1868 Lord Odo Russell, a son of the Duke of Bedford, who was created Baron Ampthill while serving as H.M. Ambassador at Berlin in 1881.

ANTRIM, Louisa, Countess of. Lady in Waiting 1890–1901. b. 1855. d. of General the Hon. Charles Grey, private secretary to the Prince Consort. m. 1875 6th Earl of Antrim.

ATHOLL, Dowager Duchess of. Lady in Waiting 1854–97, when she died at the age of 82, having been a personal friend of the Queen for 55 years. d. of H. H. Drummond of Blair Drummond. The Duke died in 1864.

BIDDULPH, Lady Elizabeth Philippa. Woman of the Bedchamber 1873–7. b. 1834, daughter of 4th Earl of Hardwicke and the Hon. Susan Liddell, 6th d. of 1st Baron Ravensworth. She married H. J. Adeane 1860, who died 1870. m. Michael Biddulph in 1877, who subsequently became Lord Biddulph of Ledbury.

BIDDULPH, Hon. Lady. Maid of Honour as Miss Seymour. Hon. Woman of the Bedchamber and Lady in Waiting to Princess Beatrice 1876–96. Widow of Sir Thomas Biddulph, a Keeper of the Privy Purse, who died 1878.

BIGGE, Lt.-Col. Sir Arthur. R.A.; K.C.B. etc. Assistant Private Secretary and Privy Purse, Groom in Waiting and Equerry. Became Private Secretary 1895 in succession to Sir Henry Ponsonby. His career at Court continued into the reign of George V. Created Baron Stamfordham.

BRIDPORT, General Alexander Nelson Hood, Viscount. Permanent

Lord in Waiting. Was Clerk Marshall to the Prince Consort. Succeeded his mother as Duke of Bronte. Father of Hon. Rosa Hood (q.v.).

CADOGAN, Hon. Ethel. Maid of Honour 1880–97, then extra woman of the bedchamber. b. 1853, d. of Hon. Frederick Cadogan and grand-daughter of 3rd Earl.

CARINGTON, Lt.-Col. Hon. William. Grenadier Guards. Equerry 1882–1901.

CHURCHILL, Jane, Baroness. b. 1826. d. of 2nd Marquess of Conyngham. m. Lord Churchill 1849. Lady in Waiting.

CLINTON, Col. Lord Edward Pelham. K.C.B. Master of the Household in succession to Sir John Cowell 1894. Son of 5th Duke of Newcastle.

COLVILLE, Col. Hon. Sir William. K.C.V.O. Master of the Ceremonies 1893, having previously been Comptroller to the Duke of Edinburgh.

DAVIDSON, Lt.-Col. Arthur. Groom in Waiting Dec. 1895. Equerry 1896.

DAVIDSON, Rt Rev. Randall. Dean of Windsor 1883. Bishop of Rochester 1891. Bishop of Winchester 1895. Later Archbishop of Canterbury till his death.

DOWNE, Viscountess. Lady in Waiting 1889. Succeeded Lady Ely.

DRUMMOND. Hon. Frances. Maid of Honour 1872–1901.

EDWARDES, Hon. Sylvia. d. of Lord Kensington. Maid of Honour 1897. m. Count Gleichen, who was a grandson of the Queen's half-sister, Princess Feodora of Hohenlohe-Langenberg. After a career in the Grenadier Guards—S. A. War, Military Attaché, Berlin—he commanded the 15th Brigade in the B.E.F., 1914, and later the 37th Division. When German titles were abandoned during the war he became Lord Edward Gleichen.

EDWARDS, Lt.-Col. the Right Hon. Sir Fleetwood, K.C.B. Assistant Private Secretary 1878–95, when he became Keeper of the Privy Purse until the Queen's death.

ELIOT, The Very Rev. P. F. Dean of Windsor June 1891.

ELY, Jane, Marchioness of. Lady in Waiting and confidential friend of the Queen 1851–90, when she died. The Queen wrote the following in the Court Circular: 'Amongst the many devoted friends and servants whose loss The Queen has in the last years had to deplore there is no one more truly regretted than Lady Ely, who was beloved and esteemed by the Queen's family and the whole Royal Household.'

ERROLL, Countess of. Lady in Waiting. m. 19th Earl, who died in 1891.

EWART, Major-Gen. Sir Henry. K.C.B. Groom in Waiting 1882, Equerry 1884–94, when he succeeded Sir G. Maude as Crown Equerry and Master of the Horse. In charge of the Royal Stud Farm, Bushey. m. 1888 Lady Evelyn Willoughby.

FITZROY, Hon. Frederica. Maid of Honour 1883–9, when she married Mr Crutchley.

GRANT, Hon. Victoria. *née* Baillie. Maid of Honour 1881–4. Extra Woman of the Bedchamber 1895, sharing duties as Private Secretary with Hon. Mrs Mallet.

HARBORD, Hon. Judith, d. of Lord Suffield. Maid of Honour 1894. Her brother, Hon. Charles Harbord, later Lord Suffield, was a Groom in Waiting in 1895.

HOOD, Hon. Rosa. Maid of Honour 1886–94. d. of Viscount Bridport. m. Mr Herbert Evans.

HUGHES, Hon. Mary. Succeeded Hon. Marie Adeane as Maid of Honour 1891. Her mother was a Liddell.

LAMBERT, Hon. Bertha. Maid of Honour 1899.

LATHOM, Earl of. Lord Chamberlain 1886–92 and again 1895. m. Lady Alice Villiers, who died 1897.

LOFTUS, Hon. Adeline (Mrs Paton). Maid of Honour in succession to Hon. Harriet Phipps, 1889–92. d. of Capt. and Lady Catherine Loftus.

LYTTON, Edith, Countess of. Lady in Waiting, in succession to the Dowager Duchess of Roxburgh June 1895. *née* Villiers. Widow of Robert Earl of Lytton. Lived to the age of 95. The Earl had been Viceroy of India and H.M. Ambassador in Paris.

McNEILL, Hon. Ina. Extra Woman of the Bedchamber 1888. Resigned 1895 on her marriage to the 8th Duke of Argyll, as his third wife.

MAJENDIE, Hon. Aline. Maid of Honour 1894. Later married Lord Grenfell.

MOORE, Hon. Evelyn. Maid of Honour 1881–1901.

PAGET, Hon. Evelyn. Maid of Honour 1874–94 when she died.

PHIPPS, Hon. Harriet. Maid of Honour 1862–89. Then Woman of the Bedchamber and Private Secretary in succession to Hon. Horatia Stopford. Born 1841, d. of Hon. Sir Charles Phipps, Keeper of the Privy Purse.

PONSONBY, General Rt Hon. Sir Henry. G.C.B. Equerry to Prince Consort 1868. Private Secretary to the Queen 1870–95. Keeper of the Privy Purse 1878–95. m. 1861 Hon. Mary Bulteel, a Maid of Honour. Died 1895 a few months after resigning office. In the Court Circular the Queen noted that he 'possessed in the highest degree the esteem and affection of his Royal Mistress'. The Queen was present at his funeral service in the Private Chapel at Windsor.

PONSONBY, Frederick (Fritz). Second son of Sir Henry. After a career in the Army and on the staff of the Viceroy, he became a notable courtier of subsequent reigns and was created Lord Sysonby. Assistant Private Secretary to the Queen 1895–1901 and Equerry. b. 1867. m. 1899 Victoria (Ria) Kennard.

ROXBURGHE, Anne Emily, Duchess of. Mistress of the Robes 1883–5. Extra Lady of the Bedchamber 1895–7. Thereafter Lady of the Bedchamber. 4th d. of Duke of Marlborough. m. 7th Duke, who died 1892.

ROXBURGHE, Susannah Stephania, Duchess of. Lady of the Bedchamber 1865–95. m. 1836 the 6th Duke of Roxburghe, who bore St Edward's Staff at the Queen's Coronation. Died 1895. 'One of Her Majesty's dearest, most valued and most devoted friends.'

SOUTHAMPTON, Ismania Katherine, Dowager Baroness. Lady of the Bedchamber 1878–1901. d. of W. Nugent. m. as second wife 3rd Lord Southampton, who died 1872.

STOPFORD, Hon. Horatia. Maid of Honour 1857–77. Then Woman of the Bedchamber in succession to Lady Elizabeth Adeane.

YORKE, Hon. Alexander (Alick). Groom in Waiting 1884–1901. Equerry to Prince Leopold until the Prince's death in 1884. b. 1847, son of 4th Earl of Hardwicke and Hon. Susan Liddell. He was brother to Lady Elizabeth Biddulph and thus uncle of Marie Mallet.

R

TREE SHOWING SOME OF QUEEN VICTORIA'S DIRECT DESCENDANTS

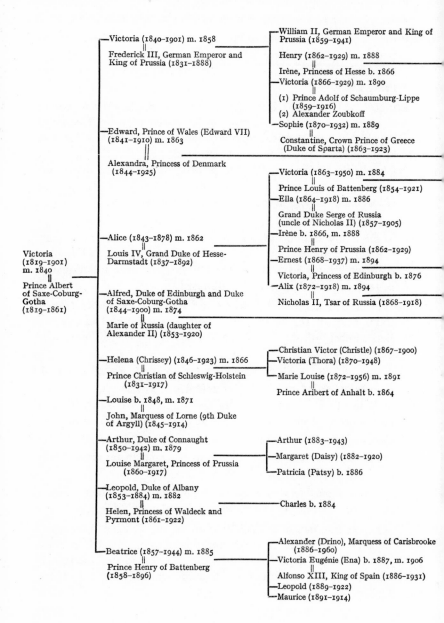

Victoria
(1819-1901)
m. 1840
‖
Prince Albert
of Saxe-Coburg-
Gotha
(1819-1861)

—Victoria (1840-1901) m. 1858
Frederick III, German Emperor and
King of Prussia (1831-1888)

—William II, German Emperor and King of
Prussia (1859-1941)
Henry (1862-1929) m. 1888
‖
Irène, Princess of Hesse b. 1866
—Victoria (1866-1929) m. 1890
‖
(1) Prince Adolf of Schaumburg-Lippe
(1859-1916)
(2) Alexander Zoubkoff
—Sophie (1870-1932) m. 1889
Constantine, Crown Prince of Greece
(Duke of Sparta) (1863-1923)

—Edward, Prince of Wales (Edward VII)
(1841-1910) m. 1863
‖
Alexandra, Princess of Denmark
(1844-1925)

—Victoria (1863-1950) m. 1884
‖
Prince Louis of Battenberg (1854-1921)
—Ella (1864-1918) m. 1886
‖
Grand Duke Serge of Russia
(uncle of Nicholas II) (1857-1905)
—Irène b. 1866, m. 1888
‖
Prince Henry of Prussia (1862-1929)
—Ernest (1868-1937) m. 1894
‖
Victoria, Princess of Edinburgh b. 1876
—Alix (1872-1918) m. 1894
Nicholas II, Tsar of Russia (1868-1918)

—Alice (1843-1878) m. 1862
Louis IV, Grand Duke of Hesse-
Darmstadt (1837-1892)

—Alfred, Duke of Edinburgh and Duke
of Saxe-Coburg-Gotha
(1844-1900) m. 1874
‖
Marie of Russia (daughter of
Alexander II) (1853-1920)

—Helena (Chrissey) (1846-1923) m. 1866
‖
Prince Christian of Schleswig-Holstein
(1831-1917)

—Christian Victor (Christle) (1867-1900)
—Victoria (Thora) (1870-1948)
—Marie Louise (1872-1956) m. 1891
Prince Aribert of Anhalt b. 1864

—Louise b. 1848, m. 1871
‖
John, Marquess of Lorne (9th Duke
of Argyll) (1845-1914)

—Arthur, Duke of Connaught
(1850-1942) m. 1879
‖
Louise Margaret, Princess of Prussia
(1860-1917)

—Arthur (1883-1943)
—Margaret (Daisy) (1882-1920)
—Patricia (Patsy) b. 1886

—Leopold, Duke of Albany
(1853-1884) m. 1882
‖
Helen, Princess of Waldeck and
Pyrmont (1861-1922)

—Charles b. 1884

—Beatrice (1857-1944) m. 1885
‖
Prince Henry of Battenberg
(1858-1896)

—Alexander (Drino), Marquess of Carisbrooke
(1886-1960)
—Victoria Eugénie (Ena) b. 1887, m. 1906
‖
Alfonso XIII, King of Spain (1886-1931)
—Leopold (1889-1922)
—Maurice (1891-1914)

234

Waldemar b. 1889

—Albert Victor, Duke of Clarence (1864–1892)
—George, Duke of York (George V) (1865–1936) ────────
  ‖
  Princess Mary of Teck (1867–1953)
—Louise (1867–1931) m. 1889
  ‖
  Duke of Fife (1849–1912)
—Victoria (1868–1935)
—Maud (1869–1938) m. 1896
  ‖
  Prince Charles of Denmark (Haakon VII of
  Norway) (1872–1957)

┌Edward (Duke of Windsor) b. 1894
├—Albert (George VI) (1895–1952)
└—Mary b. 1897

┌Alexandra (1891–1959)
└Maud (1893–1945)

Alice b. 1885
‖
Prince Andrew
of Greece

Elizabeth (1895–1903)

Olga (1895–1918)

┌—Alfred (1874–1899)
├—Marie b. 1875, m. 1893
  ‖
  Ferdinand of Roumania (1865–1927)
—Victoria (Ducky) b. 1876, m. 1894
  ‖
  Ernest, Grand Duke of Hesse-Darmstadt
  (1868–1937)
—Alexandra (1878–1942) m. 1896
  ‖
  Ernest, Prince of Hohenlohe-Langenburg
  (1863–1950)
└—Beatrice (1884–1966)
  ‖
  Infante Alfonso of Bourbon-Orleans

Carol b. 1893

Elizabeth (1895–1903)

INDEX